BEAUTY IN MONEY

BEAUTY IN MONEY

Numismatic Art and Technology of Early South India (*Up to and Including the Pallava Period*)

S. SURESH

MANOHAR
2011

First published 2011

ISBN 978-81-7304-909-5

Published by
Ajay Kumar Jain for
Manohar Publishers & Distributors
4753/23 Ansari Road, Daryaganj
New Delhi 110 002

Typeset at
Digigrafics
New Delhi 110 049

Printed at
Salasar Imaging Systems
Delhi 110 035

To the memory of my dearest parents
A.K. SETHURAMAN
and
SARASWATHI SETHURAMAN
whose supreme sacrifice forms
the foundation of all my researches

Contents

Illustrations

CHARTS

FIGURES

MAPS

*Unless otherwise stated, all photographs/drawings/maps are by the author.

PLATES

Abbreviations

ABORI	*Annals of the Bhandarkar Oriental Research Institute*
AJA	*American Journal of Archaeology*
AI	*Ancient India*
ASI	Archaeological Survey of India
ICHR	Indian Council of Historical Research
JNSI	*Journal of the Numismatic Society of India*
MCS	Madras Coin Society
ND	*Numismatic Digest*
SOAS	School of Oriental and African Studies
SSIC	*Studies in South Indian Coins*

Preface

This volume embodies my research on the topic 'Numismatic Technology, Art and Symbology of Ancient South India (Up to and Including the Pallava Period)' as an ICHR Postdoctoral Research Fellow affiliated to the Sudharsanam Centre for Art and Culture, Pudukkottai (Tamil Nadu), from December 2002 to November 2004.

I take this opportunity to offer my grateful thanks to all those who helped and encouraged me during the course of this research.

First, I am most grateful to the authorities of the ICHR for offering the fellowship that enabled me to undertake this study.

I also place on record my gratitude to the Sudharsanam Centre for Art and Culture for providing me all facilities and assistance for my research. I am specially obliged to Prof. S. Swaminathan, Director of the Centre, for his encouragement and guidance. He resolved many problems at every stage of this project.

I was blessed with opportunities to discuss the various problems pertaining to my research with a galaxy of eminent scholars such as Prof. B.N. Mukherjee, Prof. I. Mahadevan, Prof. A.V. Narasimha Murthy, Prof. B.D. Chattopadhyaya, Prof. Y. Subbarayalu, Dr. T. Sathyamurthy, Dr. R. Krishnamurthy and Prof. Prema Kasturi. I am obliged to all of them.

Several museums, both in India and abroad, have helped by providing me access to their collections and archives. I thank the authorities of all these museums, specially Dr. Rita Sharma of the National Museum, New Delhi; Ms. R. Santhi of the Government Museum, Egmore, Madras; Mr. R. Mohammad of the Government Museum, Pudukkottai; Ms. S. Mangalavathy of the Kalaimagal Kalvi Nilayam Museum, Erode; Prof. Sudharshan Seneviratne of the Department of Archaeology of the University of Peradeniya (Sri Lanka), Mr. Senarath Wickramasinghe of the National Museum, Colombo (Sri Lanka) and Mr. Joe Cribb of the British Museum, London.

Mr. S. Raman of Madras, Mr. A. Sitaraman of Tanjavur, Vidwan

I. Ramasamy of Boluvampatti (near Coimbatore) and several others kindly permitted me to examine and photograph their private collections of coins and medals. I owe a word of special thanks to all of them.

I also thank Ms. Usha Kris for doing some of the photography work for this volume.

Finally, any opinions and comments about the book are welcome from the readers.

S. SURESH

CHAPTER 1

Prologue

It is well-known that ancient coins are living testimonies to the past. Coins are an important source of information about ancient civilizations—their politics and administration, economy and trade, society and religion, art and architecture.

Basically, the coin is a utility object. It is a small piece of metal of prescribed weight, embellished with designs and/or inscriptions and manufactured on orders from an authority (king, trade-guild, etc.) for use as a currency or medium of exchange. The artistic value of a coin depends upon several factors. These include the skill and care with which the coin is minted, the purity of the metal used, the artistry of the obverse and reverse devices, including the subsidiary decorative elements such as border decorations, and the calligraphy of the legends on the coin. Thus, coins with well-produced devices, symbols and legends qualify as objects of art.

During different periods of history, in India and elsewhere, the kings and mintmasters did not evince a keen interest in producing coins of high artistic merit. Further, till the advent of mechanized minting in the modern age, the manual process of minting could not assure a precise standard or uniformity in the size, shape, weight and artistic quality of the coins belonging to a particular type or series. Yet, there were mints manned by officials and workers with an artistic bent of mind. Here, artistic coins were produced, mostly with dies carefully prepared by skilled artists. Such well-produced coins are, contrary to popular misconception, not negligible in quantity.

WHAT IS NUMISMATIC ART?

The potential of coins as a solid source of art history is beyond doubt. Numismatic art is the discipline that deals with the study of art in coinage. The major 'components' or 'aspects' constituting this rare, obscure and rather difficult discipline are as follows:

1. Examination of the obverse and reverse devices and art-motifs on coinage with particular reference to the extent to which these devices and figures exhibit plasticity, sense of proportion and illusion of depth. Also, analysis of the stylistic differences in the depiction of a single device/motif on the coins of varied dynasties/ series, as also on the coins of different rulers of a single dynasty and, in some instances, on the coins of a single ruler issued during different years of his reign and/or from different mints. For example, the elephant was the most common device on the coins of the Sangam Cōḷas, Cheras and Pāṇḍyas who ruled different regions of Tamiḷakam (Tamil Nadu-Kerala) from around 300 BC to AD 300. Yet, there are significant differences in the precise size, shape and stylistic characteristics of the elephant on the coins of each of these dynasties.
2. Study of the various countermarks seen on some of the coins of certain series/dynasties. In the south Indian context, such countermarks are often seen on the Roman coins and their local imitations that circulated in this region during the early centuries of the Christian era. The Roman coins reached south India, in large quantities, by the process of trade, and the Indians soon began to produce imitations of those coins. A few coins of the Sātavāhanas and the Ikṣvākus who ruled the Andhra region between around 300 BC and AD 300 also bear minute countermarks, at least a few of which appear to have been inspired by the devices and legends on ancient Roman coins.
3. Analysis of the significance—historical, social, religious, or any other—of the different devices/motifs/countermarks with reference to the chronology, probable place of production and geographical distribution of the coins bearing the devices/motifs. To mention one instance, the hills and river on the Sangam age Malaiyamān coins (100 BC-AD 300) are believed to represent the physical topography of their capital, Tirukoilur, in Tamil Nadu.
4. Investigation of the effects of the varied techniques of minting, and the purity of the metal of the coin, on the stylistic characteristics of the figures on the coin, and also on the artistic merit of the coin as a whole. For example, to date almost all the coins throughout

the world are machine made. Hence, the designs on these coins are clear and the edges of the coins are smooth. But prior to the seventeenth-eighteenth centuries AD, all the coins were handmade. On such coins, one or more of the devices or legends were often partially out of the flan. Also, the edges of these coins were often sharp or irregular. It is interesting to note that around the eighteenth century—the period of transition from handmade to machine made coins—certain coin types were produced by both these processes (Plates 1, 2, 3, 4). One such coin is the copper *Amman Kāśu* issued by the Tondaimān rulers of the kingdom of Pudukkottai in Tamil Nadu. This coin portrays Goddess Bṛhadāmbā or Pārvatī, the tutelary deity of the Tondaimān rulers, on the obverse, and the legend *vijaya* in Telugu on the reverse. On such coin-types produced by two totally different procedures, the effect of the minting process on the appearance of the varied devices and legends, and the general aesthetic value of the coin is startlingly discernible.

5. Study of the 'coin' within the overall context of the art and socio-cultural conditions of the period, tracing
   a. relationships between the devices/motifs on coins and those on other mediums of art (medals, seals, jewellery, sculptures and paintings). For example, the Nāyak rulers of Ikkeri or Keḷadi in Karnataka (sixteenth century AD) issued coins bearing the mythical bird *gaṇḍabhērunḍa* in imitation of the same type minted by the Vijayanagara monarch Achyutarāya (AD 1530-42); the same *gaṇḍabhērunḍa* is carved on the ceiling of the Virabhadra Temple of Keḷadi built by the Keḷadi Nāyaks.
   b. references to the devices/motifs in literature and epigraphs. For example, the Kannada work *Mānaumichaupada* refers to the beautiful Bālakṛṣṇa type coins of the renowned Vijayanagara monarch Kṛṣṇadēvarāya (AD 1509-29) as *Beṇṇemuddenāṇya* (coin of lump of butter), alluding to the ball of butter prominently featured in the hand of the god-child Kṛṣṇa on this coin. The *Mānaumichaupada* also mentions another coin called *Tirupati Haṇa* (Tirupati coin). This coin is the Veṅkaṭēśvara type minted by Kṛṣṇadēvarāya. The coin features Veṅkaṭēśvara, the presiding deity of the famous temple at Tirumala-Tirupati in Andhra Pradesh. Here, the Lord is standing below the

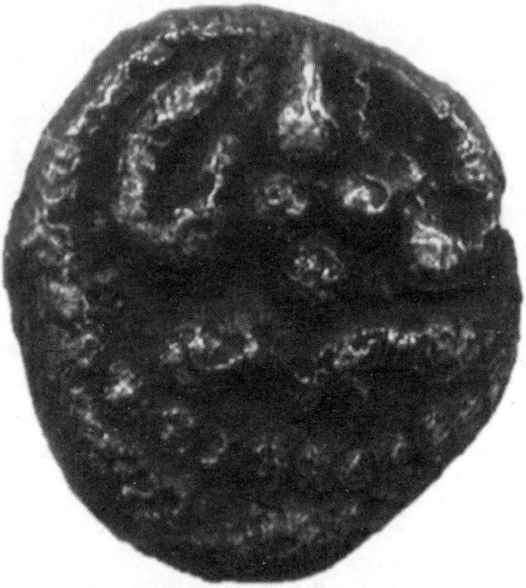

Plate 1: Pudukkottai *Amman Kāśu* (handmade)—obverse.

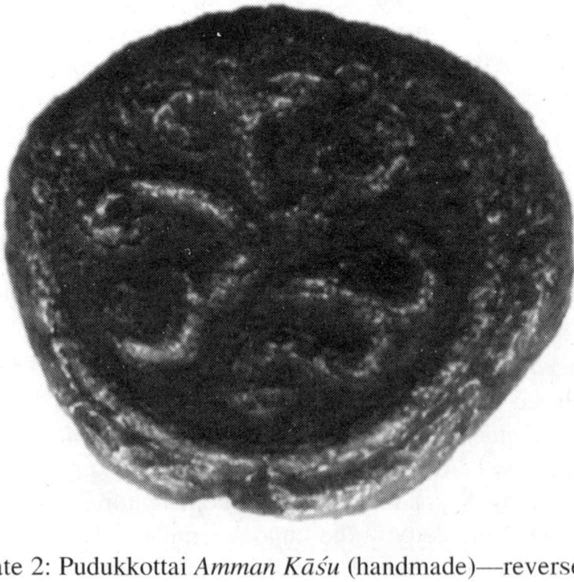

Plate 2: Pudukkottai *Amman Kāśu* (handmade)—reverse.

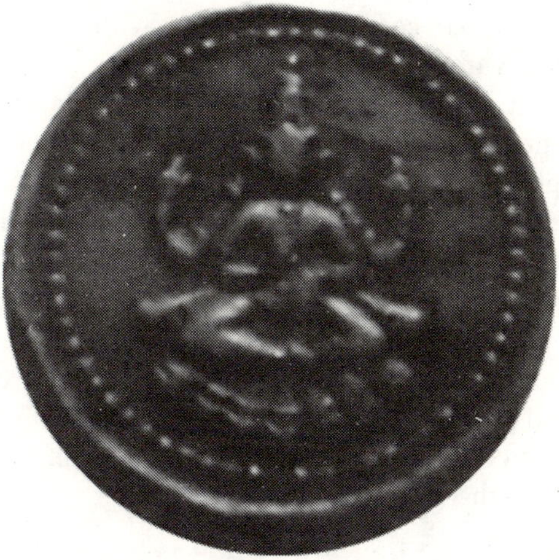

Plate 3: Pudukkottai *Amman Kāśu* (machine made)—obverse.

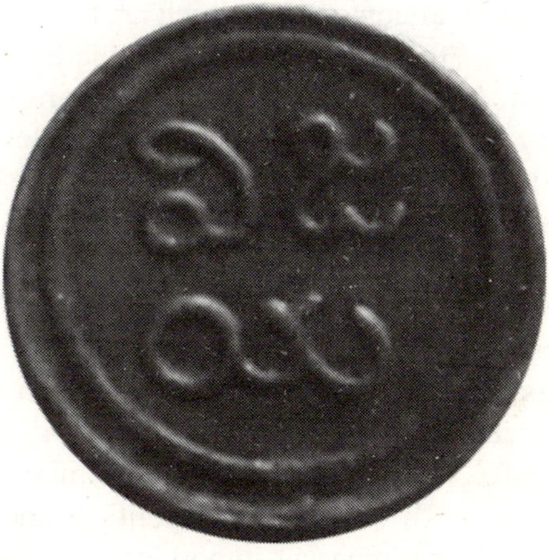

Plate 4: Pudukkottai *Amman Kāśu* (machine made)—reverse.

makara-tōraṇa. It is said that this coin was specially minted to commemorate Kṛṣṇadēvarāya's performance of the *kanakābhiṣēka* ceremony (bathing with gold coins) of Lord Veṅkaṭēśvara.

6. Assessment of the extent to which each of the coin-series exercised its influence on and, in turn, was influenced by other series/types of coinage, both indigenous and foreign. The 'influences' pertain to choice of devices, stylistic characteristics, minting technology, fabric, size and weight-standard. The coins of south India exercised their impact on and were subject to influences from the coins of western and northern India, and Sri Lanka as well. The Roman coins, too, circulated in south India during the early historical period and greatly influenced the native currency of south India. In turn, the coins of south India had a profound influence on the coins of South-East Asia.

NUMISMATIC ART: A NUMISMATOGRAPHICAL SURVEY

The recent decades have seen the emergence of new directions, conceptual frameworks, methodologies and fields of super specialization in the study of South Asian history and archaeology.[1] In the field of art-history, for example, it is now being increasingly realized that art is to be studied not as an isolated and static phenomenon but within the framework of the complex socio-cultural, economic and political contexts in which art forms evolved.[2]

Numismatics has, for long, been a 'poor, isolated cousin' of history and archaeology. In recent years, however, there has been a very slow but steady increase in the use of numismatics as a source of history. The recent revolutionary changes in the methodological approaches in historical and archaeological research are also gradually trickling down to numismatic studies.[3] Thus, numismatography is a major area of concern and interest not only to the numismatist but also the historian and the archaeologist.

Coins are, as indicated earlier, utility objects mostly produced by the state for use in day-to-day transactions, long-distance trade and, sometimes, as gifts. Hence, not surprisingly, numismatics has mainly been used for the study of economic, political and administrative histories. Although the apparent importance of the study of art in coinage, i.e. numismatic art, has, for long, been well-appreciated, the discipline is a 'newcomer' and a 'latecomer' to the international academic arena.

The actual study of numismatic art is still in its infancy, especially in India. The discipline has not attracted the attention of most scholars in the field. It has also not been included in the history and archaeology curriculum in our colleges and universities. The primary reason for this sorry state of affairs is that this little-known field of study, by its very nature, demands the researcher to be both a good art historian and a numismatist well-versed in minting technologies. Besides the discipline entails the minute physical examination of a very large number of coins in various museums and private collections. Such an exercise assumes special importance because the majority of coins are unpublished and, moreover, even in the case of published coins, the descriptions and photographs of the coins seldom reveal the tiny countermarks, and the subtle and minute stylistic characteristics of the obverse and reverse devices. This may be partially due to the low quality of the photographs and the poor quality of the paper on which they are printed. Also, unluckily, a few museums in India, for security reasons, do not provide facilities for the physical examination of their coin collections on such a large-scale and long-term basis. Further, many universities and museums simply do not have the expertise and resources for undertaking archaeo-chemical testing (micro-chemical analysis and atomic absorption spectroscopy) of coins, mainly to determine the precise minting process and the metallic composition of the coins.

The first studies on numismatic art were undertaken during the early years of the twentieth century in Europe, mainly in the U.K. Most of these studies were confined to ancient Roman coins. H. Mattingly's works (1920s; reprinted later) are among the most comprehensive publications on the subject. Mattingly's pioneering works formed the basis of many subsequent studies such as Laura Breglia's *Roman Imperial Coins: Their Art and Technique* (1968). The more recent British Museum publication (Jonathan Williams et al., eds., *Money: A History*, 1997) is an encyclopaedic survey of this museum's numismatic collections with special reference to numismatic art and technology.

B.S. Sitholey's little-known Paper (1948) on the art of Gupta coins may be regarded as one of the first-ever attempts to study Gupta numismatics, nay, Indian numismatics exclusively from the perspective of art. However, a serious and systematic study of the numismatic art of India was initiated in the 1960s by B.N. Mukherjee of the University of Calcutta. His area of interest was mainly the coinage of ancient and early medieval north India—Kuṣāṇa, Indo-Greek and Gupta (around 250 BC-AD 500). His findings are embodied in a series of monographs, the most important among which are *Nana on Lion: A Study in Kushana Numismatic Art* (1969), *Kushana Coins of the Land of the Five Rivers* (1978) and *Art in Gupta and Post-Gupta Coinages of Northern India* (1985). Mukherjee's *The Indian Gold: An Introduction to the Cabinet of the Gold Coins in the Indian Museum* (1990) also deals with the art in the coinage of different series, mainly of north India. Another publication on numismatic art is Chhanda Mukherjee's *Gupta Numismatic Art: An Artistic and Iconographic Study* (1991), based on her PhD research on the coins of the imperial Guptas at the University of Calcutta.

Although studies or books exclusively dealing with Indian numismatic art are very few, some numismatic publications incidentally include some aspects of numismatic art, often without mentioning the term 'numismatic art'. For instance, the study of different aspects of symbology and the anthropomorphic representation of deities on Indian coins has been studied by scholars such as W. Theobald (1890, 1901), A. Cunningham (1891), P.L. Gupta (1963), B. Chattopadhyaya (1967), O.P. Singh (1978) and Savita Sharma (1990).[4] Many of these works deal with the large number of symbols seen on the punch-marked coins of India. I.K. Sarma's *Coinage of the Satavahana Empire* (1980) has brief descriptions of the technique and art of the coins of this important dynasty. C. Sivaramamurti's comparatively little-known book *Numismatic Parallels of Kālidāsa* (1945, rpt. 1983) is a pioneering attempt to trace parallels between the renowned Sanskrit poet-dramatist Kālidāsa's poetic descriptions of nature and human nature, and the symbols, objects and scenes exhibited on various early Indian coins, mainly the coins of the imperial Guptas in whose times the poet lived. *Technology of Indian Coinage* by B.N. Mukherjee and P.K.D. Lee (1988) is a unique book dealing with the long history of numismatic technology in India, with some references to the art in coinage. This volume also details the technical constraints of numismatic art. Prashant Srivastava's

Aspects of Ancient Indian Numismatics (1996) mainly focuses on the commemorative medallions and victory medals from the time of Alexander (fourth century BC) down to the age of the Guptas, with brief references to the artistic value of these objects.

With a view to training a band of young scholars in the newly-emerging discipline of Indian numismatic art, the Indira Gandhi National Centre for the Arts (IGNCA), New Delhi, initiated a three-year documentation project (1991-4) entitled 'Numismatic Art of India: Documentation of Materials', with B.N. Mukherjee as the Project-Director and R.C. Sharma, former Director-General, National Museum, New Delhi, as the Project-Consultant. I was one of the full-time Research Fellows for the project. The main contribution of the project has been the creation of a computerized database pertaining to the most well-preserved Indian coins qualifying as art objects, in various museums and private collections in India and abroad. The results of the project are currently being published as a series of four volumes, featuring essays on and illustrations of the most artistic coins of specific dynasties/regions. The first two volumes of the series have been released (Mukherjee, 2007).

The above IGNCA project initiated, for the first time ever, albeit to a limited extent, the documentation of certain medieval south Indian coins, mainly Vijayanagara coins (fourteenth-seventeenth centuries AD), qualifying as art objects. This project led to the publication of a series of research papers by me.[5]

OBJECTIVES, SCOPE AND METHODOLOGY OF THE PRESENT STUDY

The above historiographical survey reveals that so far, studies on Indian numismatic art and symbology are mostly confined to the coins of north India. Hence, when I was working on the IGNCA project, B.N. Mukherjee repeatedly suggested to me the idea of a comprehensive study of the art in the coins of the earliest dynasties of south India. The present study was thus conceptualized with the guidance and inspiration received from B.N. Mukherjee, I. Mahadevan and other senior scholars.

The basic objective of the present study has been to systematically document and analyse the numismatic art and technology of ancient south India, up to and including the Pallava period. The primary focus of the study is numismatic art, while numismatic technology has been studied in relation to its effect on numismatic art. The geographical area covered under the present study includes the four southern states—Andhra Pradesh, Tamil Nadu, Kerala and Karnataka—and the union territory of Pondicherry. The period covered ranges from about 300 BC to AD 850, i.e. from the beginning of coinage in south India till the decline of the Pallavas. The study thus includes the coinage of the punch-marked series, Sangam Cheras, Sangam Cōḷas, Sangam Pāṇḍyas, Malaiyamāns, Kalabhras, Sātavāhanas, Ikṣvākus, Viṣṇukuṇḍins and, finally, the Pallavas. The choice of this rather long historical period for the present study was mainly, but not exclusively, because all these coin series exhibit a host of common characteristics with regard to weight standard, obverse and reverse devices, and style. Further, all the above south Indian dynastic issues, except perhaps those of the Pallavas and to a lesser extent, the Viṣṇukuṇḍins, circulated along with the *kārṣāpaṇas* and the Roman coins, and have been greatly influenced by these two coin series. The Pallava coins represent a 'transition' from the ancient to the medieval numismatic tradition, characterized by a more refined die-striking method of minting, different obverse and reverse motifs and weight standard, and a profusion of legends in different scripts.

It was felt that the present study would be of special academic significance as it pertains to a new field of study which is virtually unknown in universities and other institutions of higher learning in India, B.N. Mukherjee being the sole Indian scholar to have done significant research in the subject. By documenting the symbols and art motifs, and their stylistic features as seen on various coins, and investigating the extent to which these motifs and stylistic features appear in other mediums of art, the present study may also be expected to provide some fresh insights into the origin and development of numismatic art and, to a lesser extent, other forms of art, in south India, mainly Tamiḷakam. This aspect of the study would be of particular interest to art historians and numismatists as the earliest coins of the southernmost part of India, especially those of the three main Tamil kingdoms—Sangam Chera, Sangam Cōḷa and Sangam Pāṇḍya—have, until recently, not been recovered in large numbers, and hence, never been subjected to an in-depth analysis, from any perspective—technical, artistic or even historical. In this context, it may be noted that hoards containing issues of these kings are very rare, the only notable exception being the Aṇḍipaṭṭi hoard (Tamil Nadu) of 143 lead coins. The recent discoveries of such dynastic issues are mostly those found on the banks of rivers, and rarely, stratified finds. The only publication, in English, exclusively dealing with these coins is R. Krishnamurthy's *Sangam Age Tamil Coins* (1997). This is mainly an illustrated catalogue of the coins in his personal collection.

The objectives and scope of the present study necessitated the use of varied source materials. The project commenced with a study of the recent anthropological works dealing with new conceptual frameworks within which one could study art objects. Thereafter, the study of the art in the relevant coins was undertaken in two stages:

Stage I: On the basis of the published descriptions and illustrations of the various coins. It may be noted that a few coin types are known to us exclusively through the writings of the nineteenth- and early twentieth-centuries scholars such as Walter Elliot and T. Desikachari. Actual specimens of these types are, to date, unknown in any public or private collection.

Stage II: Physical examination of the coins in different museums and private collections in south India, Sri Lanka, U.K. and the National Museum in New Delhi. This formed the most interesting and original component of the present study mainly because a substantial number of these ancient coins have hitherto not been catalogued or published.

In each of the collections, as far as possible, the most well-preserved coins of each type/series were chosen for documentation and study, unless, of course, the coin was a very rare or unique specimen. While a broken coin is as good as a well-preserved coin for the study of political and economic history, for the purposes of art history, a broken and worn-out coin is comparable to a mutilated sculpture or a faded painting.

Several museums granted access to their archives and records. Interesting information about many recent, little-known and unpublished coin finds, and the technical aspects of the coins, was obtained through correspondence and personal discussions with museum curators, coin collectors, field archaeologists and metallurgists. A few new sites and coins were discovered during the course of field explorations in Kerala, Tamil Nadu, Pondicherry and coastal Andhra.

Apart from the above study of the coins, coin-photographs and coin-descriptions, literary works and inscriptions referring to coins, and coin motifs have also been consulted. Among the literary sources, the most important are the Tamil Sangam works. The use of this remarkable corpus of poems for historical research is, however, a hazardous exercise because the poems were composed and compiled by varied individuals at different times from 300 BC to AD 300. Being primarily bardic literature eulogizing kings, queens and nobles, its concern with art and coins is incidental. Nevertheless, it does provide some information on the coins that circulated in south India during those days and more significantly, limited descriptions of some of the art motifs and devices seen on these coins.

As regards stone and copper-plate inscriptions of various dynasties, these rarely refer to coins or coin motifs. However, these records are most useful for comparing their script and calligraphy with those of the legends on the coins of the respective dynasties.

Non-numismatic art historical evidences, mainly architectural and sculptural relics in stone, are very few for the Tamil Sangam kingdoms but exist in sizeable quantities for the Sātavāhanas, Ikṣvākus and Pallavas. However, we have sizeable quantities of archaeological relics such as potsherds and seals pertaining to all these dynasties. Rarely though, these archaeological relics exhibit symbols and motifs comparable to those on coins. Wherever possible, a comparison of the styles and themes of the art in stone, pottery and seals with that of the art in coinage of each period/dynasty has been attempted.

At this stage, the subtle differences in the meanings of the three terms, i.e. 'symbol', 'art motif' and 'device', as used in the present volume, may be explained. A symbol is a design or object which stands for or suggests something else. The reasons for the origin and use of different symbols may be associated with religious traditions or the existence of some sort of 'connection' or 'relationship', including accidental physical resemblance between the relevant symbol and the object which the symbol is supposed to represent. In the field of numismatics, the term 'art motif' is, not infrequently, used to convey the meaning of the 'symbol' but it should be remembered that a 'motif' need not always stand for or represent some other object or idea. Moreover, usually when a 'motif' is depicted on a coin or, for that matter, on any other medium of art including sculptures and paintings, the aim is 'artistic', i.e. to enhance the 'visual appeal' of the object on which the 'motif' occurs. However, this is not always true of the portrayal of symbols on coins or sculptures. The concept of 'device' is very different from both the 'symbol' and the 'motif'. A 'device' may refer to any object, animate or inanimate, seen on a coin; thus, the 'device' sometimes includes even the 'motifs' and the 'symbols' appearing on coins. For example, the '*svastika*-device'.

As regards the 'obverse' and 'reverse' sides of a coin, in the case of certain very ancient coins with symbols and devices on both sides, it is often difficult and confusing to precisely pinpoint the side that is the obverse. And there is no unanimity amongst scholars in this regard. The present volume largely follows the system or identifications stated in the majority of earlier writings on different coin series. For instance, in the case of the Sangam Chera, Sangam Cōḷa and Sangam Pāṇḍya coins, the side bearing the royal emblem is considered to be the reverse. But in the case of the majority of the Pallava coins, the side featuring the dynastic crest (lion or bull) is taken to be the obverse. In the case of coins bearing legends, if these occur only on one side of the coin, then that side is generally taken to be the obverse.

Throughout this volume, the name 'India', has often been used to denote not only the present republic of India but the entire Indian subcontinent, viz., Afghanistan, Pakistan, India and Bangladesh. One may note that modern political boundaries bear hardly any relevance to studies concerning the very early period of our history. Similarly, in the case of many cities and districts whose names have recently been changed, this book uses their older names which are better-known. Another reason for using these older names is that many of the publications and archaeological reports used in this study stick to the older names. For example, the names of the two major Indian cities, Bombay and Madras, have, some years ago, been changed to

Mumbai and Chennai, respectively. However, this volume retains their earlier names, viz., Bombay and Madras. Diacritical marks have not been used for well-known as well as modern names of places and persons, as also on the maps.

Each of the nine major chapters (chapters 2 to 10) in this volume deal with the art in the coinage of a particular series/dynasty of ancient south India. The punch-marked coins too have been included in the present study because of the following two reasons:

1. A large number of symbols on the punch-marked coins have been borrowed and used on the coins and other mediums of art by early south Indian dynasties.
2. A few varieties of the *kārṣāpaṇas*, from the finds at Amaravati (Andhra) and some other sites in Andhra-Tamil Nadu, are unknown anywhere outside south India. This proves that the minting of *kārṣāpaṇas* was well known in the south and also that some of the 'new varieties' of this coin-type, which may be regarded as the 'innovations' of the people of south India, were so 'localized' in their circulation that they never travelled far beyond the region where they were minted and definitely not north of the Vindhyas.

Each chapter commences with a brief historical introduction of the period in which the relevant coins were minted. This is followed by detailed discussions on the physical features, production method, art and symbology of the coins. As regards the chapter on Pallava coins, besides the historical introduction, an outline of the development of Pallava art is also included. The reason for this is that among all the major coin-series discussed in this book, the Pallava coins alone bear an amazing variety of symbols and devices, for which one can trace striking and definite similarities and parallels in other mediums of Pallava art, mainly stone sculptures. The details of these similarities and parallels have also been discussed in this chapter.

In the case of minor and little-known dynasties and feudatories, the number and the varieties or types of coins are not very large. Hence, these coins are not discussed in separate chapters. Instead, they are mostly discussed in one of the chapters dealing with a coin series closely related to these minor dynasties coins in time, space and style. For example, the coins of the Śālaṅkāyanas are included in the chapters on the Viṣṇukuṇḍin and Pallava coins.

The epilogue summarizes the conclusions derived from the study.

Photographs, charts and maps have been included, wherever appropriate. While discussing specific coins and coin-related objects, the relevant illustration numbers have been indicated within brackets.

It is sincerely hoped that this volume will be of academic interest, more for the new ideas and problems that it raises than for the fresh interpretations and conclusions that it has to offer.

NOTES AND REFERENCES

1. Examples of works revealing these new approaches and methodologies include F.R. Allchin et al., *The Archaeology of Early Historic South Asia: The Emergence of Cities and States* (Cambridge, 1995); T.R.Venugopalan, ed., *History and Theory: National Seminar Papers* (Thrissur, 1997).
2. Specimens of art historical studies based on this new approach include Asimakrishna Dasa, *Evening Blossoms: The Temple Tradition of Sāñjhī in Vṛndāvana* (New Delhi, 1996); Carmel Berkson, *The Life of Form in Indian Sculpture* (New Delhi, 2000); D.K. Chandra, *The Mystery of Art* (Delhi, 1995); Elisabeth Beck, compiled, *Sri Aurobindo on Indian Art: Selections from His Writings* (Ahmedabad, 1999); Josef James, ed., *Contemporary Indian Sculpture: An Algebra of Figuration* (Madras, 1998).
3. See Olivier Guillaume, *Analysis of Reasonings in Archaeology: The Case of Graeco-Bactrian and Indo-Greek Numismatics* (New Delhi, 1990); Osmund Bopearachchi, *Indo-Greek, Indo-Scythian and Indo-Parthian Coins in the Smithsonian Institution* (Washington, D.C., 1993).
4. For a good bibliography of these works, see Savita Sharma, *Early Indian Symbols: Numismatic Evidence* (Delhi, 1990), pp. ix-xv, 239-49.
5. S. Suresh, 'Vishnu in South Indian Coinage', in G. Kamalakar, ed., *Vishnu in Art, Thought and Literature* (Hyderabad, 1993), pp. 273-8; idem, 'Recent Archaeological Discoveries and Studies in Tamil Nadu', *Quarterly Bulletin of the School of Historical and Cultural Studies, Calcutta*, I 3-4 (1994-5), pp.11-16; idem, 'Numismatic Studies: New Methodologies and Approaches (Summary of Presidential Address delivered at the Seminar of the Madras Coin Society)', *MCS, Chennai—Special Bulletin* VIII (2001), pp. 1-3; idem, 'Countermarks on Roman Coins Found in India: Context, Chronology and Significance', *Indian History Congress: Proceedings of the LXII Session,* (2002), pp. 976-85; idem, 'Kārtikeya in Early Indian Coinage', in K.V. Ramesh et al., eds., *Śrī Puṣpāñjali (Recent Researches in Prehistory, Protohistory, Art, Architecture, Numismatics, Iconography and Epigraphy) Dr. C.R. Srinivasan Commemoration Volume* I (Delhi, 2004), pp. 95-102; idem, 'A Note on the Temple Tokens of Late Medieval South India', *MCS, Chennai—Special Bulletin* XI (2004), pp. 162-6; idem, 'The Devarāja Concept

in Ancient Tamiḷakam: Numismatic and Art Historical Evidences', in Arputha Rani Sengupta, ed., *God and King: The Devarāja Cult in South Asian Art and Architecture* (New Delhi, 2005), pp. 129-37; idem, 'Numismatic Art: A Survey With Special Reference to South India', in P. Chenna Reddy, ed., *Mahāsenasiri: Riches of Indian Archaeological and Cultural Studies (A Felicitation Volume in Honour of Dr. I.K. Sarma)* II (Delhi, 2006), pp. 525-8; idem, 'Devices on the Coins of Far South of the Early Centuries AD', in B.N. Mukherjee, ed., *Numismatic Art of India:* Vol. I: *Historical and Aesthetic Perspectives* (New Delhi, 2007), pp. 199-210. Also see Prema Kasturi and S. Suresh, 'Women in Coinage: A Socio-iconographic Study with Special Reference to South India', *MCS, Chennai—Special Bulletin* XI (2004), pp. 235-44.

CHAPTER 2

Punch-marked Coins with Special Reference to the Finds in South India

Punch-marked coins, as is well known, represent India's earliest numismatic issues. These coins are popularly known as *kārṣāpaṇas*. Pāṇini (fourth century BC), the great Indian grammarian, was the first to use this term for them. Kauṭilya's *Arthaśāstra* (fourth century BC) refers to these coins as *paṇa*. The Buddhist *Jātakas* (fourth-first centuries BC) refer to these coins as *kahapaṇa*.

Numismatists have classified the punch-marked coins into two broad categories:

1. The *Janapada* series or local series that was believed to have circulated in a limited area. The term 'local series' may be preferred because, in recent decades, there have been discoveries of new varieties of punch-marked coins confined to certain regions of south India where *janapadas* did not exist. These finds have been discussed towards the end of this chapter.
2. The Imperial series minted in many parts of India, probably on instructions from a strong central authority.

The punch-marked coins circulated as currency in different parts of the subcontinent from around the sixth century BC to the first century BC, and in some places, especially in south India, even up to the first century AD and slightly later. Thus, they were the principal currency of the Mauryan empire (fourth-second centuries BC).[1] Obviously, they were first produced in north India and they travelled to south India through traders, and Buddhist and Jain monks and pilgrims. Subsequently, they were produced in south India too. Not surprisingly, finds of punch-marked coins are more numerous and represent a wider variety of symbols and motifs in north India than in the south. But contrary to popular belief, the finds in south India are not negligible or insignificant.

In south India, the Andhra-Karnataka region, which was on the southern fringes of the far-flung Mauryan empire, has yielded several large hoards of punch-marked coins. The major hoards from this region include Karimnagar, Nasthullapur, Amaravati, Singavaram and Weepangandla in Andhra Pradesh, Raichur, Gulbarga and, more recently, Chikka Sindogi in Karnataka. Besides, such coins occur in a stratified context in excavated sites such as Amaravati, Kondapur, Bhattipprolu, Vaddamanu, Salihundam, Gudimallam and Veerapuram in Andhra, and Maski, Chandravalli, Banavasi and Vadagaon Madhavapur in Karnataka.

Even in the extreme south (Tamil Nadu-Kerala), which was definitely outside the limits of the Mauryan empire, several interesting hoards of punch-marked coins have been discovered. The major hoards from Tamil Nadu include Mambalam, Kayadi, Navalai, Pennar, Tondamanathan, Bodinayakkanur and Virasigamani. The important hoards from Kerala are Kottayam (or Elikulamkara), Eyyal, Maala and Angamali (or Kodussery). In the stratified context, significant finds of punch-marked coins come from Kaveripumpattinam, Kodumanal, TKallupatti, Alagankulam and Korkai in Tamil Nadu. The precise stratigraphy of the punch-marked coins reported from the excavated site of Bandar Pattinam, not too far from Tanjavur in Tamil Nadu, is not clear.

Besides the hoard finds and the stratified finds, stray occurrences of punch-marked coins are known from scores of sites in south India, mainly in Andhra and Tamil Nadu. The finds are heavily concentrated around Duvvuru and Nellore in Andhra (close to the Tamil Nadu border), and Tirukoilur and Karur in Tamil Nadu. Very recently, a surface-find of a batch of six punch-marked coins has been reported from Ramanathapuram, close to Ramesvaram (Tamil Nadu), almost on the peninsular tip of India. Tamil Nadu has even yielded these coins within megalithic graves in places such as Chavadipalaiyam near Coimbatore. Many of these stray finds have not been published and are now in private hands.[2]

Even the island of Sri Lanka has yielded thousands of punch-marked coins. For instance, Anuradhapura, an extensive early historical site of the island, has revealed such coins in a stratified context. Ancient inscriptions in the island refer to the use of these coins in those regions. The earliest such inscription is a Brāhmī epigraph of the late third century BC.[3]

PHYSICAL FEATURES AND PRODUCTION METHOD

The punch-marked coins are generally made of silver and rarely, of copper. Even the silver coins are often alloyed with copper, with a minor percentage of lead and iron.[4] As regards the source of the metals for these coins, copper and iron deposits were known in many places in the subcontinent, especially the Magadha region in eastern India where some of the earliest punch-marked coins were produced. Lead-silver mines existed in Afghanistan, Rajpura-Dariba, Rampura-Agucha and Zawar in Rajasthan, Ambamata and Banaskantha in Gujarat, and Agnigundala, Bandlamattu and Gavulabhavi in Andhra Pradesh.

To make these coins, the metal, together with the alloying materials, was first melted in a crucible and the molten metal was left to cool as a lump or was cast into thin flat sheets. In the case of a lump, it was later beaten out into flat sheets. The thickness of these sheets varied from 0.01 to 0.1 inches (0.3 cm). These sheets were then cut into long strips from which quadrangular blanks of the approximate desired weight were cut. For obtaining the precise weight, the blanks were clipped at the edges. This made many of the coins irregular in shape, with the edges sometimes sharp and uneven. This explains the occurrence of the *kārṣāpaṇas* in a wide variety of shapes such as square, rectangular, circular, oval and elliptical. Rarely, metal, equal to the weight of a coin, was melted and poured on the ground or on a flat board or plate, to take its own shape for a coin.

The scrap clippings from the blanks were not thrown away or wasted. They were eventually collected and melted, and globules or pellets of the desired weight were fashioned out of the molten metal. These globules were later flattened with a hammer and thus, they were converted into blanks for more coins.

As regards the silver-coated copper punch-marked coins, a slightly different method seems to have been adopted for their production. This method is called 'silver amalgam'. In this method, the copper flans were dipped into an amalgam of silver dissolved in mercury and then gently heated to just above the boiling point of mercury (357 °C). At this point, the mercury gets separated and the silver is left behind as a coating on the copper flans.

The *kārṣāpaṇa*-makers appear to have taken great care to maintain the weight standard of the coins. In fact, the name *kārṣāpaṇa* is believed to have been derived from the words *kārṣā* meaning 'a measure of weight' and *apaṇa* meaning 'custom or use', implying that the weight of the coins was decided by custom or usage. Thus, one can see distinct variations in the weight of coins produced in different regions and at different times. There has even been an opinion that the earlier coins (pre-Mauryan and early Mauryan) are larger and thinner, while the later coins (middle Mauryan and late Mauryan) are slightly smaller and thicker.[5] Many mint-fresh coins, with no traces of wear and tear, weigh around 3.3 grams. Coins as heavy as 7 grams and more have been reported. However, many of the *kārṣāpaṇas* have worn thin due to a long period of circulation as money and, hence, are of very low weight, sometimes less than half a gram.

Symbols were stamped on the blanks to transform them into coins. Probably, the blanks were heated slightly before the symbols were stamped. The symbols were stamped, one after the other, at various points on the blank, with punches, each punch having one distinct symbol. Hence, the popular name 'punch-marked coin'(Plates 5, 6).

Now, after deciding the symbols to be featured on the coins, how did the ancient people arrive at this idea of stamping or punching these symbols on the metal blanks? According to P.L. Gupta, the idea may have been borrowed from the branding of cattle during the later Vedic period (1000-600 BC)[6]—precisely the period when the first *kārṣāpaṇas* were manufactured. Significantly, prior to the advent of the *kārṣāpaṇas*, cattle was a form of wealth or currency used in commercial transactions by the people of north India. Thus, one may infer that around this time, people decided to replace cattle currency with the simpler and handier metal currency but, naturally, wanted to 'brand' the metal currency with the same symbols used for branding cattle.

The stamping of the symbols sometimes changed the very shape of the blank or the coin. If the blank was very small and was struck very hard with a single punch, the resultant coin would be a saucer-shaped or cup-shaped coin. If a bar-shaped coin was struck very hard with two punches at the two ends, it would naturally bend in the middle forming a bent-bar coin.

It was originally believed that all the punch-marked coins were manufactured by the above punching process. However, some

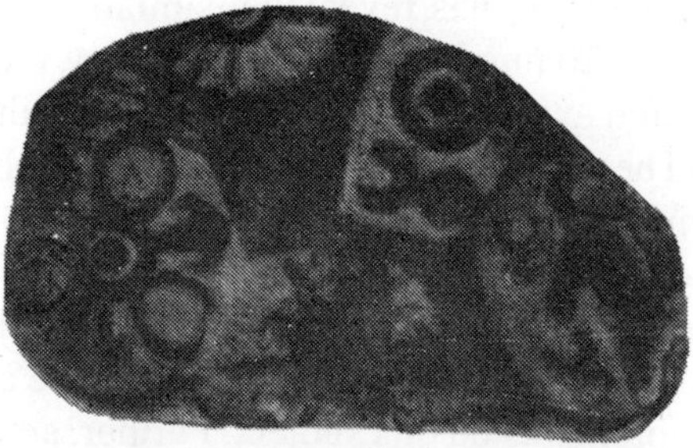

Plate 5: *Kārṣāpaṇa*—obverse.

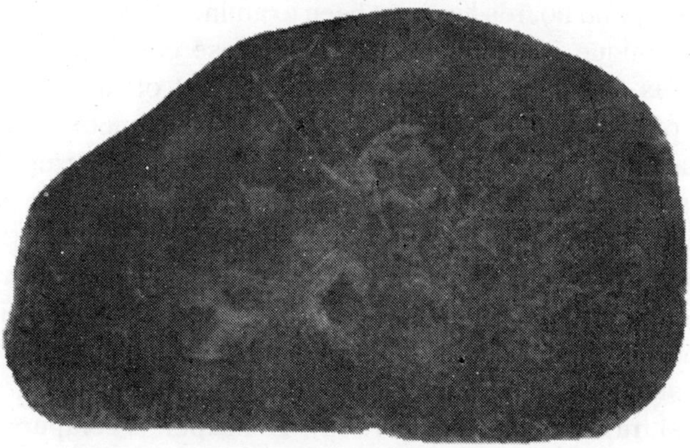

Plate 6: *Kārṣāpaṇa*—reverse.

archaeological discoveries and archaeo-chemical studies on these coins have revealed that at least some of them were produced by the casting method and a few of them, by the die-striking method.

First, we may turn our attention to the meagre evidences for the production of some *kārṣāpaṇas* by the die-striking process. There has been a unique discovery from Eran (ancient Airakaṇya) in Madhya Pradesh of a broken bronze die used for the manufacture of *kārṣāpaṇas*.[7] The die is endowed with a bevelled edge all around the 'top', and a 'hollow' at the back to keep in position the iron punch which was meant to receive the blow of the hammer. The extremely rough surface of the 'hollow' indicates the use of the die for a very long period of time. The extant portion of the die displays, in negative, the designs of the sun with a taurine at the top, an animal standing or running to the left, probably on a hill, and a six-armed symbol.

Karur (in Tamil Nadu) has revealed a similar *kārṣāpaṇa* bronze die, 9 mm thick and 20 mm in diameter.[8] The front face of the die is slightly cracked and extremely worn-out, indicating that the die was intensely used. The reverse impression of three symbols—the sun, a six-armed symbol and a dog(?) on an arched hill—all within a prominent circular depression, are discernible on the die.

Why were the *kārṣāpaṇas* sometimes produced by the die-striking method? The evidences of the dies mentioned above are too slender for any general comments on this subject. Further, actual specimens of *kārṣāpaṇas* made by this method have, till date, not been unequivocally identified, although it must be remembered that some of the *kārṣāpaṇa* hoards have not been examined from the viewpoint of the technique of the manufacture of these coins. In these circumstances, one may infer that, at some point of time, when the practice of die-striking coins had commenced, attempts were made to produce *kārṣāpaṇas* too by this process. These attempts were soon discontinued because various dynastic issues were slowly replacing the *kārṣāpaṇas* as legal tender.

As regards the use of the casting method for the *kārṣāpaṇas*, the evidences are more solid and varied, the most clinching evidence being the discovery of terracotta moulds of the *kārṣāpaṇas* from several sites such as Mathura and Jhusi (Uttar Pradesh), Adam (Maharashtra), Sisupalgarh (Orissa), Kondapur, Veerapuram and Dhulikatta (Andhra Pradesh), and Kanchi (Tamil Nadu).[9] Among them, no information is available about the find from Jhusi. Even with regard to most of the other finds, the information available is often limited and sketchy, probably because the discoverers or excavators of these objects initially did not consider these moulds to be of much historical value.

Mathura has yielded over ten coin moulds. These are round discs made from fine red-coloured baked clay. Some of these discs have coin sockets on one side while the other side is plain. Other discs have coin sockets on both sides. Thus, the complete coin mould may have consisted of at least three discs, the middle disc bearing coin sockets on both sides, while the outer discs bore coin sockets on their inner face and had a blank outer face. The precise date of these moulds are not known.

At Adam, the moulds have been recovered from stratified layers.

These fragmentary moulds are made of burnt clay, dark grey in colour. The symbols within the coin sockets are not clearly seen.

The two moulds from Sisupalgarh were also found in a stratified context. These are round discs made of grey-coloured clay. While one of the moulds is complete, the other is a fragment. Each mould shows coin sockets on one face while the other face is blank. These moulds, dated to AD 300, are more worn-out than the Mathura moulds. Obviously, the Sisupalgarh moulds were used for a longer time than the Mathura moulds.

Kondapur, a significant early historical mint town, has yielded fifty-four fragments of coin moulds in a stratified context. All of them are made of baked clay. Most of them are light buff in colour while a few are grey-coloured. They appear to have been round discs of different sizes. Most of the coin sockets are very worn and it is difficult to precisely identify the symbols on them. Stratigraphically, these moulds are dated to the second century AD.

The mould from Dhulikatta, another ancient mint town, is again from stratified deposits and is rectangular in shape. It possesses sixteen matrices for casting the *kārṣāpaṇa*-type coins. The matrices are of various shapes such as circular, oval, square and rectangular. The incuses are connected by small channels originating from a main channel to carry molten metal. The precise date of this mould is not clear.

The two moulds from Kanchi are not very widely-known. They have also been recovered in a stratified context. They are made of grey-coloured clay. One of them is a discular mould with four complete coin-matrices and two partially damaged ones, all the matrices being square-shaped. In its full form, the mould would have had six matrices and measured 6 cm in diameter. The distribution of the molten metal to each of the matrices seems to have been through narrow channels. The symbols representing the sun and the bull have been identified in one of the matrices. These symbols are the reverse impressions of the same ones seen on several of the punch-marked coins. The second mould from Kanchi, also a fragmentary one, has been unearthed from a spot close to the Jvarahareśvara temple of the city. The extant portion of this mould boasts of one coin matrice in full and three others in broken condition. All these matrices appear to be square in shape. One of the broken matrices exhibits two symbols—an elephant and the taurine symbol. The back portion of both the Kanchi moulds is plain, suggesting that these moulds may have been the bottom or top plates of one bunch of moulds used for producing the coins.

Besides the above *kārṣāpaṇa* moulds from different parts of India, such finds are now being reported from Sri Lanka as well.[10] For example, a terracotta *kārṣāpaṇa* mould has been recovered in a stratified context at Gedige (Anuradhapura) in the northern part of Sri Lanka. The mould belongs to the first-second century AD. This fragmentary mould has sockets for rectangular, circular and oval-shaped coins. The edge of the mould is slightly raised to form a rim. The mould is extremely worn-out but faint traces of the sun and elephant motifs can be seen. It has been observed that the sockets would have been made by pressing punch-marked coins on to the wet clay. The worn-out condition of the symbols in the sockets has again been stated to be the result of the use of worn-out *kārṣāpaṇas* for creating the impressions in the sockets.

Akurugoda in Sri Lanka has yielded at least two terracotta moulds. One mould has four matrices—each for a different imperial punch-marked coin. Of these four matrices, two are quadrangular, one circular and one oval-shaped. The symbols on the matrices are barely visible—one can see faint traces of the *caitya* and the six-armed symbols in one of the matrices. The molten metal reached the matrices through two prominent channels along the edge of the mould. The second mould from this site has three quadrangular matrices—each for a different imperial punch-marked coin. The symbols on these matrices are completely worn-out. The molten metal reached the matrices through a narrow channel.

Akurugoda has also revealed a unique broken rectangular stone mould containing eight matrices—six complete matrices and two broken at the edges. All the eight matrices are rectangular in shape. The symbols in the matrices are illegible. A long vertical channel is seen in the middle, with four matrices on either side of this channel. This central channel, at various points, branches into smaller channels that carry the molten metal to the various matrices. Unlike all the other *kārṣāpaṇa* moulds, this mould is made of stone and not terracotta and, hence, is unique. In any case, the Sri Lanka moulds are very similar to many of the moulds found in north India.

Many scholars have repeatedly expressed doubts about the

genuineness of the *kārṣāpaṇa* moulds. Scholars like Ajay Mitra Shastri have vehemently argued that the *kārṣāpaṇa* moulds are the contrivances of ancient forgers who unauthorizedly produced the coins for economic gain.[11]

According to P.L. Gupta, during the post-Mauryan period, various local rulers began to produce coins by the casting method.[12] With the introduction of this new currency and technique, minting of the traditional punch-marked coins slowly declined. But the *kārṣāpaṇas* continued to be accepted as legal tender for a few more centuries. At this point of time, the people conceived the idea of making *kārṣāpaṇas* by the casting process. This line of argument is supported by the fact that most of the *kārṣāpaṇa* moulds are dated to the first century BC or later.

A careful analysis of all the available evidence indicates that *kārṣāpaṇas* were legally produced by the casting method, on specific occasions, at certain places. Now for the specific evidences: Unlike a normal forger's equipment, the moulds are not confined to a particular site or group of sites or even a region but have been reported, often in a stratified context, from sites spread over several parts of the subcontinent from Mathura in the north down to Kanchi and Sri Lanka in the south. It is well known that by the first century AD, if not much earlier, the method of minting coins by the casting process had become very popular in India. Hence, it is plausible that some time during this period, the casting process, in addition to the usual punching technique, also began to be adopted for the manufacture of the *kārṣāpaṇas*, at least in some areas. The Indians could have refined their skills of casting coins by their contacts with Greeks and Romans. This is attested by the fact that there are similarities, in workmanship and construction, between the *kārṣāpaṇa* moulds and the coin moulds dated to the first century AD at Roman settlement sites in Europe and Africa.[13] Further, at Kondapur, the *kārṣāpaṇa* moulds occur in the same layers as the genuine official Sātavāhana and Western Kṣatrapa coin moulds. Even at Kanchi, the *kārṣāpaṇa* coin moulds have been recovered along with Sātavāhana coin moulds. This further proves that the *kārṣāpaṇa* moulds are genuine moulds because it is extremely unlikely for forgers' moulds to occur alongside the genuine coin moulds of the Sātavāhanas or any other ruling power. It is plausible that the cast *kārṣāpaṇas* were minted, along with the local dynastic issues by an authorized agency, probably in response to an increasing demand for the punch-marked coins in specific regions. In this connection, one may recall that the Sātavāhanas often used punch-marked coins as their silver currency, the silver issues of this dynasty being quite rare.

Kārṣāpaṇa specimens made by the casting process have also been discovered although none of the sites yielding the moulds have revealed such coins. Some examples are a single specimen of a cast *kārṣāpaṇa* which has been identified in the large Amaravati hoard (Andhra) of 7,688 *kārṣāpaṇas* and 20 cast *kārṣāpaṇas* seen in a hoard of over 400 *kārṣāpaṇas* now in the State Museum, Lucknow. The occurrence of the *kārṣāpaṇas* produced by the casting process, in association with the punch-marked coins manufactured by the usual punching technique, makes one infer that the former were treated on par with the latter and both these categories of coins were regular issues minted with royal sanction. Moreover, most of the figures and/or symbols on the *kārṣāpaṇa* moulds are stylistically similar to the figures on many of the first century BC punch-marked coins produced by the usual punching method.

The employment of the casting technique for the production of *kārṣāpaṇas* has recently been testified by the archaeo-chemical analysis conducted on a few of the punch-marked coins found at Tirukoilur in Tamil Nadu.[14] One of the coins from the site is a rectangular silver specimen with curved corners. The coin weighing 1.82 grams measures 1 cm × 1.75 cm and has a thickness of 1.5 mm. The metallographic structure of the coin, as revealed by etching the surface with potassium dichromate, is of the cast dendritic type, clearly indicating that casting was the technique of production of this coin. The composition of this coin is as follows:

Silver	-	70.81 per cent
Copper	-	25.00 per cent
Lead	-	1.25 per cent
Zinc	-	1.85 per cent

The strength and durability, i.e. the resistance to wear and tear of the coin has been increased by the deliberate addition of copper to silver. The presence of lead and zinc in the coin is explained by the fact that traces of these metals would have existed as impurities in the ores from which the silver and copper were extracted.

The second coin from Tirukoilur is a square copper issue and each side measures 1.5 cm. The coin weighs 1.82 grams and is 1.5 mm thick. Punch marks are seen on both the obverse and reverse of this corroded coin. The metallographic microstructure, as revealed by the polished unetched surface, is of dendritic type, again proving that the coin is a cast one. The spacings between the dendritic arms are large due to the slow cooling of the cast. The chemical composition of the coin, as determined by micro-chemical analysis and atomic absorption spectroscopy, is given below:

Copper	-	92.02 per cent
Silver	-	5.14 per cent
Lead	-	1.05 per cent
Zinc	-	1.08 per cent
Iron	-	0.30 per cent

The present coin is undoubtedly a copper imitation coated with silver. The lead, iron and zinc found in the coin are, most probably, impurities found in the silver ore. The coin may have been produced in or near its find-spot, i.e. Tirukoilur.

It is well known that each *kārṣāpaṇa* circulated as money for several centuries. Often, when the old symbols on the coin became effaced due to the long period of use, new symbols were stamped on it. It is plausible that a *kārṣāpaṇa,* initially made by the casting process, was, at a later date, after the original symbols on it had faded off, stamped with new symbols by the punching method.

Ancient forgeries of *kārṣāpaṇas* are not unknown. These imitation coins were made by both the usual punching as well as the casting methods. The employment of the former process for the making of forgeries is mentioned in the *Arthaśāstra* of Kauṭilya and several extant specimens of such forged *kārṣāpaṇas* produced by the usual punching technique have been identified.[15] Compared to the genuine *kārṣāpaṇas,* these imitations are lower in weight, poorer or debased in metallic content, and stylistically, too, are very different from the original coins. Some of these imitation *kārṣāpaṇas* seem to have been plated issues, i.e. a coating of silver was applied on the base metal core of the coin. The copper punch-marked coins reported from a number of sites are also sometimes believed to have been coins originally plated, the silver coating on which may have completely or partially peeled off when those coins were in use or even after they were finally buried or lost.

ART AND SYMBOLOGY

One may now note certain general features of art motifs and symbols on the punch-marked coins or *kārṣāpaṇas*. Many of these features are common to the finds in north India and south India.

General Features of Symbols and Motifs

The punch-marked coins are noted for the rich variety of symbols and motifs punched on them. If the coin has only one symbol, it is placed in the centre of the flan. When there are two symbols on a coin, they are placed side by side. When there are four symbols, they are normally in pairs of two symbols, one opposite the other. Many coins have five symbols placed haphazardly at various points on the flan. On some coins, the five symbols are placed one after the other, along the edge or rim of the flan.

Initially, the symbols were punched only on one side—the obverse—of the coin, while the reverse was left blank. There are, however, many instances where an old coin was revalidated by punching a symbol or a group of symbols on its reverse solely because the symbols on the obverse had worn out. These coins, thus, have two obverses—the old and the new!

The reverse of certain other *kārṣāpaṇas* bear minute marks or symbols that were definitely not stamped by the mint. The number of such marks on a coin varies from 1 to 12 +. These marks have been regarded as shroffs' marks or bankers' marks. Some of these marks may have been identification marks stamped by the different owners of the coins during different periods when these coins circulated as money. Thus, even on a single coin, some of these minute marks appear quite new while others are worn out. Besides, some of the later *kārṣāpaṇas* have a prominent mint-mark in the centre of the blank reverse.

Often, the size of the flan was smaller than the size of the punches. In such cases, the flan could not accommodate all the symbols, with the result that one or more symbols were only partially stamped on the flan. Sometimes, the coin maker, with a view to accommodate many symbols within a small flan, stamped one symbol over the other.

Theme and Meaning of the Symbols

Coming to the theme of the symbols and motifs, these include hills, plants, birds, animals, human figures, everyday objects, geometric designs and religious symbols. Over 2,000 symbols and motifs have been identified. Often, a single symbol occurs in different forms or versions, each version displaying subtle variations in size, shape and stylistic features. While certain symbols are seen on coins found in all places, other symbols are confined to certain areas or localities.

These symbols and their significance have been the focus of numerous studies.[16] Many of the symbols are common ones found on various objects since the pre-historic times, worldwide. Some of them definitely had some religious connotation mainly because three major religions—Hinduism, Buddhism and Jainism—flourished in different regions where these coins were minted and used. Certain symbols such as the *svastika* and *śrīvatsa* were equally sacred to all these three religions while certain other symbols may have been held sacred by a particular religion or sect.

Sources of the Symbols

Now, we may examine the various sources from which the people derived the varied symbols on the *kārṣāpaṇas*. It is accepted that the *kārṣāpaṇas* are the earliest coins in this part of the world and they have not been inspired by or modelled on the coins of any other region. In such circumstances, the earliest *kārṣāpaṇa*-makers would not have had any coin to serve as a model or prototype for them. Then how exactly did they get the idea of stamping such a wide variety of symbols on their coins? It is plausible that they simply copied the various living and non-living things around them on the coins. They would definitely have been inspired by different art objects of their period or an earlier one. For instance, many *kārṣāpaṇa* symbols such as *cakra, caitya, svastika*, bo-tree, elephant and horse are also seen on some of the earliest Buddhist monuments and sculptures (fourth century BC to second century BC) of north India.

An important but little-known observation is that some of the symbols on the punch-marked coins seem to have been derived from or at least inspired by early rock-art in the form of peckings and paintings found in central and southern India.[17] Although the exact date of some of these rock-art specimens is debatable, it is certain that the majority of them pre-date the *kārṣāpaṇas*. For instance, the symbol of the three-arched hill surmounted by a crescent appearing on innumerable *kārṣāpaṇas* is identical to the same symbol on the rock shelter at Bhimbetka in central India. The human figures appearing on the rocks at Benekal forest, Maski, Koppgallu in Karnataka, Porivarai near Karikiyur in the Nilgiris district of Tamil Nadu, and a few other sites are strikingly similar to the human figures on the *kārṣāpaṇas*. On many of these rock-art specimens and coins, the human body is in the 'S' twist form and exhibits dynamism of action. A four-armed symbol, not very different from the archaic *Ujjain* symbol, seen at Porivarai, bears remarkable stylistic affinity to the same type of symbol seen on the *kārṣāpaṇas*. Again in Porivarai, animals are mostly shown in profile as on many of the *kārṣāpaṇas*. Similarly, some of the bulls represented on the rocks at Koppgallu have stylistic affinities with the bulls on the *kārṣāpaṇas*. Several other art-motifs and symbols, including the *nandīpāda* and various geometric designs, are common to both, rock-art (mainly paintings found at sites like Kilvalai in Tamil Nadu) and the punch-marked coins.

Similarly, the arched hill symbol, the hollow cross, the *Ujjain* symbol and many other symbols seen on *kārṣāpaṇas* are known from Harappan objects, especially potsherds. Significantly, latest researches have concluded that although the Harappan civilization was at its zenith in the third millennium BC, some vestiges of the Harappan culture survived till the first millennium BC when the earliest *kārṣāpaṇas* were produced.[18]

The similarities between some of the symbols, especially the totemic ones, on punch-marked coins, and the graffiti marks on pre-Iron Age and Iron Age pottery (1300-400 BC), including the Black and Red Ware, Red Slipped Ware and the Russet Coated Ware of south India may also be noted (Chart 1). The noteworthy south

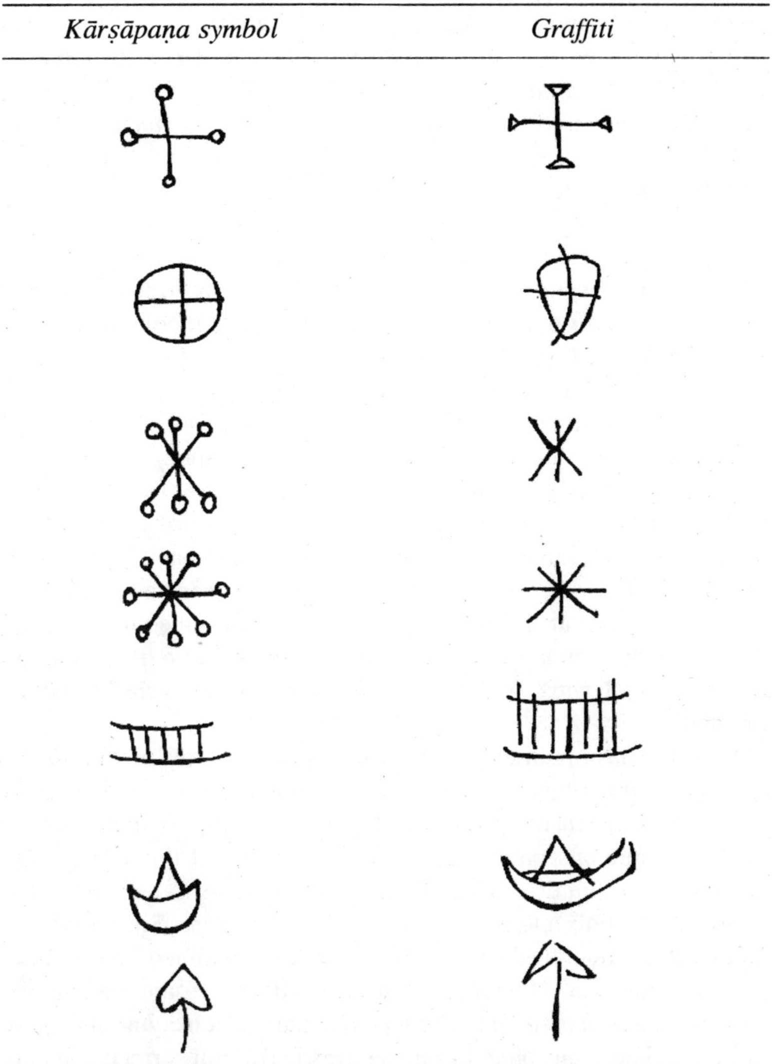

Chart 1: *Kārṣāpaṇa* symbols similar to/derived from graffiti on ancient Indian pottery (select examples).

Indian sites that have yielded graffiti-bearing pottery are T. Narsipur in Karnataka, and Kanchipuram, Vallam, Uraiyur, Tirukkampuliyur, Alagarai, Karur, Kodumanal, Alagankulam, Adichanallur and Korkai in Tamil Nadu.[19] Graffiti resembling the Sun, crescent-moon, *svastika,* wheel, bow, arrow, *triśūla* (trident) and many other objects appearing on the ceramics are almost identical to the corresponding symbols on the *kārṣāpaṇas* found in Andhra-Tamil Nadu and other places. Recent archaeological excavations at Adichanallur have revealed an interesting graffiti resembling a stag. In this instance, too, the animal with its long straight horns and upturned tail is strikingly identical to the stag represented on the *kārṣāpaṇas*.

It may be conjectured that the early people were very familiar with the above symbols which were frequently portrayed first on pottery and later on coins. Some of the pottery symbols have been copied, without any change whatsoever, on coins. The other pottery symbols have been slightly modified while being featured on the coins. The modifications include the addition of short strokes or pellets, mostly at the extreme corners of the symbol. The addition of pellets, dots or short strokes may have been either for decorative purposes or to indicate the sacredness or supernatural power of the symbol. Significantly, while pottery bearing the above graffiti are confined to a few regions and sites, *kārṣāpaṇas* bearing the graffiti-inspired symbols are found at many places in the subcontinent. It is likely that the coins produced in certain places travelled, through traders and pilgrims, to the other sites where they were buried or hoarded.

Scholars have pointed out that some of the symbols on the *kārṣāpaṇas* and other objects have originally been derived from letters or alphabets of ancient scripts, mainly the Brāhmī script.[20] Such symbols include auspicious ones such as the *svastika* and the *nandīpāda*. According to some studies, the *svastika* symbol is derived from either the Brāhmī letter *ma* or the Brāhmī letter *pu*. Similarly, the *nandīpāda* symbol has been taken to be a combination of the Brāhmī letters *na* and *ma*. However, these derivations are not acceptable because the *svastika*, *nandīpāda* and many such symbols were portrayed on various objects long before the Brāhmī script came into vogue.

Artistic Value of the Symbols

Being the earliest and rather 'experimental' coins of the land, *kārṣāpaṇas* are generally not of much artistic merit. The very process of manufacture of these coins, as described earlier, did not lend itself to artistic finery. The majority of the symbols and motifs on these coins appear like thumb-nail sketches, devoid of plasticity or a sense of movement. However, there are notable exceptions such as the motif of the hare, sometimes shown holding a pup in its mouth. Here, the hare is most realistically depicted in the act of running or jumping.

As the art of writing was not very widespread when the earliest *kārṣāpaṇas* were produced, these coins do not bear any legends or inscriptions. Even during the Mauryan and post-Mauryan periods, when the art of writing had reached a fair level of evolution, *kārṣāpaṇas* continued to be produced without any legends on them. There have, however, been opinions that at least some of the symbols on these coins may be pictographs or logographs that have not been deciphered or read because, in most cases, they have not been positioned in an orderly way either along the edges of the coin or in a series of lines, one below the other, as noticed in the coins of later periods.[21]

KĀRṢĀPAṆAS IN SOUTH INDIA: WITH REFERENCE TO SYMBOLS AND ART

As noted above, *kārṣāpaṇa* finds in north and south India mostly display common stylistic and other features. However, some of the finds from south India exhibit certain distinct features. At this stage, it may be pointed out that precise details of the symbols and motifs on some of the *kārṣāpaṇas* in the south Indian finds, reported in the nineteenth and early twentieth centuries, were never recorded. The present whereabouts of some of these coins are not known. Thus, valuable information about some of the south Indian finds is lost.

Regarding specific instances of the special features of south Indian finds, the lone *kārṣāpaṇa* recovered from the lowest levels (layer 5) of the archaeological digs at Peddavegi (ancient Vengipura in Andhra) features an irregular line (?) instead of any of the usual symbols on the obverse.[22]

Of the 7,688 *kārṣāpaṇas* of the Amaravati hoard (Andhra), at least 48 coins show distinct symbol-characteristics, unknown among the finds in north India.[23] Again, two of the 164 *kārṣāpaṇas* found at

Kottayam (Kerala) bear distinct combinations of symbols, different from the *kārṣāpaṇas* in other places.[24] A stray rectangular silver-plated base metal *kārṣāpaṇa* from Tiruvananthapuram (Trivandrum) in Kerala also exhibits certain unusual symbols such as the somewhat stylized carp, along with the usual ones like the bull and the six-arched hill on the obverse and an enigmatic *aṅkuśa* (elephant goad) on the reverse.[25]

The Angamali hoard (Kerala) is a peculiar one containing 783 coins that typologically belong to different centuries. Some of the coins in this hoard bear certain indistinct symbols that are unknown to any other punch-marked coin so far. A few coins in the hoard do not bear any symbol—probably these were blanks meant to be punched with symbols, or else the symbols on them may have been completely wiped off due to excessive usage of the coin. In this context, it may be noted that many of the *kārṣāpaṇas* in south India—hoard finds, stratified finds and other finds—are frequently so worn that the symbols on them cannot be clearly identified.

In the case of the Navalai hoard (Dharmapuri region of Tamil Nadu) of 333 base silver *kārṣāpaṇas*, some of the coins bear impressions of figures seen on Roman coins. A few coins of this hoard bear impressions of the standing figures of Gaius and Lucius as seen on the 'Gaius and Lucius Caesares reverse' type coins of the Roman emperor Augustus (27 BC-AD 14). A few other coins of this hoard bear the figure of Livia seated on a stool, as depicted on the 'Pontif Maxim' type of the Roman emperor Tiberius (AD 14-37). Incidentally, these are the two commonest types of Roman coins occurring in south India. It has been opined that the figures on Roman coins were transferred or impressed on the *kārṣāpaṇas* by the process of oxidization that took place when both these categories of coins (Roman and *kārṣāpaṇa*) were tightly packed or hoarded together below the ground.[26] However, this line of argument is not convincing because the hoard does not contain a single Roman coin. Hence, it is plausible that the Roman figures were deliberately stamped on the archaic and worn-out *kārṣāpaṇas* to use them as currency along with the Roman coins in the region. In any case, this is the sole instance, in India, of *kārṣāpaṇas* bearing Roman figures.

Coming to the more recent finds from Tamil Nadu, complete details about the interesting finds from the Pāṇḍyan port-town of

Alagankulam (near Ramanathapuram) are not available. Besides the Roman artefacts, the site has yielded two heavily-corroded indigenous square coins, one of copper and the other of silver, in a stratified context. The former coin was recovered at a depth of 2.75 m below the surface and the latter at a depth of 3.30 m. The silver coin is definitely of the punch-marked variety and the symbols on it are very faintly visible. The copper coin, although not properly identified, may also be of the punch-marked series. This coin displays, among other symbols, a tree-in-railing. Surface collections from the site include another square copper coin portraying, on the obverse, a well-executed elephant and a goad along with auspicious symbols (*maṅgala lakṣaṇas*) such as the wheel and *pūrṇaghaṭa*, while the reverse displays an arrow mark. This reverse symbol may represent a fish, in which case the coin could be safety attributed to the Sangam age Pāṇḍyas (300 BC-AD 300) whose dynastic crest was the fish. All these coins seem to have been issued and used during the early centuries of the Christian era.

The two *kārṣāpaṇas* from Kodumanal—one recovered from stratified deposits and the other a surface find—exhibit a few rare symbols of which at least some were hitherto unknown on punch-marked coins throughout India[27] (Figures 1, 2). Among the two Kodumanal *kārṣāpaṇas*, the one obtained from the stratified context, at a depth of about 68 cm below the surface, in the habitation mound of the site, is thinner in section and larger in size than the coin recovered from the surface. Both the coins are well-preserved. The coin from the stratified layers weighs 2.68 grams. Only four symbols are discernible on the obverse of this coin whereas its reverse exhibits

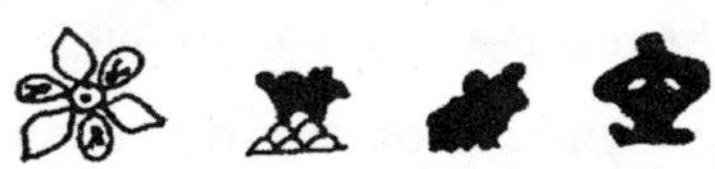

Figure 1: Symbols on the *kārṣāpaṇa* found in Kodumanal (Tamil Nadu)—stratified find (obverse symbols).

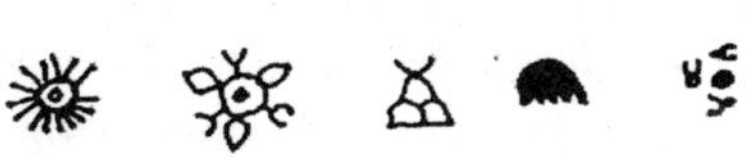

Figure 2: Symbols on the *kārṣāpaṇa* found in Kodumanal (Tamil Nadu)—non-stratified find (obverse symbols).

five minute symbols, of which one resembles a tree while the rest are unidentified. The obverse symbols of this coin are:

1. A circle with a pellet in the centre; the circle is surrounded by six symbols, three of which somewhat resemble an arrowhead or umbrella, while the other three are taurine symbols within an oval.
2. A five-arched hill surmounted by a dog or a bull.
3. A bull which is stylistically quite different from those seen on Mauryan *kārṣāpaṇas*.
4. A human figure. Here again, the present figure is more stylized than the human figures appearing on punch-marked coins from other regions.

The absence of the usual sun-symbol on the present coin is not surprising because *kārṣāpaṇas* bearing the symbol of the human figure normally do not depict the Sun-symbol.

The second *kārṣāpaṇa* from Kodumanal weighs 3.11 grams. The five obverse symbols on this coin are as follows:

1. Sun symbol.
2. Six arms—three arrowheads and three taurines—around a circle with a conspicuous dot in its centre.
3. Three-arched hill with a crescent at the top.
4. A rare symbol identified as the 'human hand' but this symbol may also be taken to represent a crudely drawn quadruped (bull?).
5. Four taurines around a central solid circle. This symbol, in a slightly smaller size, has also been depicted on the reverse of the present coin; the reverse does not exhibit any other symbol.

Almost all the symbols on the Kodumanal *kārṣāpaṇas* are stylistically very different from those seen on the punch-marked coins found at Andhra and in north India, the symbols on the Kodumanal coins being of a lower standard artistically. The poor quality of the execution of the symbols on the Kodumanal *kārṣāpaṇas* is most startlingly illustrated in the case of the beast depicted atop a five-arched hill on one of the coins from the site described above. The animal may be identified as a bull mainly because the depiction of a bull standing atop a five-arched hill is very common on punch-marked coins reported from several sites. However, the horns of the 'bull' on the present Kodumanal coin are too short and have not been realistically delineated. The absence of the hump on the back of this animal, and its peculiar sagging tummy and extremely short tail, make it appear to be a dog which, however, is rather uncommon on *kārṣāpaṇas*, that too standing on a hill. The animal on the present Kodumanal coin is certainly not a hare which has been frequently portrayed on the top of hills on punch-marked issues found in several Andhra-Karnataka sites. One may recall that this symbol on the Kodumanal *kārṣāpaṇa* is identical, in every way, to the same symbol on the *kārṣāpaṇa* die recovered from Karur in Tamil Nadu. It could, thus, be concluded that the above Kodumanal coins were manufactured in or near that site, in imitation of the Mauryan *kārṣāpaṇas*. The maker of the Kodumanal coins, probably a local citizen, does not appear to have been very skilled in the punching of the various symbols.

A few noteworthy parallels between the symbols on the Kodumanal *kārṣāpaṇas* and those on other ancient artefacts have come to light. Kodumanal itself has yielded, from a habitation layer below the levels from which the punch-marked coin (noted above) was obtained in a stratified context, the base of a red ware ceramic container on which a group of three taurine symbols have been scratched. Significantly, the figures on the ceramic are stylistically identical to the taurines on the *kārṣāpaṇas* recovered from the site.

It may be recalled that the three-arched hill surmounted by a crescent, seen on one of the Kodumanal *kārṣāpaṇas*, is a very common symbol appearing on punch-marked coins reported from all parts of India. The symbol was extensively used by the Mauryans and was, in all probability, the insignia of Mauryan sovereignty. This is corroborated by the fact that several other material vestiges of the Mauryas, both artefactual and architectural, including the Sohgaura copper-plate inscription (320-300 BC), portray this important symbol.[28]

It is clear that new varieties of punch-marked coins, displaying new symbols or modified versions of symbols occurring on the Mauryan *kārṣāpaṇas*, were produced in considerable numbers in south India, especially the Tamil country. The study of the stylistic differences between the figures on the *kārṣāpaṇas* found in different places amply reveals the subtle regional variations in the artistic merit of this well-known coin-series.

IMPACT OF THE *KĀRṢĀPAṆAS* ON LATER COINAGE

As *kārṣāpaṇas* were minted in very large numbers and circulated for a very long period (at least over 800 years) in large areas of the Indian subcontinent, their impact on other coin-series was probably immense. Among the latter, some were produced and used along with *kārṣāpaṇas* in certain regions, while others were minted after the *kārṣāpaṇas* ceased to be a currency. Thus, *kārṣāpaṇa* symbols and stylistic features can be seen on the coins of the Western Kṣatrapas, Sātavāhanas, Sangam Cheras, Sangam Cōḷas, Sangam Pāṇḍyas and many other early Indian dynasties. The devices and art motifs on many of these dynastic coins were modified, enlarged or refined versions of the symbols on the *kārṣāpaṇas*. To mention but one instance, the symbol of the three-arched hill with crescent seen on the Sātavāhana coins seems to have been borrowed from the *kārṣāpaṇas*. Several Sātavāhana lead coins from the archaeological digs at Kondapur (Andhra) bear this symbol, sometimes with a pellet within each of the arches and, in rare instances, with a dot above the crescent on the obverse. No legends can be seen on these coins. More recently, Kanganahalli (Karnataka) has revealed Sātavāhana lead coins, showing the three-arched hill surmounted by a crescent and a legend on the obverse. The reverse of all these coins from both the sites usually displays the *Ujjain* symbol.

The profound impact of *kārṣāpaṇas* on later Indian coinage will be made clearer in the subsequent chapters that deal with the coins of some of the major early south Indian dynasties in detail.

Not many are aware that the *kārṣāpaṇa* symbols were not only being reproduced on various coins by coin makers or die-cutters, but these symbols also occasionally appear as minute countermarks on various indigenous and foreign coins in many parts of India. In particular, the Roman coins found in south India sometimes bear countermarks, many of which are derived from the symbols on the *kārṣāpaṇas*[29] (Chart 2). Roman coins countermarked with *kārṣāpaṇa* symbols have occurred at many sites such as Akkanpalle, Nagavarappupadu, Nasthullapur and Peddabankur in Andhra, Budinatham in Tamil Nadu, and Nedumkandam in Kerala. The *kārṣāpaṇa* symbols seen on Roman coins include the *svastika*, *śrīvatsa*, *nandīpāda*, *cakra*, the sun, the crescent moon and the bull symbol.

It is clear that Roman coins with *kārṣāpaṇa* symbols are more in

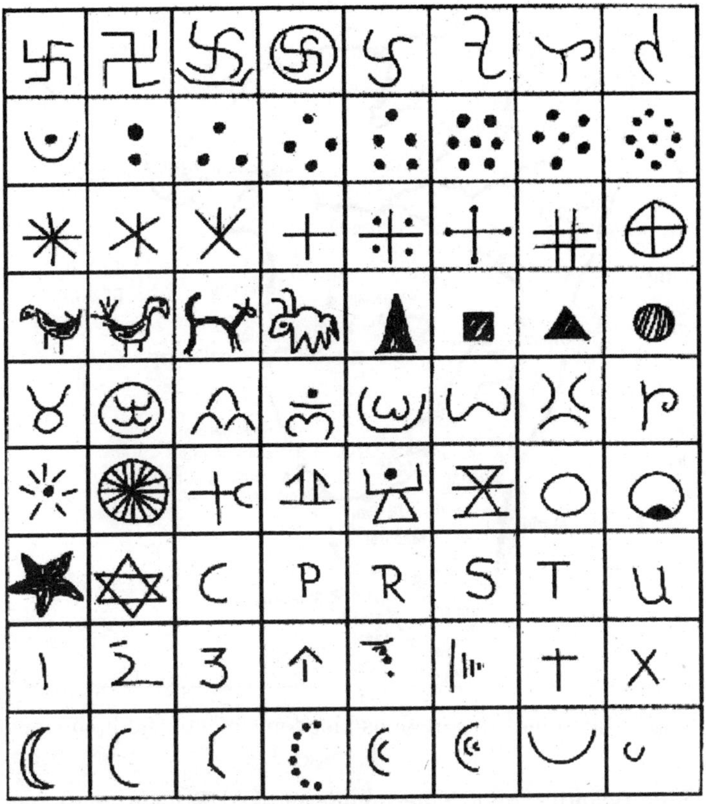

Chart 2: Important countermarks on Roman coins found in India.

the Andhra country than in the Tamil country. A probable reason for this is that punch-marked coins were in more intense circulation and for a much longer time-period in the former region than in the latter. This view is corroborated by the fact that finds of *kārṣāpaṇas* are more numerous in the Andhra country than in the Tamil country. In this context, it may also be pointed out that many of the *kārṣāpaṇa* finds in Tamil Nadu appear to have reached those sites from north India via Andhra by the process of inland trade. In fact, at Nasthullapur in Andhra, countermarked Roman coins are found in association with 8 *kārṣāpaṇas*. Surprisingly, the symbols on these 8 *kārṣāpaṇas* are unknown among the countermarks on any of the Roman coins in India.

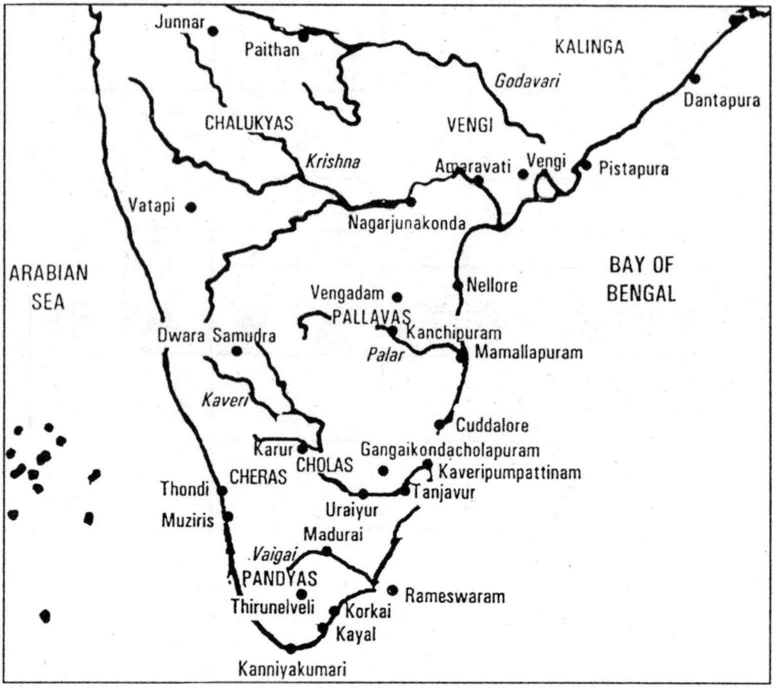

Map 1: Important sites/regions/kingdoms mentioned in this book.

Significantly, among the countermarked Roman coins, certain *kārṣāpaṇa* symbols predominate in a specific area or site. For example, religious symbols such as the *nandīpāda*, *svastika* and *cakra* are all confined to the Roman coins from Akkanpalle in Andhra. Although these symbols are equally sacred to the Hindus, Buddhists and even the Jains, on circumstantial and contextual evidence, it is now clear that the symbols on the Akkanpalle coins are undoubtedly connected with Buddhism.[30] All the denarii from the site are of the first century AD—a period when Buddhism was very popular in the Andhra region. Further, it has now been established that Buddhist monasteries, in Andhra and elsewhere, actively participated in the Indo-Mediterranean maritime trade, and Buddhist monks and pilgrims were familiar with and had access to Roman coins.

Roman coins countermarked with *kārṣāpaṇa* symbols mostly

belong to the first century AD and not later. An apparent reason for this is that the second-third centuries AD saw a marked decrease in the circulation of punch-marked coins in all parts of India and the decline of early Buddhist centres in Andhra.

As regards the purpose of these countermarks, they may have been intended to authenticate foreign coins as local currency and, thus, were 'authority symbols'. Incidentally, the practice of counter-stamping foreign coins to validate them as local money has been in vogue throughout history. It is, however, more likely that these marks were identification marks of the owners of the coins. One may recall that such ownership marks are seen on the reverse of certain *kārṣāpaṇas* themselves.

NOTES AND REFERENCES

1. The bibliography for the punch-marked coins is vast. For a detailed account of these coins, see P.L. Gupta, *Coins* (New Delhi, 2000), pp. 8-22; P.L. Gupta and T.R. Hardaker, *Ancient Indian Silver Punch-marked Coins of the Magadha-Maurya Kārṣāpaṇa Series* (Nashik, 1985). For a good historiographical survey of these coins, see A.N. Lahiri, 'Numismatography of Punch-marked Coins', in C. Mani, ed., *A Macro Study of Early Indian Coins* (Delhi, 1999), pp. 33-44.
2. For the important *kārṣāpaṇa* finds in Andhra see P.L. Gupta, *Punch-marked Coins in the Andhra Pradesh Government Museum* (Hyderabad, 1960); idem, *The Amaravati Hoard of Silver Punch Marked Coins* (Hyderabad, 1963). For the *kārṣāpaṇa* finds in Karnataka, see A.V. Narasimha Murthy, 'Numismatic Studies in Karnataka', *SSIC* I (1991), pp. 99-120; idem, *Some Aspects of Early Historic Archaeology and Numismatics of Karnataka* (Madras, 1991), pp. 31-3. For the finds from Kerala, see P.L. Gupta, *The Early Coins From Kerala* (Trivandrum, 1988); T. Sathyamurthy, 'Angamali Hoard of Silver Punch-marked Coins', *SSIC* IV (1994), pp. 45-50. For the major finds in Tamil Nadu, see K. Rajan, 'A Chronological Note on the Punch-marked Coins of Tamil Nadu', *SSIC* I (1991), pp. 17-22; R. Nagaswamy, 'Alagankulam: An Indo-Roman Trading Port', in C. Margabandhu, K.S. Ramachandran, A.P. Sagar and D.K. Sinha, eds., *Indian Archaeological Heritage, Shri K.V. Soundara Rajan Felicitation Volume* I (New Delhi, 1991), pp. 247-54; Natana Kasinathan et al., *Alagankulam: A. Preliminary Report* (Madras, 1992), pp. 14-15.

   Details regarding the finds from Karur, Tirukoilur (Tamil Nadu) and many other sites listed here were obtained from A. Sitaraman, Tanjavur and K.A. Thirugnanasampandam, Erode. Their private collections include coins from these sites. I am most grateful to them for permitting me to study these coins.

Among the museums in south India, the Government Museum, Egmore, Madras, and the Andhra Pradesh State Archaeological Museum, Hyderabad, have very large collections of punch-marked coins.

3. For a good discussion on the *kārṣāpaṇa* finds in Sri Lanka, see Osmund Bopearachchi, 'Archaeological Evidence on Changing Patterns of International Trade Relations of Ancient Sri Lanka', in Osmund Bopearachchi and D.P.M. Weerakkody, eds., *Origin, Evolution and Circulation of Foreign Coins in the Indian Ocean* (New Delhi, 1998), pp. 133-78.
4. For a brief survey of the metallic composition and production technique of the *kārṣāpaṇas*, see P.L. Gupta, 1988 (supra n. 2), p. 1. Also see P.L. Gupta, 2000 (supra n. 1), pp. 8-22.
5. For the weight-standard of the *kārṣāpaṇas*, see O. Bopearachchi, 1998 (supra n. 3), pp. 133-78; P.L. Gupta, 1988 (supra n. 2), pp. 1-5.
6. P.L. Gupta, 2000 (supra n. 1), p. 9.
7. The die was discovered by Alexander Cunningham between 1875-80. For a detailed analysis of this find, see A.M. Shastri, 'Presidential Address (International Colloquium on Coinage, Trade and Economy)', in Amal Kumar Jha, ed., *Coinage, Trade and Economy* (Nashik, 1991), pp. XI-XXIII.
8. P.V. Radhakrishnan, 'A Punch-marked Die From Karur', *SSIC* IV (1994), pp. 51-6.
9. A comparative study of the moulds from different sites is available in P.L. Gupta 1960 (supra n. 2), pp. 130-5; Upendra Thakur, 'Mints and Minting in India', in C. Mani, ed., *A Macro Study of Early Indian Coins* (Delhi, 1999), pp. 117-35. Also see B.B. Lal, 'Śiśupālgarh 1948: An Early Historical Fort in Eastern India', *AI* 5 (1949), pp. 62-102; G. Yazdani, 'Excavations at Kondapur: An Andhra Town *c.* 200 BC-200 AD', *ABORI* XII (1941), pp. 171-85. The find from Dhulikatta (Andhra) is not widely-known. For this find, see V.V. Krishna Sastry, ed., *Annual Report of the Department of Archaeology & Museums, Government of Andhra Pradesh—1976-77* (Hyderabad, 1978), p. 16. Incidentally, this publication is not easily available or widely consulted. For the moulds from Kanchi or Kanchipuram, see K.V. Raman and P. Shanmugam, 'Terracotta Coin Moulds From Kanchipuram', *SSIC* I (1991), pp. 23-9.
10. S. Deraniyagala, 'The Citadel of Anuradhapura 1969: Excavations in the Gedige Area', *Ancient Ceylon* 2 (1972), pp. 48-170; Osmund Bopearachchi and Rajah M. Wickremesinhe, *Ruhuna: An Ancient Civilisation Re-visited: Numismatic and Archaeological Evidence on Inland and Maritime Trade* (Colombo?, 1999), pp. 31, 110.
11. A.M. Shastri, 1991 (supra n. 7), pp. XI-XXIII.
12. P.L. Gupta, 1960 (supra n. 2), pp. 134-5. Here, the author tries to prove that the moulds were not part of the forgers' equipment.
13. I learnt about the Roman coin moulds during my research at the Department of Coins and Medals of the British Museum, London, in 1990, 1994,

1997 and 2010. I discussed these moulds with A. Burnett and Joe Cribb of the Museum. I am grateful for the information and suggestions that they gave me.

14. V. Jeyaraj, 'Physico-chemical Examination of Two Punch-marked Coins', *SSIC* II (1992), pp. 159-63.
15. For more details of such forgeries, see A.M. Shastri, 1991 (supra n. 7) XI-XXIII. For some more interesting references to counterfeiting of coins in the *Arthaśāstra*, see L.N. Rangarajan, *Kautilya: The Arthashastra* (New Delhi, 1992), pp. 75, 228. Also see P.L. Gupta and T.R. Hardaker, 1985 (supra n. 1).
16. The great scholars who studied the *kārṣāpaṇas* and the symbols on them include Alexander Cunningham, W. Theobald, D.B. Spooner and many others. Bibliographies of the studies on *kārṣāpaṇa*-symbols have appeared in a series of publications and, hence, are not repeated here. For a good summary of these studies and fresh interpretations of some of these symbols, see Savita Sharma, *Early Indian Symbols: Numismatic Evidence* (Delhi, 1990).
17. I visited the major rock-art sites of Tamil Nadu and Karnataka between April and June 2004. The biggest and one of the most important sites in this region is Porivarai, near the tribal village of Karikiyur in the Nilgiris district of Tamil Nadu. The painted panel here measures around 53 m × 15 m in size. The site is located deep inside a thick forest infested with wildlife. Hence, the site is not widely-known and has, so far, not been adequately documented and studied.

    N. Kasinathan, former Director, Tamil Nadu State Department of Archaeology, Madras, has exhaustively studied and published several specimens of early rock-art (except the one in Porivarai) in Tamil Nadu. I was benefited by several fruitful discussions on the subject with him in 2002.

    One of the most interesting accounts of Indian rock art is V.S. Wakankar, 'Rock Art of South India', in C. Margabandhu, K.S. Ramachandran, A.P. Sagar and D.K. Sinha, eds., *Indian Archaeological Heritage: Shri. K.V. Soundara Rajan Felicitation Volume* I (New Delhi, 1991), pp. 63-90. The value of this paper is enhanced by the large number of neat line-drawings. Also see Avvai Natarajan and Natana Kasinathan, *Art Panorama of Tamils* (Madras, 1993), pp. 29-34.
18. For a detailed analysis of the Harappan culture elements in later periods, see F.R. Allchin et al., *The Archaeology of Early Historic Sourh Asia: The Emergence of Cities and States* (Cambridge, 1995), mainly chapters 1-7.
19. For a detailed study of graffiti on ancient Indian pottery, see S. Gurumurthy, *Ceramic Traditions in South India (Down to 300 AD)* (Madras, 1981); idem, *Deciphering the Indus Script (From Graffiti on Ancient Indian Pottery)* (Madras, 1999).
20. The physical similarities between some of the Brāhmī alphabets and religious symbols have been analysed by a number of scholars. For a fairly

comprehensive survey of these writings, see A.L. Srivastava, 'Use of Auspicious Motifs in Indian Epigraphs', *Bulletin of the Assam State Museum* V (1985), pp. 1-18.

21. S. Gurumurthy, 1999 (supra n. 19), p. 177.
22. For more details about the coin finds from Peddavegi, see I.K. Sarma, 'Coins From Peddavegi Excavations (1985-87)', *SSIC* VI (1996), pp. 49-65.
23. For full details about the *kārṣāpaṇa* hoard from Amaravati, see P.L. Gupta, 1963 (supra n. 2).
24. For full details of the *kārṣāpaṇa* hoard from Kottayam, see P.L. Gupta, 1988 (supra n. 2).
25. Beena Sarasan, 'An Unique Punch Marked Coin of Venad', *SSIC* XV (2005), pp. 30-4.
26. P.V. Radhakrishnan, 'Chronology of Silver Punchmarked Coins in South India', *SSIC* VIII (1998), pp. 27-34.
27. Kodumanal has been repeatedly explored and excavated, mainly by the Department of Epigraphy and Archaeology of the Tamil University, Tanjavur. I am grateful to Y. Subbarayalu and K. Rajan of the university for allowing me to examine the objects from the site on various occasions from 1991 to 2003.
28. Some of these objects are in the Government Museum, Patna. See P.L. Gupta, 1960 (supra n. 2) p. 50.
29. For a detailed analysis of the Roman coins found in India, the countermarks on them and their significance, see S. Suresh, *Roman Antiquities in Tamil Nadu* (Madras, 1992), pp. 30-1; idem, 'Roman Vestiges in Kanchipuram', in Nanditha Krishna, ed., *Kanchi: A Heritage of Art and Religion* (Chennai, 1992), pp. 56-61; idem, 'Early Roman Finds in Madras City', in G.J. Sudhakar, ed., *Aspects of Madras: A Historical Perspective* (Chennai, 1993), pp. 13-16; idem, 'Roman Coins Found in India: A Study of the Countermarks', Paper presented at the international seminar on Trade and Economy of Ancient Sri Lanka, India and South-East Asia: Archaeological and Literary Evidence (Colombo, 1999); idem, 'Roman Denarii Hoard From Koneripatti, Tamil Nadu', in S. Rajagopal, ed., *Kaveri- Studies in Epigraphy, Archaeology and History (Prof. Y. Subbarayalu Felicitation Volume)* (Madras, 2001), pp. 267-72; idem, 'Religion and Trade: Spread of Jainism in Ancient Andhra Desa and Tamiḷakam', in Haripriya Rangarajan, G. Kamalakar and A.K.V.S. Reddy, eds., *Jainism: Art, Architecture, Literature and Philosophy* (Delhi, 2001), pp. 321-7; idem, *Symbols of Trade: Roman and Pseudo-Roman Objects Found in India* (New Delhi, 2004), pp. 52-8; idem, 'Muziris to Arikamedu: Roman Trails in South India', Paper presented at the international conference on Arikamedu Archaeological Heritage: Cultural and Technological Valorisation' (Pondicherry, 2004); idem,'Early Roman Trade With South Asia: A Study Based on Recent Explorations in South India and Sri Lanka', Paper

presented at the international seminar on Tamil Nadu and Sri Lanka: New Evidence on Maritime and Inland Trade (Madras, 2004); idem, 'Epigraphical Evidences for the Roman Trade and Roman Artifacts in Ancient India—With Special Reference to South India', Paper presented at the Second Symposium on Tamil Epigraphy: Historical Sources and Pluridisciplinary Perspectives (Paris, 2006); idem, *Arikamedu: Its Place in the Ancient Rome-India Contacts* (New Delhi, 2007); idem, 'Two Unpublished Roman Aurei from Pudukkottai Hoard, Tamil Nadu', *SSIC* XVII (2007), pp. 33-7; idem, 'The British Museum Collection of Roman Republican Coins Found in India', *SSIC* XVIII (2008), pp. 20-4; idem, 'A Rare Roman Republican Coin Found in India', *SSIC* XIX (2009), pp. 32-4; idem, 'Two Unpublished Roman Denarii found at Kodumanal, Tamil Nadu', *SSIC* XX (2010), pp. 37-9; S. Suresh and M. Nambirajan, 'The Single Surviving Roman Coin from a Rare Hoard in Goa', *SSIC* XX (2010), pp. 44-8. Also see S. Suresh and Prema Kasturi, *Cambodia: What it Got From South India? (A Historical-cum-Archaeological Survey)* (Madras, 2009).

30. S. Suresh, 'Counter-marks of Buddhist Symbols on the Roman Coins Found in Andhra Desa', in G. Kamalakar and M. Veerender, eds., *Buddhism: Art, Architecture, Literature and Philosophy*, vol. II (Delhi, 2005), pp. 481-6.

CHAPTER 3

Coins of the Sangam Cheras

When the Mauryas and Kuṣāṇas were ruling north India (fourth century BC to third century AD), south India was ruled by the Sātavāhanas, Cheras, Cōḷas and Pāṇḍyas. The Sātavāhanas mainly ruled over parts of Maharashtra and the Karnataka-Andhra regions. The Cheras, Cōḷas, Pāṇḍyas and a few minor chieftains ruled the region south of the Sātavāhana territory.[1] This region was called Tamiḷakam because the language spoken here was Tamil. Tamiḷakam was bound by the Venkatam or Tirupati hills in the north and Cape Comorin in the south. To the west lay the Arabian Sea and to the east, the Bay of Bengal. The region thus mainly included the present-day states of Tamil Nadu and Kerala.

The Tamil kings were great patrons of art and literature. At the Pāṇḍya palace in Madurai (Tamil Nadu), scholars and poets from different lands assembled to participate in academic debates and discussions. This gathering of Tamil scholars was called the *sangam*. The *sangams* were held frequently between 200 BC and AD 300. Hence, historians call this period the 'Sangam Age' and the prefix 'Sangam' is frequently appended to the three main dynasties—Cheras, Cōḷas and Pāṇḍyas—of this region. This is the only instance where a historical period has been named after an academic conference.

The Chera kingdom comprised present-day Kerala and parts of western Tamil Nadu—the Kongunādu or the Coimbatore region. The location of the capital of this kingdom was, until recently, hotly debated by scholars. Some scholars felt that Tiruvanjikkalam in coastal Kerala was the Chera capital while others opined that Karur, on the banks of the river Amaravati, a tributary of the Kāverī in Tamil Nadu, was the capital. The discovery of Sangam Chera inscriptions at a site called Pugalur near Karur and the recurrent discoveries of thousands of Sangam Chera coins in and around this town have now proved, beyond doubt, that Karur was the royal capital.

The important Sangam Chera rulers included Neḍun Cheral Ādan, Senkuttuvan and Perun Cheral Irumpoṛai. Senkuttuvan is said to have invaded north India and to have even crossed the river Ganga to procure stones from the Himalayas for erecting a statue of Goddess Kannagi in the Chera land. He was a contemporary of Gajabāhu I (AD 173-95), the ruler of Sri Lanka. The Chera power slowly declined after the second century AD.

The coins minted by the Sangam age Cheras seem to be the earliest among those issued by the Sangam age Tamil kings. Compared to the issues of other Tamil dynasties of the Sangam period, finds of the Chera coins are limited in number.

The majority of the Chera coins have been recovered from the bank of the river Amaravati in Karur.[2] A few coins have been reported from Parur and some other places in Kerala. Recently, a single Sangam Chera coin was found at the newly-discovered site of Pattanam, on the southern side of the river Periyār in Kerala. Incidentally, Pattanam provides the sole evidence for a full-fledged urban settlement on the Malabar coast and has tentatively been identified with Muziris—the famous port of the Sangam Cheras. A single specimen of a Sangam Chera coin has been reported from Kantarodai in northern Sri Lanka.

PHYSICAL FEATURES AND PRODUCTION METHOD

The majority of the known Sangam Chera coins are of copper, while a few specimens are of base silver and, very rarely, lead. With regard to the source of the metals, copper mines are known in south India and Sri Lanka as well. Further, as attested by the *Periplus* (first century AD?), south India imported copper along with tin and lead from the Roman empire.[3] Silver was, however, very scarce in south India, especially in Tamil Nadu-Kerala, and it is said that the local Tamil rulers often melted foreign silver coins, mainly the Roman denarii, reaching their territories, to obtain silver for their coins and jewels.

The copper coins are either circular, rectangular or square in shape, whereas the lead coins are rectangular or square and the silver ones are invariably circular. Recently, an attractive oval-shaped copper coin has also come to light. Some of the coins are irregular in shape. In this connection, it is interesting to note that the ancient Tamil poems describe coins in the shape of certain fruits.[4]

As regards the size of the quadrangular coins, many of the rectangular coins measure 2 cm × 1.8 cm or 1.8 cm × 1.6 cm. In the case of many of the square coins, each side measures 2.2 or 2.3 cm. There are a few smaller rectangular and square coins, where each side measures less than 1 cm, and some larger coins where each side measures around 2.5 cm. The weight of these coins ranges from less than 1 gram to over 11 grams but the average weight ranges from 1.7 to 2.7 grams. Many of the low weight coins appear worn-out clearly indicating that they lost weight when they were in intense use as money.

Coming to the circular coins, they measure, whether in silver or copper, around 1.5 to 1.9 cm in diameter. As regards weight, the silver circular coins weigh between 1.7 and 2.3 grams while the copper circular coins are much heavier, their weight ranging from 4 to 6.7 grams. The sole oval-shaped copper coin weighs 5.6 grams.

Most of the Sangam Chera coins, whether in silver, copper or lead, were die-struck on a thin sheet. These kings, however, produced a few silver coins by the punch-marking technique. It has been opined that the obverse and reverse of the Chera silver portrait coins, mostly bearing the Tamil-Brāhmī script legend *Mākkōtai*, were minted in two separate pieces and joined by molten lead paste.[5] This view is based on the assumption that these coins, as seen in some private collections, are merely the 'obverse pieces' of the coins while the 'reverse pieces' have, at some point of time, got detached from the 'obverse pieces'. Incidentally, none of these 'reverse pieces' have yet been discovered or identified. The presence of traces of lead coating on the blank reverse of these 'obverse pieces' has been cited to support the above line of argument. The unusually rough surface of the reverse of these pieces further strengthens this argument.

Besides minting their own coins, the Cheras also appear to have counterstruck some of the silver punch-marked coins and Roman denarii for use as money in their territory. R. Krishnamurthy has published a 'Gaius and Lucius Caesares reverse' type of Roman emperor Augustus (27 BC-AD 14), counterstruck, on the obverse, with the bust and legend of the Chera king, Mākkōtai.[6] As to the procedure of counterstriking, the Roman coin was initially heated and the dotted border on it was completely cut-off when the coin was hot. Using a die with a portrait of Mākkōtai, the coin was counterstruck on the obverse. Another die, a blank one, was used to counterstrike the reverse. Usually, during such a process, if the coin was sufficiently hot and the force applied during counterstriking was adequate, the original designs on the coin were bound to be completely obliterated and the designs on the new die were automatically impressed on the coin. However, if the coin was not sufficiently hot or if the force applied while counterstriking was not sufficient or uniform throughout the surface of the coin, some portions of the original designs or legends were likely to remain on the flan, even after the counterstriking. In the present coin, traces of the original Augustus legend are seen on the obverse, and the faint outline of the figures of Gaius and Lucius is noticeable on the reverse.

The difference in weight between the Mākkōtai coin (2.1 grams) and the Augustus denarius (3.8 grams) is obviously due to the cutting away of the dotted border of the denarius during the process of counterstriking. The reason for slicing off the border may have been to save the precious silver for melting the cut bits and using it to mint more Chera coins. In this connection, one may recall that silver was very scarce in ancient Tamiḷakam. It is equally plausible that the Cheras wanted to produce silver coins weighing around 2.1 grams to imitate the weight standard of the Western Kṣatrapas who, in the first century AD, minted numerous silver coins of almost the same weight.

More recently, Karur has yielded a silver *kārṣāpaṇa* bearing, on the obverse, five symbols, the last being the bow and arrow—a symbol rare but not unknown on punch-marked coins. The reverse of this coin features another bow and arrow—a symbol hitherto unknown on the reverse of any *kārṣāpaṇa*. It has been argued that the Cheras counterstruck the reverse of this *kārṣāpaṇa* with a die bearing the bow and arrow symbol which was their royal insignia.[7] During this process of counterstriking, the original symbol on the reverse may have been completely wiped off. The margin of the circular Chera die is partially seen on the reverse of this *kārṣāpaṇa*. This coin may again reconfirm the extreme scarcity of silver in ancient south India so much so that the local rulers sometimes used silver coins from other regions as money in their kingdom, after duly counterstriking them with one or more of the local symbols or motifs, either on the obverse or reverse or on both sides. Counterstriking the foreign coins for use as local money was far easier and less expensive than melting them and using the metal thus obtained for minting local coins. Yet, as noted earlier, the ancient south Indians did often melt foreign silver coins for procuring the silver in them.

Several mints, located in different parts of the Chera empire, may have been engaged in the production of new coins, and the counter-striking of Roman coins and *kārṣāpaṇas* for use as currency. Judging from the rich variety of numismatic discoveries—stratified, hoard and surface finds—in every part of the Chera capital of Karur, this town itself appears to have had more than one mint during the days of the Sangam Cheras. The Chera king or an officer appointed by him issued clear instructions regarding the metal, size, shape and weight of the different coins, and the devices to be featured on the coins so as to ensure some uniformity in the coins produced by various mints.

It may be noted that die-struck coins were unknown in Tamiḷakam prior to the Cheras. Then, how did the Cheras learn this intricate process of minting and counterstriking coins? Probably, they learnt it from the Western Kṣatrapas during the course of trade between these two kingdoms. There is also every likelihood of the Sangam Cheras having learnt the sophisticated skills of die-cutting from the Romans whose die-struck Republican coins began to reach, as products of trade, the Chera territory at least from the first century BC onwards.[8]

ART AND SYMBOLOGY

Several interesting symbols and devices appear on the Sangam Chera coins.

Obverse Devices

Elephant

One of the commonest obverse devices on the quadrangular copper issues is the elephant, usually standing to the right. On several coins, it is the principal device appearing at the centre of the flan but there are many coins where it is in a corner. The animal invariably appears stout and majestic. Some coins feature the elephant without tusks.

In some instances, its trunk is raised. On a few coins, the elephant is not realistically portrayed and appears like a horse but is identified as an elephant by its long trunk and tusks.

An unusual coin features a tall, slender lamp-stand with a lamp in front of the huge elephant. This appears to be a terracotta lamp in the form of a small shallow bowl or cup, common in south India even now. The single flickering flame emanating from the lamp has been most clearly delineated. The positioning of the sacred lamp in front of the elephant is probably meant to indicate the worship of the animal. Rarely, two warriors are seen riding the elephant. On a unique coin, the elephant is seen standing on a huge platform or pedestal, with an intricately designed flag mast in front of it. Probably, this coin features an important royal elephant or a war elephant honoured after its successful return from war.

It may be recalled that the breeding of elephants was very common in the ancient Chera land. The Cheras and other ancient rulers of the Tamil country recognized the importance of the tusker in warfare, as described in ancient Tamil texts such as the *Puraṇānūru.*[9] The elephants on most of the early Chera coins are typical war-elephants (*komban yānai*), possessing long, strong and sturdy tusks with a sharp and pointed tip.

The elephant played a vital role not merely in wars but also in the economy of the Cheras. The animal was used as a beast of burden in the rural areas. Further, ivory was one of the main items of export from the Chera port of Muziris to Rome.[10] The Cheras gifted elephants to brave warriors. The animal was considered the king of the forested hills of the Cheras. Even now, they are quite common in this region that possesses one of South Asia's largest habitats of the wild elephant.

Horse

Many Chera coins feature the horse instead of the elephant on the obverse. The horse is featured standing to the right or left. Sometimes, the front legs of the animal are raised as if the horse is galloping or else is trying to munch the leaves or fruits of a very tall tree. Several coins feature a trough resting on a thin pedestal, just below the mouth of the horse. This may indicate that the animal is eating grains or drinking water stored in the trough. On some coins, the pedestal is plain but, in other specimens, it is fluted and carved.

A rare coin features a horse standing to the right, face drooping and mouth almost touching a long plain cylindrical column. This column has been identified as a *yūpastambha* (sacrificial post) and hence, this coin is interpreted as a special issue minted by a Chera ruler to commemorate his performance of the *aśvamedha yajña* (horse sacrifice). But the *yajñakuṇḍa* (sacrificial pit), normally seen on *aśvamedha* type coins of other dynasties, is not appearing on the obverse or reverse of this coin.

Bull

Sometimes the obverse of Chera coins shows the bull instead of the elephant or the horse. The bull is standing to the right with its long and sharp horns clearly delineated. On some coins, the horns are straight and erect while on certain other coins, they are curved. Sometimes the bull is garlanded and decorated.

Lion

An extremely limited number of copper coins feature the lion on the obverse. These lion type coins occur in both circular and quadrangular shapes. This is one of the rarest instances in south Indian numismatics where the same type occurs in two different shapes. Probably this coin type was first issued around the first century AD when the Cheras and many other south Indian dynasties were slowly trying to change over from the quadrangular to the circular shape for their coins.

On Chera coins, unlike the elephant, bull or horse, the lion is standing to the front on a circular seat, platform or abacus. It is flanked by a *śaṅkha* (conch) on a mast to its right and a *cakra* (wheel) on a mast to its left. Above the lion is the bow and arrow—the royal emblem of the Cheras. The conch and the wheel on this coin may allude to the Hindu god Viṣṇu who is invariably represented with these objects. In that case, this is one of the earliest representations of symbols or objects connected with Viṣṇu on a coin. Interestingly, Ujjain in central India has yielded a little-known glass seal representing the seated lion flanked by the conch and the wheel.[11] Stylistically, the motifs on this seal and the Chera coin are strikingly similar. This seated lion on the seal is also stylistically comparable to the seated lion carved on the rounded drum or abacus on the capital of the columns erected by the Mauryan emperor Aśoka (272-35 BC). The seal was obtained in the stratified context from the Sātavāhana layers and is believed to have been produced on instructions from a Sātavāhana king, or one of his officers or feudatories. Significantly, the Sātavāhanas were ardent worshippers of Viṣṇu.[12] This Chera coin may be a commemorative one featuring symbols of religion and royalty surrounding the lion, the king of animals, symbolizing nobility, regal strength and power.

Goddess Yamuna

An extremely rare Chera rectangular copper coin depicts goddess Yamuna.[13] She is two-armed and is standing to the front. The agitated folds of the loose garment (sari?) worn by her have been delineated through a series of short zig-zag strokes. She wears circular ear-ornaments, bangles and anklets. She is standing on a tortoise. Her right hand holds two small water pots hanging from a rope or sling. Her left hand holds a dagger. A palm tree (*panai maram*)-in-railing is seen to her right. The tree is typically long. It is not straight but slightly bent because of the exigencies of space on the flan. To the left of the goddess are a cock and a long staff.

This coin has immense religious, artistic and historical significance. The portrayal of the river goddess on the coin shows the reverence with which the Cheras treated the rivers. One may remember that the Chera capital of Karur was located on the banks of an important river named Amaravati, then called Ānporunai, a tributary of the more famous Kāverī. Further, the palm tree featured on the coin was the tutelary tree of the Cheras. It is featured at the end of a little-known one-line Tamil Brāhmī cave inscription (third century AD?) found at Edakal in Kerala. Interestingly, this is the earliest inscription to bear the dynastic name Chera. The tree is also seen on megalithic pottery found in sites such as Sanur and Uraiyur in Tamil Nadu, and also on a unique metal seal obtained during the excavations of a unique megalithic burial complex at Anaikoddai in Sri Lanka. The palm tree is very common in the Chera region and certain other parts of south India to this day. The present coin is among the earliest examples of the portrayal of the anthropomorphic form of a Hindu deity on a coin in south India. It is also the sole instance of the depiction of a goddess on a coin by a Tamil king of the Sangam age.

Royal Portrait

The royal portrait coins of the Sangam Cheras form a distinct group. While the majority of the Sangam Chera coins are made of copper, are quadrangular in shape, and are usually without inscriptions or legends, the portrait coins are always circular in shape, bear a legend, and occur mostly in silver and rarely in copper.

One of the copper portrait coins displays a rectangular doorframe, probably surmounted by a beam made of huge stone blocks. Within this frame, a warrior (king?) is seen, standing to the front at the doorstep. The facial features have not been clearly delineated. In fact, the face appears merely as a circular protrusion on the flan. The figure is clad in a round cap, coat or jacket, and long trousers that have been folded up—garments absolutely foreign to ancient south India. The long object in his right hand may be a weapon. The figure betrays unmistakable Graeco-Roman influence. The dress of the soldier or king is very similar to the description of the dress of a *yavana* (Roman?) gatekeeper or bodyguard in an early Tamil text named *Mullaipāṭṭu*: 'With their wide and puffed skirts, folded up and sustained by a whip, with their stiff corset. . . .'[14]

The most enigmatic Sangam Chera portrait coins are the silver ones. Over twelve specimens of this type, probably the remnants of a small ancient hoard emerging piecemeal, have come to light from the Chera capital of Karur. These coins portray, on the obverse, the bust of the Chera king turned to the right; the legend, in Tamil Brāhmī script above the bust reads *Mākkōtai* (Plate 7) or *Kuṭṭuvaṇkōtai.* The form of the bust on these coins is quite plastic. The facial features are sharp and clear. Even the minute features such as the eyelashes and sometimes, the thin moustache, have been delineated through a series of thin strokes by a skilled die-cutter.

It has been observed that at least three of the bust coins with the legend *Mākkōtai* are definitely of the same ruler, each of these coins featuring him during different stages of his life—youth, middle age and old age. The coin featuring the aged king even shows the wrinkles in his sagging cheeks. Obviously, these three coins were issued by

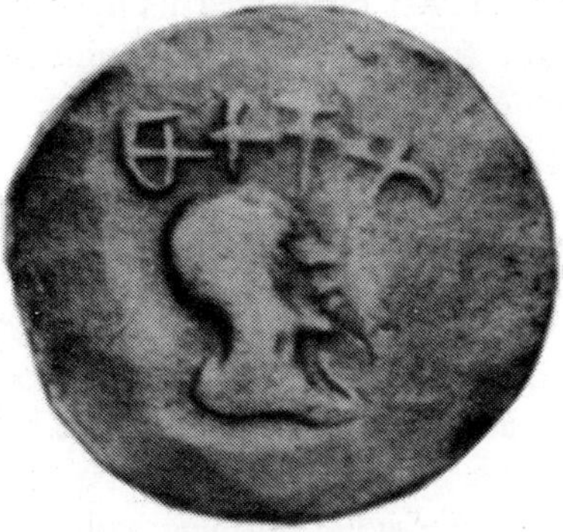

Plate 7: Sangam Chera coin—bust with legand *Mākkōtai* obverse.
(Photo: A. Sitaraman, Tanjavur)

a single king during different years of his long reign. However, the figure on many of the other *Mākkōtai* coins does not seem to be of the same person, and the exact size of the bust also varies from coin to coin. Again, the legends on some specimens of this type show significant paleographic variations. Thus, it may be concluded that Mākkōtai was a family name of the Sangam Chera dynasty and successive rulers of this line issued these portrait type coins with the same legend.

One may recall that the earliest portrait coins of the world were issued by the Greeks around the fourth century BC.[15] The Greek numismatic art traditions greatly influenced the Romans who succeeded the Greeks in Europe. The Romans issued the largest variety of portrait coins, displaying astounding variations in stylistic features.[16] In the Indian subcontinent, the Indo-Greeks, who ruled in the north-western region, minted the first portrait coins. Shortly after, the Western Kṣatrapas of western India began to issue portrait coins based on the Indo-Greek model. In due course, inspired by the Western Kṣatrapa coins, the Sātavāhanas began to mint their own portrait coins.

The Chera portrait coins are, stylistically and otherwise, different from the Sātavāhana and Kṣatrapa portrait coins. Hence, they do not seem to have been inspired by the Kṣatrapa or Sātavāhana coinage. Instead, the Cheras would have imitated the Roman portrait coins that began to reach their land as early as the second-first centuries BC by the process of trade. This hypothesis can be further substantiated by the following points of similarities between the early Roman and the Chera portrait coins:

1. The Chera bust has a clean-shaven head. Many early Roman coins display this feature.
2. The Chera portrait is turned to the right and has a protruding nose with a pointed tip, very much like the royal head on Roman issues.
3. The drapery wrapped round the neck of the bust on Chera coins is almost identical to the drapery round the neck of the busts on many Roman coins.
4. The Chera ruler as depicted on these coins is not adorned with any jewellery. Augustus and Tiberius, too, have often been portrayed on coins without any ornaments.
5. Many of the Chera portrait coins and Roman coins exhibit a dotted or beaded border along the edge of the flan.
6. The diameter of both the Roman and Chera coins is around 1.8 cm.
7. The weight of the known Mākkōtai and Kuṭṭuvaṇkōtai coins (1.7 to 2.2 grams) is almost half the weight of the Roman silver coin (3.4 to 3.9 grams). But if, as stated earlier, these Chera coins are only the 'obverse pieces' of the coin, then the weight of the Tamil coin would be almost equal to a Roman denarius, on the assumption that the 'reverse piece' of these Chera coins would be equal in weight to the 'obverse piece'.

Other Principal Obverse Devices

The obverse of a few Chera quadrangular coins feature, instead of an animal or a deity or a royal portrait, certain other devices such as a tree-in-railing, or else four three-petalled flowers radiating from a circle with a conspicuous dot at its centre; taurine symbols are seen in between the flowers. These obverse devices are not very different from similar ones seen on *kārṣāpaṇas*.

Combination of Principal Obverse Devices

Normally, the above-mentioned devices do not occur together on the obverse, However, there are coins featuring both the elephant and the tree-in-railing, and, very rarely, the elephant and the bull.

.ces

vices, the obverse features several
often above or below the main device.
-hed or six-arched hill, sometimes sur-
.uted pillar with a rectangular base, battle
trident, bow and arrow, thunderbolt, dumb-
alled flower, garland, triskelion, conch, wheel,
.ed *svastika*, *pūrṇaghaṭa*, five-pointed star, sun,
.er, cock, peacock, tortoise, snake and fish. Some
devices like the snake and the fish are quite common
ıike the human figure, the cock and the peacock are
.skelion is the rarest symbol that is clearly seen only on
.angam Chera coin so far.

.tanding human figure seen on a few coins is highly stylized.
.gure is seen at the edge of the coin, next to a tree or flagstaff.
.quently, the human figure is partially out of the flan. The fish is
.alistically depicted, often in the sea or in a river. The sea or the river is indicated by wavy lines. Here, the sea may represent the Arabian Sea that bordered the Chera kingdom on the west. The river may be Amaravati, on whose banks the Chera capital was located, or Periyār, the biggest river of the kingdom, or else any of the smaller rivers, some of them tributaries of the Periyār, flowing through the Chera land. Significantly, the mighty Periyār has been vividly described and eulogized in early Tamil poems dealing with the Sangam Chera kings.[17] On some coins, the fishes are shown inside a square or rectangular tank. A very rare coin shows a row of fishes within a narrow long-winding canal, skilfully indicated by two parallel curves below the elephant.

The snake with its sharp fangs and sinuous body is also realistically portrayed. Sometimes fishes are depicted in between the bends of the body of the long snake.

A rare Chera coin portraying the bow (Chera emblem), tiger (Cōḷa emblem) and fish (Pāṇḍya emblem) may be interpreted as representing Chera superiority or supremacy over the other two powers. Appropriately, the bow is placed above the fish and the tiger on this coin.

Religious symbols such as the *svastika* and *śrīvatsa* generally occur only on some coins where the elephant is the principal obverse

device. A few religious symbols s
rarely occur on the horse obverse
usually absent on coins where the m
lion, tree-in-railing or flowers radiating
auspicious symbols are noticed on coins
the bull together on the obverse. The tiny
shown in a row above the elephant or the horse
coins, up to six such symbols appear above the a
which is one of the commonest auspicious symbo
is sometimes delineated in dots. In one instance, th
on a stalk or pillar.

Reverse Devices

Bow and Arrow

The reverse of the Chera quadrangular copper coins mostly bear the symbol of the bow and arrow, which was the royal emblem of the Cheras from very early times (Plate 8). A single coin bears two sets of these symbols. Sometimes the *aṅkuśa* (goad) is shown above, below, or on the right or left, of the bow and arrow. Some

Plate 8: Sangam Chera coin—bow and arrow reverse.

coins exhibit a taurine at the end of the arrow or else two taurines, one on either side of the arrow. Some other coins feature a single taurine and a group of fishes surrounding the bow and arrow, with two fishes within the bow, one on either side of the arrow.

An uncommon coin displays two *svastikas*—one right-handed and the other left-handed—one on either side of the arrow. These are not the usual forms of the *svastika* but have curved arms, and are sometimes seen on chalcolithic pottery, punch-marked coins and as countermarks on Roman coins in Andhra. In a very rare instance, the reverse of a Sangam Chera coin displays a part of the Ujjain symbol which may have been borrowed from the *kārṣāpaṇas* or the early Sātavāhana issues. Unlike the obverse, the reverse motifs and devices on Chera coins are sometimes enclosed by a linear circle, a dotted circle, a dotted quadrangle or, in one case, a triple border—a dotted circle enclosed by a linear circle which, in turn, is enclosed by a larger dotted circle.

As regards the Chera circular coins, the silver coins have a blank reverse but the copper ones depict, besides the bow and arrow, taurine and fishes, six-arched hills, the tortoise and the river, represented by a wavy line. One may recall that the latter three devices are common on the obverse of Chera coins.

On most Chera coins, the bow and arrow is realistically depicted but on some specimens, the device is stylized to the extent that the bow appears stiff and sometimes it is in the shape of a triangle, totally devoid of the usual curves and elasticity. On others, the posterior end of the arrow is curved or twisted.

What made the Sangam Cheras adopt the bow and arrow, an important weapon in primitive warfare, as their royal insignia and portray the same on an overwhelming majority of their coins? Probably they were inspired by the bow and arrow symbol seen on megalithic pottery and some rare *kārṣāpaṇas*, at least one specimen of which, as stated earlier, was found in the Chera capital of Karur. It is plausible that the Cheras even had access to the bow and arrow device coins of the Sātavāhanas and Kuras who ruled the region north of the Chera territory during the early historical period. The Cheras would also have been aware of Kṣatrapa Nāhapāṇa's (second century AD) famous coins bearing the arrow. Interestingly, a stylized representation of the bow and arrow, very similar to the one seen on Chera coins, is engraved in the middle of an early Vaṭṭeḻuttu cave inscription (fifth century AD) at Sittannavasal near Pudukkottai in Tamil Nadu, a site within the Pāṇḍya kingdom and quite far from the Chera kingdom.

It may be noted that no dynasty has featured the bow and arrow on such a large number of coins, and in such a prominent manner, as the Sangam Cheras. The Cheras have been intimately identified with the bow and arrow and are sometimes called *Villavar* (bow men).

Lion

The copper coins featuring goddess Yamuna on the obverse portray a lion on the reverse. The huge animal is seated to the left. The tail is represented not by linear curves but by a series of small circles or dots. It is raised and twisted. Yamuna is sometimes considered another form of goddess Durga whose mount is the lion.

Legends

Legends, mainly confined to the silver and copper circular coins, are in the Tamil language and, as indicated earlier, in the Tamil Brāhmī script. They furnish the names or titles of the kings. For example, the legend *Kolippuṛai* may be a title assumed by the Chera ruler after his conquest of the area covered by the Kolli hills in the Salem region of Tamil Nadu.[18]

Many of the legends are placed along the margin or edge on the upper half of the flan, from left to right. In the case of the silver bust type coins, the legend is sometimes placed just above the head and, from a distance, appears like a spiked crown or helmet over the royal head. The legends are well-incised but do not display any artistic flourishes or calligraphic features unlike those on the coins of certain later dynasties. Stylistically, the Chera coin legends could be compared with the early Tamil Brāhmī cave inscriptions found in Mangulam (second century BC?) and other sites in Tamil Nadu.

NOTES AND REFERENCES

1. For a general account of the political, economic and social history of the Cheras, Cōḷas and Pāṇḍyas, see K.K. Pillay, *A Social History of the Tamils* I (Madras, 1975); C.E. Ramachandran, *Ahanānūru in its Historical Setting*

(Madras, 1974). Also see K.A. Nilakanta Sastri, *A History of South India: From Prehistoric Times to the Fall of Vijayanagara* (New Delhi, 2002), pp. 104-31. For a general survey of the history and coins of Tamil Nadu region, see R. Nagaswamy, *Tamil Coins: A Study* (Madras, 1981).

2. Coins of the Sangam Cheras are being frequently picked up from the dry bed of the river Amaravati near Karur. Some of these coins are sold as scrap metal by the vessel merchants of Karur. Local private collectors acquire most of these finds or else, the coins reach antique markets abroad. Until recently, these discoveries did not attract academic attention. Not surprisingly, these coins are rare in museum collections. I am thankful to S. Raman (Madras), A. Sitaraman (Tanjavur), K.A. Thirugnanasampandam (Erode) and Vidwan I. Ramasamy (Boluvampatti near Coimbatore) for showing me their personal collections of coins and also for providing me valuable information regarding these new finds.
3. The *Periplus* 56 lists metals such as antimony, copper, tin and lead as imports to India.
4. For more details and translations of some of these verses, see Vidwan I. Ramasamy, 'Ancient Chera Coin Found (Globule)', *JNSI*, LIII 1&2 (1991), pp. 64-5. Here, the author describes a gold punch-marked Chera coin in the shape of a margosa fruit. I have physically examined the coin. It is somewhat oval-shaped and is not of gold but copper.
5. R. Krishnamurthy, 'Mākkōtai Coins', *SSIC* II (1992), pp. 89-93.
6. R. Krishnamurthy, 'A Note on Counterstruck Silver Coin of Mākkōtai', *SSIC* VIII (1998), pp. 35-9.
7. P. Vijayaraghavan, 'A Further Note on the Silver Punchmarked Chera Coin From Karur', *SSIC* XI (2001), pp. 60-1. Also see P. Vijayaraghavan, 'A Punch-marked Chera Silver Coin From Karur', *SSIC* X (2000), pp. 28-31.
8. Recent research has established that the maritime trade between south India and the Mediterranean regions began around 300 BC. For a detailed discussion on the date of the commencement of the trade, see V. Begley, 'Arikamedu Reconsidered', *AJA* 87 (1983), pp. 461-81; idem, 'Rouletted Ware at Arikamedu: A New Approach', *AJA* 92 (1988), pp. 427-40; idem, 'Ceramic Evidence for Pre-*Periplus* Trade on the Indian Coasts', in V. Begley and Richard Daniel De Puma, eds., *Rome and India: The Ancient Sea Trade* (Madison, 1991), pp. 157-96; S. Suresh, *Symbols of Trade: Roman and Pseudo-Roman Objects Found in India* (New Delhi, 2004), pp. 28-30, 153-4.
9. The *Ahanānūru* and the *Puraṇānūru* are among the earliest Tamil poems (first century BC?) with descriptions of wars and war-strategies of the period. In particular, the latter work has beautiful descriptions of the king's elephants: 'The king has elephants which fight as if they were ramming mountains. . . .' For more details regarding the elephant in the ancient Tamil kingdoms and references to this animal in the *Puraṇānūru*, see Beena Sarasan, 'An Unique Punch Marked Coin of Venad', *SSIC* XV (2005), pp. 30-4, mainly p. 33 fn. 2.

10. An ancient papyrus discovered in Vienna mentions the shipment of nard, ivory and textiles from Muziris (Kerala) to Alexandria (Africa). See H. Harrauer and P.J. Sijpesteijn, 'Ein neues Dokument Zu Roms Indienhandel: P. Vindob. G 40822', *Anzeiger der Akademie der Wissenschaften, Wien, Philologisch-historische Klasse* 122 (1985), pp. 124-55. Also see L. Casson, 'P. Vindob G 40822 and the Shipping of Goods From India', *Bulletin of the American Society of Papyrologists* 23 (1986), pp. 73-9; idem, 'New Light on Maritime Loans: P. Vindob G.40822', in Ranabir Chakravarti, ed., *Trade in Early India* (New Delhi, 2001), pp. 228-43.
11. I am grateful to I. Mahadevan for drawing my attention to this seal.
12. For more details regarding the religious beliefs of the Sātavāhanas, the religious motifs on their coins and the published references on this subject, refer to Chapter 7 of this book.
13. P. Shanmugam and S. Raman, 'A River Goddess (?) Coin From Karur', *SSIC* XI (2001), pp. 62-4.
14. This poem gives a graphic description of the appearance, physical features and dress of the *yavanas* or foreigners in the Tamil country. It is said that the *yavanas* were so strong, well-built and fearsome-looking that they were employed as gatekeepers or watchmen by the kings in Tamiḻakam (*Mullaipāṭṭu* 59-62).
15. For a brief survey of the portraiture on ancient coins, see T. Sathyamurthy, *Catalogue of Roman Gold Coins (In the Collections of Department of Archaeology, Kerala)* (Thiruvananthapuram, 1992), p. 8; R. Krishnamurthy, *Sangam Age Tamil Coins* (Madras, 1997), pp. 101-3.
16. For more details on the art in Roman coins, refer to Appendix IV of this book.
17. The most important reference is found in the *Ahanānūru*. One verse (149, 7-11) of this work refers to the *yavana* ships arriving at Muziris which is located at the spot where the Periyār joins the sea. 'The ships, stirring the white foam of the Periyār river, sail in with gold and sail off with pepper . . .'.
18. This legend has been read and interpreted in different ways by many scholars like R. Nagaswamy, I. Mahadevan and P. Shanmugam. See R. Nagaswamy, *Roman Karur: A Peep into Tamils' Past* (Madras, 1995), pp. 9-10; I. Mahadevan, *Early Tamil Epigraphy: From the Earliest Times to the Sixth Century AD* (Madras, 2003), pp. 62, 118; P. Shanmugam, 'Two Inscribed Coins of the Sangam Age Cheras', *SSIC* XV (2005), pp. 53-7.

CHAPTER 4

Coins of the Sangam Cōḷas

The kingdom of the Sangam Cōḷas mainly consisted of parts of northern and central Tamil Nadu with the epicentre of power in the Tiruchi-Tanjavur region of central Tamil Nadu.[1] The Cōḷas had two capitals—Uraiyur (near the city of Tiruchirappalli or Tiruchi) was their main capital while the port-city of Kaveripumpattinam (also called Kaveripattinam, Cōḷapattinam or Kolapattana) served as the secondary one. Uraiyur was known for its fine cotton textiles, while Kaveripumpattinam was a major trading port and harbour.

The important Cōḷa rulers included Karikālan, Nedun Kiḷḷi, Nalan Kiḷḷi, Koperum Cōḷan and Chenganan but their precise dates are unknown. Among them, Karikālan was the greatest. The name 'Karikālan' means either 'charred leg' or 'hunter of elephants'. Thus, it is said that he lost one of his legs in a fire accident and was an expert in subduing enemy elephants during war. Probably his favourite pastime was elephant-hunting. He built the Kaḷḷanai dam across the river Kāverī near the city of Tiruchi. After his death, the power of the Sangam Cōḷas rapidly declined.

Many coins of the Sangam Cōḷas have been recovered from Karur and Tirukoilur in Tamil Nadu.[2] Obviously, Cōḷa coins reached the Chera capital of Karur during the course of trade. Archaeological digs at the coastal sites of Kaveripattinam and Arikamedu (near Pondicherry) have revealed Sangam Cōḷa coins.[3] A few coins also occur in Sri Lanka. An interesting coin of this dynasty was reported in a stratified context from the distant site of Khuan Luk Pat on the west coast of Thailand.[4] It is rather surprising that no Sangam Cōḷa coin was found during archaeological excavations at their capital city of Uraiyur.[5]

PHYSICAL FEATURES AND PRODUCTION METHOD

The majority of Sangam Cōḷa coins are made of copper and a few the copper obtained from copper mines spread in different parts of south India. Tamiḷakam did not have large lead deposits. Hence, the Cōḷas may have imported the lead found in Rajasthan, Bihar and Andhra or, more likely, from Myanmar (Burma). As indicated in the last chapter, south India also imported copper and lead from Rome. The early lead coins of the Mahārathis and the Sātavāhanas (second-first centuries BC?) and later, the lead imitations of the first century AD. Roman coins, all found in the Maharashtra-Andhra region, may have inspired the Sangam Cōḷas and, to a limited extent, the Sangam Cheras too, to produce lead coins.

The Cōḷa copper coins come in various shapes such as squares, rectangles, circles and semi-circles. The majority of these coins are, however, rectangular in shape. The length of each side of the quadrangular coins ranges between 1.1 and 2.2 cm, with a single rectangular specimen measuring 2.7 cm × 2.6 cm. The weight of these coins ranges from less than 1 gram to over 7 grams; the average weight is 4.5 grams. However, the big coin, measuring 2.7 cm × 2.6 cm, weighs 14 grams. The diameter of the copper circular coins ranges from 1.2 to 1.7 cm. The weight of these coins ranges from 1 to 3 grams.

A unique semi-elliptical Sangam Cōḷa copper coin has also been discovered. This coin seems to have been produced by neatly cutting an elliptical metal blank into two pieces, almost equal to one another. The diameter of this coin is 1.5 cm and its weight is 1.7 grams. It is plausible that this coin was initially a large elliptical one, later cut into two to maintain the weight standard.

The lead coins are always circular in shape. These circular coins are far bigger than the circular copper coins. The diameter of the lead coins ranges from 2.5 to 3.2 cm. Their weight ranges from 8.5 to 12.5 grams. Probably the very light coins lost weight during the long period when they circulated as legal tender. This argument is further supported by the fact that most of the lighter issues appear extremely worn.

Many of the coins are die-struck but a few specimens have been manufactured by the process of punching, commonly used for the production of *kārṣāpaṇas*. One rectangular copper coin exhibits both these minting processes—the obverse has been die-struck, following which the reverse motif has been punched on the flan.[6] The unusually heavy coin (weighing 14 grams) and a few more Cōḷa coins were, like the Sangam Chera silver portrait coins, apparently produced in two pieces—the obverse piece and the reverse piece—both of which were fused back to back.

The Sangam Cōḷas did not mint silver coins due to the scarcity of silver in south India. Unlike the Sangam Cheras, the Cōḷas did not think of counterstamping the Roman denarii or the *kārṣāpaṇas* for use as local coinage in their land. Instead, they often used foreign silver coins as local currency, without effecting any countermark on them.

The Sangam Cōḷas appear to have had mints at Uraiyur, Kaveripattinam and a few other places in the kingdom. All the mints followed certain common guidelines regarding the design and weight of the coins. These would have been framed by the Cōḷa king or senior officials in charge of the mints and the currency.

ART AND SYMBOLOGY

The symbols and motifs on the Sangam Cōḷa coins are many but do not display such a rich variety as those on the Sangam Chera coins.

Obverse Devices

Elephant

The obverse of over 99 per cent of Sangam Cōḷa coins depicts a well-built elephant as the principal device. The animal is standing to the right or left. Its trunk mostly hangs downwards and terminates in a beautiful inward or, rarely, outward twist. On a large majority of the coins, the animal does not possess tusks. In fact, the lead coins never display the tusked elepant.

Sometimes the elephant is standing on a platform. On a few coins, it is shown on a six-arched hill as if it is struggling to climb the hill. A rare lead coin shows the animal holding a ball (coconut?) in its trunk. On most of the copper coins, an umbrella, sometimes richly decorated, is normally seen above, behind or, rarely, in front of the elephant. On many coins, an ornamented chariot, which, in some instances, is driven by one or two horses, is shown in front of the elephant. The superstructure of the chariot has not been clearly delineated on any of the specimens. Some of them appear to be tall with a conical top. The chariot wheels, some of them huge and having several spokes, are prominently represented. On a few coins, the wheel with a conspicuous axle is shown to represent the entire chariot.

Unlike some of the Sangam Chera coins that exhibit warriors riding on the elephant, the Cōḷa coins never show any warrior on or near the animal. Like the Cheras, the Cōḷas, too, accorded great reverence to elephants that played a major role in their wars and economy. The animal was frequently featured in local folklore.

Horse

On several Cōḷa elephant type coins that do not feature the chariot, a horse is shown standing behind the elephant and, on one coin, standing in front of and facing it. On all these coins, a pillar or column is seen between the horse and the elephant. This may represent the *yūpastambha* (sacrificial post), in which case the coin may be taken to represent the *aśvamedha yajña* (horse sacrifice) performed by the Sangam Cōḷa rulers. Significantly, the reverse of one such Cōḷa coin shows a circular *yajñakuṇḍa* (sacrificial pit) with four rectangular projections on one side.

Besides being featured along with the elephant, the horse is also depicted on some coins as the principal obverse device. On coins where the main device is the elephant, the horse is, not surprisingly, shown as a small creature, often stiff and lifeless. On many of these coins, only a part of its body is depicted. Even on coins featuring the horse as the main device, the animal appears rather stiff, without any sense of movement. The eyes, mane and other finer details of the body have not been delineated. The animal, with its long legs that do not have any bends or folds, appears to be standing erect on the ground and not galloping or moving. At least for the *aśvamedha* type coins, such a manner of depiction may have been intended to convey that the animal was to be shortly sacrificed and hence, appears sad and lifeless, without vigour and strength. One may recall that some of the famous *aśvamedha* coins of the imperial Guptas (fourth-fifth centuries AD) feature the horse in the same way.[7]

Bull

The bull is rarely seen on Sangam Cōḷa coins. On the obverse of one coin, it is seen behind the elephant. Its front legs are lifted up as it strains to eat the leaves on a tall tree-in-railing. On another coin without the elephant, the bull is shown climbing a six-arched hill in order to reach the leaves of a tree-in-railing. On rarer specimens, the obverse exhibits a humped bull to the right with two taurines below it. On all these coins, the bull is quite plastic in its form. Its horns and bushy tail have been realistically delineated.

Tree-in-railing

Apart from being featured along with the elephant and/or the bull, the tree-in-railing is sometimes featured as the sole device on the obverse of certain Cōḷa coins. On these, the tree-in-railing is flanked by two taurines, one on each side. On some coins, the tree is full of round fruits.

Subsidiary or Smaller Obverse Devices

Apart from principal devices such as the elephant, horse and bull, the obverse of Cōḷa coins bear many smaller devices such as the three-arched and six-arched hill, river, five-petalled flower jutting out of a basin, full-bloomed lotus, crescent (sometimes with a dot within it), sun, *śrīvatsa*, conch, *triśūla* (trident), triangle-headed spear, bow and arrow, battle axe, pitcher with a long spout, flag mast, human footprint, tortoise or turtle, and fish. It may be noted that the tree-in-railing occurs both as a sole obverse device and as a small ancillary device along with various other devices on the obverse of different coins. Various other unidentified quadrangular as well as oval-shaped symbols are faintly seen on some of these coins, mostly above the elephant device.

In most cases, subsidiary devices surround the main device on each coin. While some are realistically depicted, others are highly stylized. Sometimes the same device is depicted in different forms on varied coins. To cite an instance, fishes are mostly depicted in a realistic manner but are sometimes featured as small zig-zag lines. They are mostly exhibited moving, one behind the other, within a tank, canal or river. The river is, as usual, represented by two wavy lines, parallel to each other. Here, it may denote the river Kāverī on whose banks the Cōḷa capitals—Uraiyur and Kaveripattinam—were situated.

Among the religious symbols on these coins, those connected with Śaivism deserve special mention. Such symbols include the *triśūla*, one of the attributes of God Śiva and the triangle-headed spear closely connected with Kārttikeya, Murugā or Kumāra, the son of Śiva. In this context, one may note that Uraiyur, was a centre of Śaivism from very early times. Murugā was a popular deity in this region and the Tamil Sangam poems contain copious references to him, his iconographic features and the way in which he was worshipped by men and women.[8]

Among other sacred symbols, a distinct variety of the sun symbol, without rays or spokes but encircled by taurines, is seen above the elephant and six-arched hill on a rare Cōḷa coin. This variety of the sun symbol is occasionally seen on *kārṣāpaṇas*, too. Another variety of the sun with rays represented by thin strokes, almost identical to the symbol seen on numerous Mauryan *kārṣāpaṇas*, appears behind or above the elephant on some Cōḷa coins. A third variety of the sun symbol with rays shown as solid bars, unknown to the Mauryas and the *kārṣāpaṇas*, also appears on some of the Cōḷa coins. This variety of the sun symbol (rising sun?) is usually depicted partly hidden by the elephant, just above its head. The latter two varieties of the sun symbol are also occasionally displayed on the reverse of the Sangam Cōḷa coins, normally above the main device. The repeated depiction of the sun symbol and, rarely, the lotus flower, again closely associated with the sun, on Sangam Cōḷa issues may be associated with the fact that the Cōḷas belonged to the Solar race (*Sūryavaṁśa*). In the same vein, the frequent depiction of the crescent or the lunar symbol on imperial Gupta coins is linked to the lunar origin of that dynasty.[9]

A rare Cōḷa lead coin features a lifelike human footprint in front of the elephant, next to the trunk. This may have some religious connotation. It may represent the feet of the Buddha (*Buddhapāda*). Significantly, a representation of the *Buddhapāda* in stone has been recovered from layers of the first century BC-first century AD, during archaeological digs at Kaveripattinam, the secondary capital of the Sangam Cōḷas.[10] Such footprints are, however, very rare on early Indian coins.

On one of the Cōḷa coins with the horse as the main device, the bow and arrow symbol appears above the animal. Incidentally, this is the only Cōḷa coin bearing this symbol. However, the bow and arrow on this coin is quite different from the same motif commonly seen on Sangam Chera coins. The bow on the Cōḷa coin is bigger, heavier and thicker than that on the latter coins.

Among other ancillary motifs, the flag mast has been shown in an inverted position on a Cōḷa coin. One is not able to think of any particular reason for placing the flag mast in this position. Probably this was an unintentional mistake on the part of the die-cutter.

Reverse Devices

Tiger

The reverse of the Sangam Cōḷa coins mostly portray a tiger prancing or moving, usually to the left and sometimes to the right (Plate 9).[11] Wide variations are seen in the size and shape of the animal on different coins. Although the anatomical features have not been

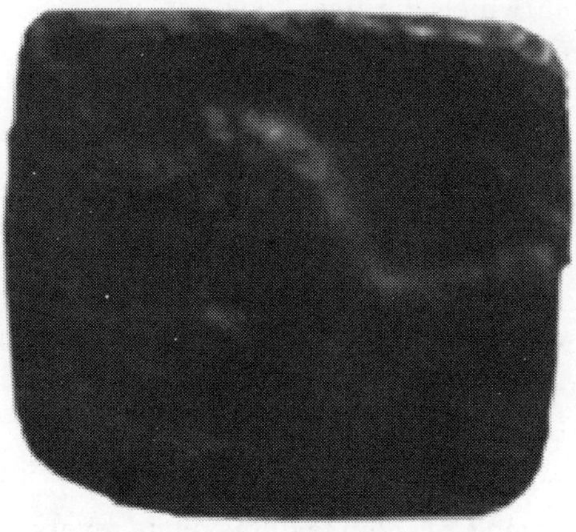

Plate 9: Sangam Cōḷa coin—tiger reverse.

clearly brought out, the sense of movement has been most effectively conveyed through bends in all the four legs, the lifting up of the forelegs, the wide open mouth, and the uplifted and twisted tail. On many coins, the right foreleg is raised to a great height while the left foreleg is raised slightly above the ground. Often, the tail is raised above the body in an 'S'-shaped twist. The animal mostly appears ferocious.

On a few coins, a peacock is perched on top of a flag mast in front of the tiger. The curved beak and rich plumage of the bird are clearly seen. On a sole specimen, a tree-in-railing is shown in front of the tiger. Sometimes religious symbols such as the sun and, rarely, the crescent, lamp and *śrīvatsa* occur either above or in front of the animal. Occasionally, the tiger is surrounded by a square border or double-border of small dots or circles (strings of pearls?) or taurine symbols.

The depiction of the tiger on Sangam Cōḷa coins has to be viewed in the light of the fact that it was the royal emblem of the dynasty. There are numerous references to the tiger in the Tamil Sangam literature (second century BC-second century AD).[12] It is significant that the tiger figure on Sangam Cōḷa coins is a replica of its vivid description in literary works. The Cōḷa king, according to the Sangam work *Puraṇānūru*, was adorned with shawls and armour bearing the tiger emblem. The ruler was supposed to protect his subjects in the same manner in which the tiger took care of her cubs. The tiger emblem was engraved on the doors of the Cōḷa forts as also on other forts captured by them. The animal has also been featured on many jewels and seals of the period. A gold finger ring, recovered from Karur, bears a Brāhmī inscription reading *Bramhasahasa* and below it, the figure of a tiger facing left, remarkably identical to the tiger seen on many Cōḷa coins.[13] The ancient people of Tamiḷakam considered the tooth of the tiger a talisman and tied it to a long thread or chain that was worn like a necklace. Kings and warriors often wore the teeth of the tigers that they hunted.

Eagle

An unusual Sangam Cōḷa coin features on its reverse, instead of the tiger, an eagle holding a pair of leaves or a small snake in its beak. The full body of the bird has not been portrayed. The long neck and beak alone have been depicted. A *yajñakuṇḍa*, a series of minute, indistinct, circular symbols, and a flag staff are seen around the bird.

NOTES AND REFERENCES

1. For a general account of the political, economic and social history of the Sangam Cōḷas, see K.K. Pillay, *A Social History of the Tamils* I (Madras, 1975); C.E. Ramachandran, *Ahanānūru in its Historical Setting* (Madras, 1974). Also see, R. Krishnamurthy, *Sanga Kāla Cōḷar Nāṇayangal* (Tamil) (Madras, 1986), pp. 1-6; idem, *Sangam Age Tamil Coins* (Madras, 1997), pp. 1-11, 109-11; K.A. Nilakanta Sastri, *A History of South India: From Prehistoric Times to the Fall of Vijayanagara* (New Delhi, 2002), pp. 104-31.
2. Like the Sangam Chera coins, Sangam Cōḷa coins are also rare in museum collections. I am grateful to S. Raman (Madras), A. Sitaraman (Tanjavur), K.A. Thirugnanasampandam (Erode) and Vidwan I. Ramasamy (Boluvampatti near Coimbatore) for showing me their personal collections of the Sangam Cōḷa and other coins.
3. K.V. Raman, 'An Early Chola Coin From Arikamedu', *SSIC* III (1993), pp. 87-8. Also see T. Sathyamurthy, 'Numismatic Evidences From Archaeological Excavations: Chennai Circle', *SSIC* XV (2005), pp. 110-18.
4. P. Shanmugam, 'Two Coins of Tamil Origin From Thailand', *SSIC* IV (1994), pp. 95-100.
5. The site was excavated for four seasons from 1964-5 to 1969 by the Department of Ancient History and Archaeology of the University of Madras, Madras. For details of the digs, see K.V. Raman, ed., *Excavations at Uraiyur (Tiruchirappalli) 1965-69* (Madras, 1988).
6. For more details of this coin see R. Krishnamurthy, 'A Rare Sangam Period Chola Coin', *SSIC* I (1991), pp. 31-2.
7. B.N. Mukherjee, *Art in Gupta and Post-Gupta Coinages of Northern India* (Lucknow, 1985), pp. 21-2. Also see Pratapaditya Pal, 'A Sacrificial Horse and a Mysterious Script', *South Asian Studies* 3 (1987), pp. 47-52. Incidentally, the Guptas also produced stone sculptures of *aśvamedha* horses, exhibiting the same physical characteristics and emotions as the *aśvamedha* horses on the coins. One such stone sculpture found at Khairigarh (Uttar Pradesh region) is now in the State Museum, Lucknow. As per inscriptions on the sculpture, this is the replica of the horse sacrificed at the *aśvamedha* performed by the Gupta king, Kumāragupta I (AD 415-56). It is plausible that the sculptor was also the die-cutter of these coins.
8. *Tirumurugāṟṟupaḍai* is the most important Sangam period text dealing with Murugā worship. For more details, see R. Champakalakshmi, 'From Kuṟiñci

to Tamiḷakam: The Universalisation and Emergence of Sacred Geography in the Cult of Murukaṇ', Paper presented at the first international conference seminar on Skanda-Murukan (Madras, 1998). For a bibliography of Kārttik-Murugā in Tamil and English, see G. John Samuel et al., eds., *The First International Conference Seminar on Skanda-Murukan-1998 Souvenir* (Madras, 1998), pp. 155-70.

9. Chhanda Mukherjee, *Gupta Numismatic Art: An Artistic and Iconographic Study* (Delhi, 1991), p. 71.
10. K.V. Raman, 'Excavations at Pumpuhar', in *The Handbook (II International Tamil Conference)* (Madras, 1968), pp. 238-40. The *Buddhapāda* slab is now preserved in the office of the ASI caretaker for the site. It is made of limestone and also features other auspicious symbols such as the *svastika* and the *pūrṇaghaṭa.*
11. Brajadulal Chattopadhyaya, *Coins and Currency Systems in South India c.* AD *225-1300* (New Delhi, 1977), p. 52. Here, the author raises doubts about the identification of the reverse figure as the tiger. According to him, the figure appears to be a 'typical lion . . . such as those which appear on Pallava coins'. Hence, he tentatively assigns some of the coins, originally attributed to the Sangam Cōḷas, to the Pallavas.
12. For an exhaustive account of the early Tamil literary references to the tiger and other devices on Sangam Cōḷa coins, see R. Krishnamurthy, 1986 (supra n. 1), pp. 53-65. Also see S. Suresh, 'Defence Architecture in the Early Tamil Country', *Proceedings of the Indian History Congress: Forty-ninth Session, 1988* (Delhi, 1989), pp. 657-61.
13. A.M. Shastri, 'An Unique Identity Ring From Karur', *SSIC* XI (2001), pp. 57-9.

CHAPTER 5

Coins of the Sangam Pāṇḍyas

The Sangam Pāṇḍya kingdom comprised the regions of Madurai, Ramanathapuram and Tirunelveli in southern Tamil Nadu. The kingdom was situated immediately south of the Cōḷa kingdom, the river Kāverī often forming the boundary between the two. Thus, the Pāṇḍyas were the rulers of the southernmost tip of India and were closest to the island of Sri Lanka.[1]

Madurai, also called Kūḍal, was the capital of the Pāṇḍyas. Marungurpattinam or Alagankulam and Korkai were the chief ports of the kingdom. The Pāṇḍyas carried on brisk trade with Rome, Sri Lanka and South-East Asia from these ports. It is said that a Pāṇḍya king even sent an ambassador to the court of the Roman Emperor Augustus (27 BC-AD 14).

The important Sangam Pāṇḍya rulers were Palyāgasālai Mudukudumi Peruvaḷuthi, Kadalulmaintha Iḷam Peruvaḷuthi, Veḷḷiambalattutunjiya Peruvaḷuthi and Āriyapadaikadantha Neduncheḷian. The name of the last-mentioned king literally means 'Nedunchеḷian who conquered the Āryan army', probably indicating his conquest of some north Indian kingdom. The precise dates of all these kings are not known. In any case, it is clear that by AD 300, the Pāṇḍya kingdom declined along with the Cheras and Cōḷas.

Sangam Pāṇḍya coins have been discovered at Madurai and a few other places within the Pāṇḍya territory. They were also found at Karur, the Chera capital.[2] A large number were reported from many sites such as Kantarodai in Sri Lanka. The historic site of Anuradhapura in Sri Lanka has yielded a Sangam Pāṇḍya coin in a stratified context.[3] The contention that these finds in Sri Lanka may be the issues of a Sri Lankan Tamil ruler has been disproved.[4] The Pāṇḍya coins reached these distant places by the process of trade.

PHYSICAL FEATURES AND PRODUCTION METHOD

The Pāṇḍyas issued coins mostly in copper and sometimes in silver. As regards their source of copper, besides the imports from Rome, they would have obtained the metal from different mines in south India and Sri Lanka as well.[5] Indeed, the very name of Tāmbraparṇī, one of the major rivers of the Pāṇḍya kingdom, is said to be derived from the Tamil word 'Tāmbaram' meaning 'copper', indicating the occurrence of this metal on its banks. Recent archaeological evidences have further proved that the Pāṇḍya region was particularly rich in copper deposits. Adichanallur (24 km from the city of Tirunelveli, close to the Tāmbraparṇī) has revealed copper deposits that were used during the early historical times. Incidentally, this site also revealed iron deposits. The site has been recently subjected to large-scale archaeological digs.[6]

As silver deposits were unknown in the Pāṇḍya region, these rulers should have melted the silver *kārṣāpaṇas*, Roman denarii and also, possibly, the Sātavāhana silver coins reaching their territory. Such a hypothesis is reinforced by the fact that *kārṣāpaṇas*, Roman coins and even Sātavāhana coins exercised profound influence on the Sangam Pāṇḍya coins. The extent of this influence will be made clear in the following section on the art and symbology of the Sangam Pāṇḍya coins.

The Sangam Pāṇḍya coins are mostly quadrangular—square or rectangular, and, occasionally, hexagonal in shape. In some instances, two corners of the quadrangular coin are clipped off to obtain the desired weight and, in the process, the coin becomes a hexagon. Circular coins are extremely rare among Sangam Pāṇḍya issues. There has, so far, been only one well-recorded circular coin of this dynasty.

As regards the quadrangular and hexagonal coins, the length of each side ranges from 0.25 to 2.8. cm. Wide variations are also discernible with regard to the weight of these coins. Specimens as light as 0.5 gram, and as heavy as 12.2 grams have been reported, although an overwhelming majority weigh between 3 to 5 grams. In general, these Sangam Pāṇḍya coins are thicker and heavier than many of the Sangam Chera and Sangam Cōḷa coins. The sole well-documented circular Sangam Pāṇḍya coin is made of copper, and its diameter is 1.4 cm and weight 1.6 grams.

Most of the Sangam Pāṇḍya coins are die-struck. There are thousands of punch-marked coins too. While all the die-struck coins are of copper, the punch-marked coins are of silver as well as copper. Many of the latter are, except for their reverse symbol, identical to the *kārṣāpaṇas* found north of Tamil Nadu.

The Sangam Pāṇḍyas seem to have had several mints mostly located in and around their capital Madurai.

ART AND SYMBOLOGY

Among the coins of the early Tamil kingdoms, those of the Sangam Pāṇḍyas exhibit the maximum number of symbols and art motifs. The variegated symbols and devices on these coins do not lend themselves to any clear-cut classification and seem to have been inspired by different sources, including the Mauryan *kārṣāpaṇas.*

OBVERSE DEVICES

Kārṣāpaṇa Symbols on Kārṣāpaṇa-like Coins

All Sangam Pāṇḍya punch-marked coins display five distinct symbols on the obverse. These coins include 1,124 of the 1,138 silver coins of the well-known Bodinayakanur hoard; of the remaining 14 coins in the hoard, 13 are either blank pieces or pieces on which the symbols have worn out, and 1 coin has been identified as a Mauryan *kārṣāpaṇa.*

Among the symbols on the Pāṇḍya punch-marked coins, the commonest ones are the sun and the *ṣaḍaracakra*, which is a circle with a dot in the centre and enclosed by six arms—three arrowheads and three taurines. The other important symbols seen on the obverse of these coins include the *stūpa* or the temple symbol, foliage, tree-in-railing, tree without railing, *triśūla*, axe, taurine, dog or hare holding a pup in the mouth, fish and duck. Many of these are identical to similar symbols seen on *kārṣāpaṇas* elsewhere. The sole evidence for attributing these punch-marked coins to the Sangam Pāṇḍyas is the reverse device which is a fish—the dynastic crest of the Pāṇḍyas. Also, the weight (1.2 to 2.8 grams) of these punch-marked coins is much lower than the Mauryan *kārṣāpaṇas* that normally weigh around 3.3 grams. Incidentally, these Pāṇḍya punch-marked coins are the only *kārṣāpaṇas* unequivocally attributed to a local dynasty of south India.

Elephant

Leaving aside the Pāṇḍya punch-marked coins which form a distinct group, one of the commonest obverse devices on Pāṇḍya coins is the elephant, standing mostly to the right and, rarely, to the left (Plate 10). The animal is well-delineated. The trunk hangs down and gently curves inwards. Minute details such as the folds on the skin of the legs and the braid of hair at the end of the tail have been skilfully chiselled. On most coins, the tusks appear slender but are pointed and sometimes prominently bent upwards. Unlike on the Sangam Chera and Sangam Cōḷa coins, the elephant on many of the Pāṇḍya coins is richly decorated. On some coins, the elephant wears a garland of flowers or a spiked chain round the neck. On rare coins, the head of the elephant is adorned with a small shawl or blanket, sometimes with geometric designs on it. Often, a warrior is seen standing in front of or riding on the animal. Frequently, two warriors are seated on the elephant. In such cases, the warrior at the back has an umbrella or parasol above him. Probably he was a king or prince while the warrior in the front was an ordinary soldier driving the elephant. On many of these coins, a third warrior is also seen standing in front of the tusker, sometimes holding an umbrella or a war weapon. On a rare specimen from Sri Lanka, this third warrior appears to be a female. Probably due to constraints of space, none of these warriors have been realistically featured. In many cases, the mere outline of the body is portrayed. The various anatomical

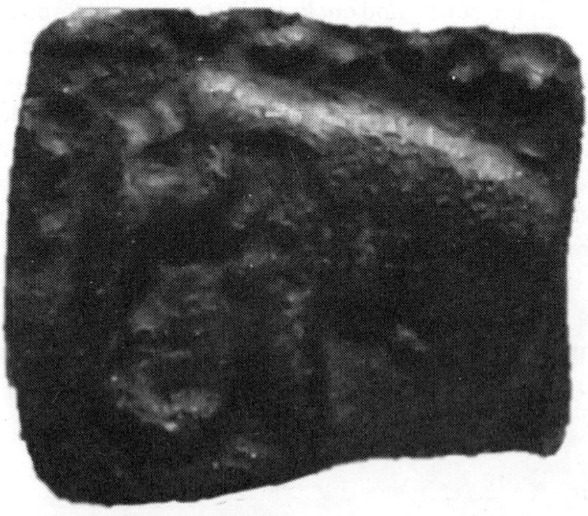

Plate 10: Sangam Pāṇḍya coin—elephant obverse.

characteristics and the dress are hardly discernible. On a rare coin, however, the warrior in front of the elephant wears a peculiar conical cap with a flap at the back. A rarer coin found in Sri Lanka shows a crown adorning the head of the warrior (king?) seated on the elephant. The upper part of this crown exhibits a row of arrow-like sharp projections.

A careful study of all the Pāṇḍya elephant type coins reveals the crucial role played by the elephant in the wars of those days. In fact, most of these coins portray the animal along with kings or warriors and, sometimes, with the royal flag mast with a huge flag fluttering in the wind.

Horse

A sizeable number of Pāṇḍya coins feature the horse as the principal obverse device instead of the elephant. The horse obverse type coins of the Pāṇḍyas can be broadly classified into two main sub-varieties:

1. The quadrangular *aśvamedha* type coins in which the horse is shown standing, mostly to the right and, rarely, to the left. The horse mostly appears dull and lifeless, standing still with drooping head and sorrowful eyes, apprehending imminent death at the sacrifice—very similar to the horse on the *aśvamedha* type coins of the Sangam Cōḷas and imperial Guptas. On these Pāṇḍya coins, the *yūpastambha* (sacrificial post) is placed in front of the animal. On most coins, the *stambha* is heavily carved and decorated with umbrella-like projections at various points on its shaft or upper part. On some coins, however, the *stambha* is plain and tall like a lamp-post. A thick rope connects the horse with the *stambha*. One end of the rope is tied to the neck or the right foreleg of the animal while the other end is tied to the *stambha*. On some coins, however, the rope extends far beyond the *stambha*, and terminates at the foot of the three-arched hill in a corner of the flan. The *yajñakuṇḍa* is circular, quadrangular, pentagonal, or hexagonal in shape and is placed near the edge of the flan, far from the horse. Other auspicious devices and symbols including the tree-in-railing, the sun symbol and the *nandīpāda* are also featured on most coins of this type

The Tamil Sangam literature clearly states that the Sangam Pāṇḍya kings including Palyāgasālai Mudukudumi Peruvaḷuthi performed various Vedic sacrifices.[7] Even the Sanskrit poet Kālidāsa (fourth-fifth centuries AD), in his *Raghuvaṃśa*, describes a Pāṇḍya king blessed, for his successful performance of the *aśvamedha* sacrifice, by the great sage Agastya who lived in Tamiḷakam during the Sangam age.

2. In the quadrangular or hexagonal coins featuring the horse, sometimes encircled by the Tamil Brāhmī legend *Peruvaḷuthi*, a common surname or last name in the Pāṇḍya royal family, the horse is standing mostly to the left. The horse on these coins is artistically far superior to that on the Pāṇḍya *aśvamedha* type coins. It appears more lifelike and plastic. The mane and the hairy tail have been clearly indicated. A sense of movement has been most effectively conveyed by slight bends on all the four legs. Often, a tank or trough with tortoises in it is seen below the mouth of the horse. Probably the horse is drinking water from the tank.

Bull

Another important obverse device on the Sangam Pāṇḍya coins is the standing bull. Most coins feature a single bull, standing to the right. On many coins, the curved and pointed horns and the sagging skin on the neck of the animal have been beautifully portrayed.

Tortoise

As indicated earlier, on the Sangam Chera coins, the tortoise occasionally occurs as a subsidiary device on the obverse and the reverse. On Sangam Cōḷa coins, the tortoise is rarely portrayed as a subsidiary device on the obverse. On Sangam Pāṇḍya coins, however, it repeatedly occurs both as a subsidiary and as the main or sole device on the obverse and, sometimes, as the main device on the reverse, too.

On Pāṇḍya coins featuring the tortoise as the main obverse device, a single specimen of the creature is prominently displayed within a shallow rectangular tank. On the obverse of many other coins, up to four small tortoises occur mostly within a quadrangular or circular tank.

It is plausible that the Pāṇḍya tortoise coins were inspired by the *kārṣāpaṇas* and Sātavāhana coins bearing the same creature. In this connection, one may note that the tortoise occurs on *kārṣāpaṇas* belonging to many hoards such as at Amaravati, Mambalam and Virasigamani in south India. Significantly, the Virasigamani hoard comes from the heart of the Pāṇḍya region.

The repeated and prominent portrayal of tortoise on Pāṇḍya coins may also have some religious significance. According to the *Ahanānūru*, a Tamil Sangam text, the tortoise played a vital role in religious sacrifices.[8] We know that the Pāṇḍya kings performed such sacrifices. Further, the tortoise is also closely associated with the Hindu deity Viṣṇu.[9]

The tortoise may also have been important for the economy of the Pāṇḍya kingdom. The *Periplus* (first century AD) categorically mentions tortoise-shell as a major item of export from Tamiḷakam, and the islands along the coast of Tamiḷakam, to the Mediterranean region.[10]

Temple

Among the coins of the Tamil kings of the Sangam age, the Sangam Pāṇḍya coins alone feature the temple device. The temple on these coins is mostly a domed structure, often erected on a high plinth. The dome is supported by a series of pillars or columns. Some temples have roofs with overhanging eaves. On a few coins, the temple appears like a hut with an umbrella-shaped thatched roof.

One may recall that the punch-marked coins display at least 9 varieties of domed edifices (temples or *caityas*) and 1 flat-roofed structure. One of these 9 domed edifices, closely resembling a Buddhist *stūpa*, is seen on the obverse of many Sangam Pāṇḍya punch-marked coins, too. Such architectural devices are also seen on Mauryan artefacts. Slightly later, the Audumbaras and Trigartas of north India issued coins bearing a domed temple. The temple on the Audumbara coins is very similar to that on Sangam Pāṇḍya coins. At the same time, the temple on Pāṇḍya coins bears a close resemblance to the pillared and domed temple of Vesta on Roman coins. Significantly, a Nerovian (AD 54-68) aureus of the Vesta temple reverse type has been reported from Valuvally in Kerala. It is likely that the Pāṇḍyas featured the temple on their coins after observing the temple devices on the *kārṣāpaṇas* and Roman coins circulating in their land.

The temple on Audumbara coins has been interpreted as dedicated to Śiva. The temple on Pāṇḍya coins, too, may be for the same deity because Madurai, the capital of the Pāṇḍyas, has been associated with Śiva and his consort Pārvatī from an early period of history. Further, Sangam Pāṇḍya coins feature many other devices and symbols like the bull and axe, traditionally associated with Śiva.

Royal Bust

Like the Sangam Cheras, the Sangam Pāṇḍyas minted royal bust type coins too. The busts on the Pāṇḍya coins are always turned to the right and appear to be of sturdy, muscular men with bulbous, round cheeks. The sheath of muscles rippling under the skin of the well-formed chin and neck exude strength, robustness and vitality.

The busts on some of the Pāṇḍya coins portray a single ruler at different stages of his life—youth, middle age and old age. Thus, this Pāṇḍya ruler has issued a large number of bust coins throughout his long reign. The busts on many other Pāṇḍya coins show significant variations in the positioning of the royal head, facial features and jewels. This indicates that several Pāṇḍya rulers issued bust type coins; while some rulers issued such coins at regular intervals, others issued them probably on one or two occasions.

The Pāṇḍya busts are invariably enclosed within a circle of dots or beads. One may recall that several bust coins of the Sātavāhanas, Cheras and Romans display this feature, which may have been a common ornamental feature on ancient coinage. It has, however, been suggested that the circle of dots encircling the Pāṇḍya bust may be a string of pearls, especially because the Sangam Pāṇḍyas produced high-quality pearls that were exported to distant lands.[11] The *Periplus* also mentions pearls as one of the exports from south India to Rome.[12]

While discussing the Sangam Chera bust coins, we had put forward the hypothesis that these coins were modelled on the Roman bust coins and had listed reasons for this hypothesis. The Sangam

Pāṇḍya bust coins are, however, very different from the Sangam Chera coins. The specific differences between these two categories of bust coins are as follows:

1. While Chera bust coins are round and made of silver, the Pāṇḍya bust coins are invariably square or squarish in shape and are made of copper.
2. The busts on all the Chera coins are clean-shaven but the busts on Sangam Pāṇḍya coins always have a heavy crop of hair or else the head is covered by a crown.
3. Chera busts often have drapery wrapped round the neck. None of the Pāṇḍya busts have this.
4. All the Chera busts are not adorned with jewellery but many of the Pāṇḍya busts wear elaborate jewellery.
5. Chera bust coins always have a legend above the bust but none of the Pāṇḍya bust coins bear any legend.
6. The weight (4-4.5 grams or higher) of Pāṇḍya bust coins is much higher than the Chera bust coins.

In the light of these facts, one may infer that Pāṇḍya bust coins were partly inspired by the Roman coins reaching their territory and, to a greater extent, by the Sātavāhana bust coins. The aquiline nose, half-closed eyes and the thin lips of the Pāṇḍya busts appear to have been derived from the Roman busts. As for the Sātavāhana influence on the Pāṇḍya coins, it is well known that the Sātavāhanas had close commercial contacts with the Sangam Pāṇḍyas. This is clearly attested by the Tamil Sangam literature.[13] Further, there have been a series of recent discoveries of Sātavāhana coins and coin moulds in Tamil Nadu, including Madurai, the capital of the Pāṇḍyas. Of course, none of these coins and moulds is of the bust type. Some Sangam Pāṇḍya coins, like the Sātavāhana coins, even bear legends in the Prakrit language and Brāhmī script.

The Pāṇḍya busts have close stylistic affinities with the portraits on Sātavāhana coins. The following are the main points of similarity between these two categories of bust type coins:

1. The busts on many Pāṇḍya coins have been positioned in such an angle that the eyes of the ruler are gazing upwards or heavenwards. Several Sātavāhana coins and a few Roman coins, too, exhibit the same feature.

2. None of the Pāṇḍya and Sātavāhana busts are clean-shaven. The head usually has a huge crop of hair, neatly combed and arranged in perfect ringlets. Or else, the head is covered with a helmet-like round crown, richly ornamented, especially at the edges.
3. Many of the Pāṇḍya and Sātavāhana busts have distended ears with ear-ornaments.
4. Many of the Sātavāhana busts and some Pāṇḍya busts have a prominent crest jewel or diadem (*lalāṭamakuṭa*) in the middle of the forehead. This diadem is tied to the back of the head with a string, chain or fillet. Such a head-band of a different design is not uncommon on Roman coins too.

Other Principal Obverse Devices

A limited number of Sangam Pāṇḍya coins feature certain obscure devices as the sole or principal device on the obverse. Some of these devices are unknown to the early coins of any other dynasty or series in India.

A limited number of Pāṇḍya coins bear either the tree-in-railing or the *ṣaḍaracakra*—a circle with a dot in the centre and enclosed by six arms—three arrowheads and three taurines—as the sole obverse device. Both these are stylistically akin to the same devices featured on many *kārṣāpaṇas*. However, these devices on the Pāṇḍya coins are much bigger in size than those on the *kārṣāpaṇas*. One of the Pāṇḍya coin obverse devices is the five-arched hill, with a plant or tree growing on top of it. A slightly different version of the same device occurs on the *kārṣāpaṇas*, too. The main difference between the Pāṇḍya device and the *kārṣāpaṇa* device lies in the arrangement of the five arches forming the hill, and the size and shape of the tree and its leaves.

A rare Pāṇḍya coin features an abnormally big fish with its mouth wide open. The beautifully executed fish exudes a three-dimensional effect. Four taurines are seen below it. The fish faces the right and the taurines, left.

Another enigmatic Pāṇḍya coin shows a set of kitchen utensils—probably part of a dinner set. These utensils include a ribbed bowl, a dish with a pedestal and a wine cup with a long handle. The ribbed bowl on this coin is similar to the Roman glass bowl recovered in fragments from the first century AD levels at the Indo-Roman trading station of Arikamedu near Pondicherry.[14] The wine cup also bears unmistakable classical influence and is very similar in shape to the terracotta wine cups recovered, again from early historical levels (first century BC or first century AD), at Kanchipuram in northern Tamil Nadu.[15]

A unique device occupies the obverse of the only well-recorded circular coin of the Sangam Pāṇḍyas. This is the anchor of a ship or a boat, neatly engraved in the middle of the flan.

Combination of Principal Obverse Devices

Many Pāṇḍya coins feature the above motifs and devices in various combinations. For example, several coins feature the horse and the bull, often facing each other with a tree-in-railing in between. The significance of the axe planted on either side of the tree-in-railing on such coins is not clear. Another variety of Pāṇḍya coins shows the horse below the bull, both standing to the right. As indicated earlier, the tortoise motif occurs in combination with most other principal obverse devices such as the elephant, horse and bull.

Subsidiary or Smaller Obverse Devices

The subsidiary or smaller devices on Pāṇḍya coins include the three-arched hill surmounted by a crescent, six-arched hill, river, round flower made of dots, three-petalled flower, various ornamental floral designs, axe, spear, dagger, *triśūla*, pot or vessel, drum, *aṅkuśa*, wheel, *pūrṇaghaṭa*, lamp, *śivaliṅga*, conch, crescent with its ends pointing upwards, crescent with its ends pointing downwards, round moon, sun, triskelion symbol, *śrīvatsa*, right-handed and left-handed *svastikas*, taurine, crocodile, fish, and a bird resembling the vulture or the eagle.

A few Sangam Pāṇḍya coins feature the *śivaliṅga* on the obverse. It is represented by a conspicuous circle or square within a quadrangle (pedestal?) whose sides are indicated by thick bands. The *liṅga* occurs in association with the tortoise within a tank. Incidentally, this is the first ever representation of a *liṅga* on a coin. The worship of the *liṅga* had become very popular in Tamiḷakam during this age, as indicated by the excavation of a *liṅga* at the sanctum of a Śiva temple (200-100 BC) at Gudimallam in Andhra, very close to the present-day border between Tamil Nadu and Andhra states.[16] Apart from the *liṅga*, it is likely that many other objects and symbols like the temple, axe, bull and tortoise on Pāṇḍya coins may be, as indicated earlier, associated with the worship of Śiva in this region. Significantly, a rare coin features, in front of the elephant, a triangle-headed spear, an attribute of Kārttikeya. Next to it is the trident, an attribute of Śiva. Besides the *śivaliṅga*, the Pāṇḍya coins bear various smaller religious devices and symbols such as the *svastika*, which is sometimes represented with its arms curved.

An interesting group of religious devices are the pots or pitchers that appear along with other well-known religious devices and symbols such as the coconut, *śrīvatsa* and conch. These pots are mostly ovoidal and sometimes semi-circular in shape with a thick and prominent neck. They are covered with a crescent-shaped lid such that the ends of the crescent point upwards. On some coins, instead of these pots, we see a *pūrṇaghaṭa* which is a simple spherical or conical pot with no neck and with a bunch of mango leaves jutting out of its mouth.

Up to seven auspicious symbols and devices, including one of the above pots, appear in a row on the elephant obverse coins, mostly above the elephant. Sometimes Tamil Brāhmī letters like *ko* and *ma* appear in between these sacred symbols. Plausibly, these Tamil Brāhmī letters were also accorded some sanctity by the Pāṇḍyas.

Apart from these religion-oriented pots, Pāṇḍya coins feature several small but interesting kitchen vessels and pots as subsidiary devices. Sometimes a pot is featured below the mouth of a bull. Probably this was meant to indicate the bull eating grains or drinking water contained in the pot. Such pots are round and have a narrow neck and flared mouth. Some of them have a pedestal. One Pāṇḍya coin features a pair of handleless tall conical jars with a tiny circular mouth at the top. These jars are identical to the terracotta conical jars found from early historical levels at a series of sites such as Tiruverkadu, Kanchi, Vasavasamudram, Arikamedu and Karaikadu in south-eastern India (Tamil Nadu-Pondicherry region).[17]

Another important subsidiary device on Pāṇḍya coins is the famous three-arched hill surmounted by a crescent. This device is prominently displayed on coins featuring the temple device. Several sub-varieties of the former device, characterized by the occurrence of a dot within each arch, or else the replacement of the top crescent either by the tree-in-railing or by the absence of any top-device, also appear on these coins. It is clear that the Pāṇḍyas borrowed the device from the Mauryan *kārṣāpaṇas* and Sātavāhana coins reaching the Pāṇḍya land. In due course, the Pāṇḍyas introduced several interesting modifications and innovations in the portrayal of this device on their coins.

Among the faunal devices on Pāṇḍya coins, the crocodile is a rare one. The creature is shown lying within a tank next to the temple device on the obverse of a Pāṇḍya coin. The mouth of the crocodile is wide open.

One may observe that among all the coins issued by the early rulers of Tamiḷakam, the Pāṇḍya coins alone feature a profusion of water-bodies (sea, river, tank, pond), aquatic creatures (various varieties of the fish, crocodile) and naval devices (anchor of a boat or a ship). These devices may be taken to represent the naval power and the seafaring abilities of the Pāṇḍyas whose kingdom lay at the confluence of the three seas—the Arabian Sea, the Indian Ocean and the Bay of Bengal. Significantly, one of the Pāṇḍya kings is believed to have lost his life at sea during a naval battle and, hence, was accorded the title *Kadalulmaintha* or 'one who died in the sea'.

Reverse Devices

Fish

The reverse of most of the Sangam Pāṇḍya coins portray the fish which was their dynastic emblem (Plate 11). Unlike some of the fishes seen on the obverse of Pāṇḍya coins, those on the reverse are never portrayed in a realistic fashion but are highly stylized. Often, the fish is shown as a mere cross, sometimes within a curve or as an angle or triangle. On certain other coins, the fish is represented by a symbol identical to the letter V, a small V inside a bigger V, two Vs intersecting each other at one or more points. Sometimes a wavy line indicating the sea or the river appears above the fish. Rarely, a tree-in-railing appears next to the fish. Rarer still, a taurine symbol occurs within or just next to the fish. A unique specimen found in Sri Lanka shows a three-arched hill above the fish.

Plate 11: Sangam Pāṇḍya coin—fish reverse.

The precise reasons that prompted the Pāṇḍyas to feature the fish in such varied stylized ways are not clear. These stylized and sometimes awkward-looking fishes are more astonishing because those on the obverse are mostly featured in a realistic fashion, although such stylized fishes also rarely occur, as a subsidiary device, on the obverse.

The precise meaning and significance of this stylized fish were not understood by early scholars.[18] Some did not identify this device as a fish at all. They felt that this symbol represents some Buddhist motif or the wheel of Viṣṇu. Others felt that this device was reproduced from some graffiti marks seen on early pottery recovered from many south Indian sites, including Adichanallur within the Pāṇḍya region. It has been observed that one variety of this stylized fish closely resembles a brandmark for cattle among certain Tamil communities in the Anuradhapura region (Sri Lanka) that has revealed such coins. Some scholars strongly felt that the symbol resembles a crocodile. Other scholars even opined that this device represents the plan or layout of the Pāṇḍya kingdom or of Madurai, the capital city. Most scholars now agree that this device is definitely the fish, although such a stylized fish does not occur on any other coin series or even on any other object (seal, pottery, etc.) of the Sangam Pāṇḍyas.

Tortoise

The reverse of the Pāṇḍya bust coins do not feature the fish alone. Instead, they feature a thick-walled rectangular tank containing two or five tortoises or four tortoises and a fish which, with its fins and open mouth, has been clearly portrayed in a realistic fashion. The absence of the stylized fish, the royal emblem, on these royal portrait coins appears strange. But then, the choice of the tortoise device for the reverse of these coins reinforces, as indicated earlier, the importance of this creature in the Pāṇḍya society and economy.

Legends

Some Pāṇḍya coins bear legends on the obverse. These legends like those on the Sangam Chera coins, are in the Tamil language and Tamil Brāhmī script. But a few of the Sangam Pāṇḍya coins bear two legends, one after the other. On these coins, one legend is in the usual Tamil language and Tamil Brāhmī script, and the other, in the Prakrit language and Brāhmī script.[19]

The legend reads from left to right and is usually placed along the border of the flan. Thus, it almost encircles the horse seen on these coins, although portions of the legend are often out of the flan. The legend reads *Peruvaḷuthi* in Tamil and *Peruvaḷuthisa* in Prakrit, Peruvaḷuthi being a common surname or last name of many Pāṇḍya kings. Sometimes this name is repeated twice, one after the other.

On some elephant obverse coins, certain letters of the Tamil Brāhmī script occur in between auspicious symbols. As stated earlier, these letters may have been accorded some religious sanctity. Or else, they may be the initials of a Pāṇḍya king. For example, some coins bear the letters *pa*, *ma* and *ko* that may denote the Pāṇḍya ruler named Pāṇḍyan Māran Ko.

Stylistically, these legends can be compared to the Tamil Brāhmī inscriptions at Sittannavasal (Tamil Nadu) (second century BC), some of the Brāhmī cave inscriptions of Sri Lanka (first century AD) and the legends on the coins of Vāsiṣṭhiputra Pulumāvi (late first or early second century AD) of the Sātavāhana dynasty.

NOTES AND REFERENCES

1. For a general account of the history, economy and society of the Sangam Pāṇḍyas, see R. Krishnamurthy, *Pāṇḍiyar Peruvaḷudi Nāṇayangal* (Tamil) (Madras, 1987), pp. 1-12; idem, *Sangam Age Tamil Coins* (Madras, 1997), pp. 1-14; K.A. Nilakanta Sastri, *A History of South India: From Prehistoric Times to the Fall of Vijayanagara* (New Delhi, 2002), pp. 104-31. Also see K.K. Pillay, *A Social History of the Tamils* I (Madras, 1975).
2. Unlike the Sangam Chera and Sangam Cōḷa coins, the Sangam Pāṇḍya coins are not very scarce and are seen in museum collections. The Government Museum, Egmore, Madras, has a good collection of such coins. Besides, Sangam Pāṇḍya coins are also seen in the private collections of A. Sitaraman (Tanjavur) and S. Raman (Madras).
3. Many of the Sri Lankan finds are in the National Museum, Colombo.
4. P. Pushparatnam has examined many Sangam Pāṇḍya coins found in Sri Lanka. He opines that they 'have been issued by local Tamil rulers who established Tamil kingdoms in the island . . . these rulers issued these coins probably in memory of their Pāṇḍya ancestors'. P. Shanmugam has categorically disproved this contention. See P. Pushparatnam, 'Sankam Age Coins Found in Sri Lanka', Paper presented at the international seminar on Tamil Nadu and Sri Lanka: New Evidence on Maritime and Inland Trade, (Madras, 2004); P. Shanmugam, 'Sangam Pāṇḍya Coins in Sri Lanka', *SSIC* XIV (2004), pp. 30-40.
5. Until recently, there were hardly any copper mines in Sri Lanka and, hence, many scholars asserted that during the ancient times, the island imported copper for producing coins and other objects. In recent years, however, copper deposits have been located in the island and it has been proved that the smelting of copper was known to the local people, even during the early Iron Age. According to Sudarshan Seneviratne, South Asia's largest copper-magnetite deposit south of the Bihar-Orissa region is in Sri Lanka. Brāhmī inscriptions in the island specifically refer to guilds of coppersmiths. See S. Seneviratne, 'The Ecology and Archaeology of the Seruwila Copper-Magnetite Prospect, North East Sri Lanka', in Jonathan Mark Kenoyer, ed., *From Sumer to Meluhha: Contributions to the Archaeology of South and South West Asia in Memory of George F. Dales, Jr. (Wisconsin Archaeological Reports 3)* (Madison, 1994), pp. 261-80; idem, S. Seneviratne, 'The Ecology and Archaeology of the Seruwila Copper-Magnetite Prospect, North East Sri Lanka', *The Sri Lanka Journal of the Humanities* XXI 1&2 (1995), pp. 114-45.

6. The site has been recently (2004-5) excavated by the Chennai Circle of the ASI.
7. For a discussion on the early literary references to the Pāṇḍyas performing Vedic sacrifices, see R. Krishnamurthy 1997 (supra n. 1), pp. 13, 26, 34.
8. R. Santhi, 'Sangakāla Pāṇḍyarkaḷin Cheppu Kāśugal (Tamil)', *MCS Special Bulletin* VIII (2001), pp. 12-15. For the relevant verse from the *Ahanānūru* and its transliteration, see R. Krishnamurthy 1997 (supra n. 1), pp. 33-4.
9. Many Hindus believe that Viṣṇu appeared as a tortoise in one of his incarnations. In another incarnation, he was a fish. The wheel is one of his chief attributes. The tortoise, fish and wheel are frequently seen on the coins of the Sangam Pāṇḍyas, probably indicating their attachment to this deity.
10. The *Periplus* 56 mentions tortoise-shell found in 'Chryse island or taken among the islands along the coast of Damirica', as an item of export from south India to Rome. These refer to the tiny islands in between India and Sri Lanka. They appear to have been part of the Sangam Pāṇḍya kingdom.
11. R. Krishnamurthy 1997 (supra n. 1), p. 46.
12. The *Periplus* 56 mentions 'great quantities of fine pearls' exported from south India to Rome. As the Pāṇḍya kingdom was most famous for its pearls, one can safely presume that these pearls came from this kingdom.
13. For more details on Sātavāhana contacts with Tamiḷakam, see S. Rajavelu, 'A New Copper Coin of Satakarni From Madurai', *MCS Special Bulletin* XI (2004), pp. 200-2. For more details on the Sātavāhana coin moulds and coins found in Tamil Nadu, refer to Chapter 7 of this book.
14. R.E.M. Wheeler, A. Ghosh and Krishna Deva, 'Arikamedu: An Indo-Roman Trading-Station on the East Coast of India', *AI* 2 (1946), pp. 17-124.
15. K.V. Raman, 'Further Evidence of Roman Trade From Coastal Sites in Tamil Nadu', in V. Begley and Richard Daniel De Puma, eds., *Rome and India: The Ancient Sea Trade* (Madison, 1991), pp. 125-33.
16. I.K. Sarma, *Religion in Art, and Historical Archaeology of South India: Contacts and Correlations* (Madras, 1987), pp. 34-46.
17. For a detailed analysis of these conical jars, see S. Suresh, *Symbols of Trade: Roman and Pseudo-Roman Objects Found in India* (New Delhi, 2004), pp. 108-11. Also see R. Nagaswamy and A. Abdul Majeed, *Vasavasamudram (A Report on the Excavation Conducted by the Tamil Nadu State Department of Archaeology)* (Madras, 1978), pp. 11, 21-2; S. Suresh, 'Roman Vestiges in Kanchipuram', in Nanditha Krishna, ed., *Kanchi: A Heritage of Art and Religion* (Madras, 1992), pp. 56-61; idem, *Roman Antiquities in Tamil Nadu* (Madras, 1992), pp. 47-9; idem, 'Early Roman Finds in Madras City', in G.J. Sudhakar, ed., *Aspects of Madras: A Historical Perspective* (Madras, 1993), pp. 13-16.
18. I had an interesting discussion with I. Mahadevan on this subject. For some peculiar interpretations of this motif, see C.H. Biddulph, *Coins of the*

Pandyas (Varanasi, 1966), pp. 6-7; H.W. Codrington, *Ceylon Coins and Currency, Memoirs of the Colombo Museum*, Series A, No. 3 (Colombo, 1924, rpt. 1975), pp. 19-20; K.N.V. Seyone, *Some Old Coins Found in Early Ceylon (Sri Lanka)*, Part III-XI (Colombo?,1998), pp. 51-2.

19. R. Krishnamurthy does not accept that any of the Sangam Pāṇḍya coins bear Prakrit legends. According to him, all the legends on these coins are in Tamil. See R. Krishnamurthy, 1997 (supra n. 1), p. 23; idem, 'Sangam Age Pāṇḍya Coins With Legend Peruvaḷuthi in the National Museum, Colombo', *SSIC* XV (2005), pp. 58-63.

CHAPTER 6

Coins of the Malaiyamāns

While the Cheras, Cōḷas and Pāṇḍyas were the three main rulers of Tamiḷakam, there were a number of minor chiefs who were loyal to one of them. These chiefs often switched their loyalty from one power to the other. The most well known among the chiefdoms were the Malaiyamāns or Malaiyans of Tirukoilur or Kovalūr and the Adigamāns of Tagadūr in Tamil Nadu.

The Malaiyamāns exercised control over Malaiyamān Nāḍu, which included parts of present-day Pondicherry and the adjoining South Arcot region of Tamil Nadu, with the town of Tirukoilur (193 km from Madras city) as their capital.[1] Compared to the other chieftains, the Malaiyamāns were very powerful. The famous port of Arikamedu was under their control for some years.

The important Malaiyamān rulers were Malaiyamān Tirumudi Kāri and Choḷiya Enadi Tirukaṇṇan. The Sangam text *Puraṇānūru* describes, in glowing terms, the military achievements of Tirumudi Kāri. He is said to have defeated a north Indian king who invaded Tamiḷakam. Kāri was initially loyal to the Cōḷas but later shifted his allegiance to the Cheras.

We do not know the precise dates of any of the Malaiyamān rulers and presume that their power declined before AD 300.

The Malaiyamāns minted several interesting coins.[2] It is not clear as to whether any of the other chieftains in Tamiḷakam also issued coins.[3] Hundreds of Malaiyamān coins have been discovered from the area ruled by them, mainly in and round their capital Tirukoilur. No coin of this dynasty has been discovered anywhere beyond the frontiers of their territory.

PHYSICAL FEATURES AND PRODUCTION METHOD

All the Malaiyamān coins are of copper. The chieftains would have obtained this metal from the mines in Tamiḷakam, or the Mediterranean region through the port of Arikamedu. Being a chieftain and not a major power, the Malaiyamāns probably could not afford to mint coins in silver that was very scarce and expensive in south India in those days.

As regards the shape of the Malaiyamān coins, both rectangular and square coins are known but the former predominate. Each side of the quadrangular Malaiyamān coins measures between 1 to 2.5 cm. The weight of these coins ranges between 1.1 and 6.1 grams; the majority of the specimens, however, weigh around 2 to 4 grams. A sole oval-shaped Malaiyamān coin also exists.[4] It is 2.4 cm long, 1.2 cm wide and weighs 2 grams.

The coins were die-struck on thin copper sheets, and hammered and cut to the requisite shape.

ART AND SYMBOLOGY

Compared to the coins of the Sangam Cheras, Cōḷas and Pāṇḍyas, the coins of the Malaiyamāns exhibit a limited number of devices and symbols. This may be partially explained by the fact that while the Cheras, Cōḷas and Pāṇḍyas were large and powerful kingdoms, the Malaiyamāns were mere chieftains, although powerful at times, ruling over a small area. All their coins appear to have been minted from a single mint located at Tirukoilur, the Malaiyamān capital. They, as indicated in the following sections, often simply portrayed the different objects within their territory on their coins.

Obverse Devices

Horse

The main device on the obverse of most of the Malaiyamān coins is the horse, standing mostly to the right and sometimes to the left (Plate 12). On most coins, the animal has been well-delineated. The mane and the long, sharp ears have been clearly portrayed. A sense of movement has been conveyed by the slight bends in the legs of the animal. Rarely, the head of the animal bends so low that the mouth almost touches the neck. On some coins, the tail is abnormally stiff and long, almost touching the ground. On most coins, however, it is short, hairy and appears sinuous.

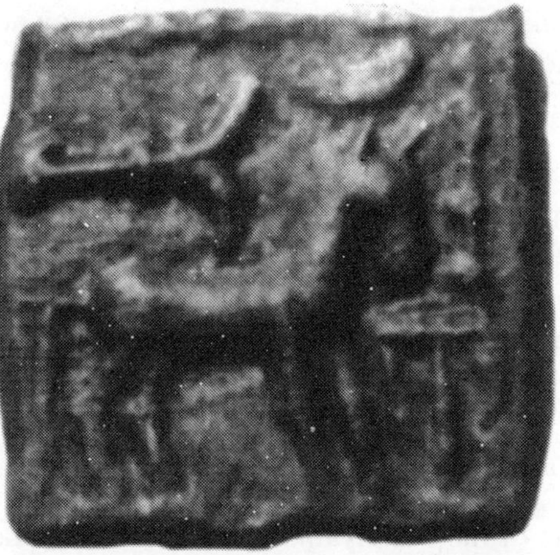

Plate 12: Malaiyamān coin – horse obverse
(Photo: A. Sitaraman, Tanjavur)

Stylistically, the horse on Malaiyamān coins is closest to that seen on many Sangam Chera coins. One may infer that the majority of the Malaiyamān horse coins or, at least, the earliest among such coins, were minted when these chieftains were under the overlordship of the Cheras. Significantly, a few Malaiyamān coins portray the bow and arrow—the royal insignia of the Cheras—in front of the horse on the obverse. However, the Sangam Cōḷa or Pāṇḍya emblems—the tiger and fish, respectively—have never been featured on any Malaiyamān coin.

Coming to the reasons for the prominence accorded to the horse on Malaiyamān coins, the Sangam literature indicates that Tirumudi Kāri, the greatest Malaiyamān ruler, was an excellent horseman.[5] He maintained many high-quality horses in his palace and gave his name Kāri to his favourite horse. This horse was affectionately called Kāri-kudhirai, *kudhirai* meaning 'horse' in Tamil. Probably he minted the first Malaiyamān coins, or the first horse type Malaiyamān coins featuring his favourite horse, during the years when he was loyal to the Cheras. His successors may have continued this device on their coins.

None of the Malaiyamān horse coins appear to be *aśvamedha* type coins because they do not display the *yūpastambha* or the *yajña-*

kuṇḍa. Being small chieftains, the Malaiyamāns may not have been capable of performing the *aśvamedha* sacrifice.

Goad and Staff

On a few coins, the obverse depicts the *aṅkuśa* and a staff or stick instead of the horse. On such coins, the goad and stick are placed vertically, parallel to each other. Sometimes, a dot or pellet is seen close to the goad. On many coins, both the goad and stick are in high relief.

Subsidiary or Smaller Obverse Devices

The horse coins of the Malaiyamāns feature various subsidiary or smaller devices and symbols such as the tree-in-railing, oak-wreath, dotted lines, *nandīpāda*, crescent moon, sun, *aṅkuśa*, stick or sceptre, bow and arrow, flag mast ornamented with dot-like carvings, tripod or three-legged stool, square stool, ornate pillar, and the head of a bull. Most of these occur above or in front of the horse and, rarely, behind the horse.

Among the smaller symbols and devices, the *nandīpāda* occurs on a large number of coins. It is beautifully portrayed, sometimes with tiny dots surrounding it, above the horse. This *nandīpāda* has remarkable stylistic affinities with the *nandīpāda* seen on the silver coins (first century BC?) of the Audumbaras, Kunindas and Yaudheyas of north India.

Among other subsidiary symbols and motifs, the stool and pillar deserve special mention. Often, a stool or pillar is placed in front of the horse, below the mouth of the animal. The stool is either three-legged or four-legged or in the form of a huge, solid, square box. On some coins, instead of the stool, we see a carved pillar or pedestal with a triangular or round base. A vessel, basin or trough is usually placed on the stool or pillar. There are significant differences in its size and shape on different coins. The vessel or trough is mostly either spherical or oval in shape. Sometimes it is rectangular or trapezoidal and has a flat bottom. Rarely, it is closed at the top probably with a huge lid. The vessel may be for storing grains or water for the horse.

On a few coins, the flag mast is seen in front of the horse. In one instance, the mast has a big rectangular flag fluttering above the head of the animal. An enigmatic coin features the head of a bull in front of the horse. While the horse is standing to the right, the bull's head faces front. The ears and horns of the bull are very clear. The horns are long and curved such that their tips almost touch each other.

On a very small number of Malaiyamān coins, an oak-wreath is seen mostly above the horse. The Malaiyamāns may have been prompted to portray this non-Indian device on their coins after seeing it on many Roman coins.[6] In this connection, one may recall that the Malaiyamāns, along with the other south Indian powers, traded with Rome. The Indo-Roman trading port of Arikamedu was under Malaiyamān control for some time. Further, Tirukoilur, the Malaiyamān capital, was a major trade centre mainly due to its strategic location on the banks of a river in between Arikamedu and inland trade centres such as Uraiyur and Karur. Thus, we find thousands of Roman and Roman imitation gold and copper coins in Tirukoilur. Archaeological excavations have even revealed rouletted ware and the fragment of a Roman amphora at the site.[7]

Reverse Devices

Hillocks, Road and River

The reverse of almost all known Malaiyamān coins, with a few exceptions, feature hillocks, the river and the road in varied angles and positions (Plate 13). Usually three and sometimes two hills are represented in a row. On some coins, there are gaps (passes?) between the hills. Normally, the river originates from one of the hills but rarely, it starts from the gap between two hills or from two adjoining hills. It is generally shown as two curves or wavy lines, parallel to one another, or a single wavy line. Frequently, the river is shown disproportionately larger than the hills. Many rivers bear a series of dots or tiny circles denoting fishes. In most instances, close to the river, there is a mound, normally four-sided. A little distance away, a mud track or road is shown by two parallel lines or a single straight line. On most coins, the road is somewhat parallel

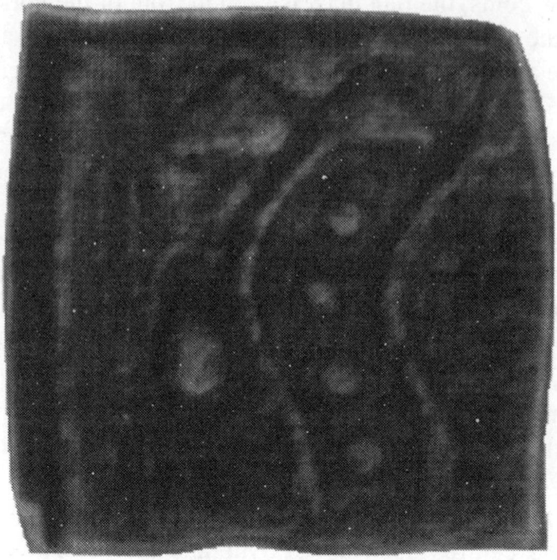

Plate 13: Malaiyamān coin—hill, road and river reverse.
(Photo: A. Sitaraman, Tanjavur)

to the river. On many coins, one or more of the above devices (hillocks, mound, road, river) are missing or partially out of the flan. In fact, a few coins feature the river or road as the sole reverse device. It is plausible that all these devices were struck on each coin but some features went out of the flan because of the carelessness of the die striker. It is also likely that some of these devices wore out when the coins were used as money or after they were buried underground.

The precise significance of these reverse devices is not clear. Probably they represented the physical topography of the Malaiyamān chiefdom, particularly their capital Tirukoilur. The hills on the coins may denote the Mullur hills that were part of the Malaiyamān territory. Further, it is widely believed that the Malaiyamāns originally hailed from a hilly region, as indicated by their family name *Malaiyamān* or *Malaiyan* that may have been derived from the word *Malai* that means 'hill' in Tamil. The river on the coins may be the Pennar on whose banks Tirukoilur is situated. When the Pennar reaches Tirukoilur from the hills, it takes a sharp bend that has been clearly shown on most coins. Close to this bend, there is a rocky outcrop which may be the mound appearing on the coins. The road seen on them may be one of the ancient highways that connected Tirukoilur with other trade centres such as Arikamedu, Kanchipuram, Karur and Uraiyur. Significantly, in ancient and medieval Tamiḷakam, highways often ran parallel to the river.

A few coins portray a triangle-headed spear to the right of the hills and the two vertical wavy lines denoting the river. This spear may indicate a temple for Murugā on the foothills closer to the river because it was an attribute of this god. One may recall that Murugā was a very popular deity in Tamiḷakam in those days and Murugā temples have mostly been located on the hills, foothills, or on a small hillock or mound.

The identification of some of the lines on the reverse of Malaiyamān coins as the *aṅkuśa* and the sceptre[8] is not acceptable because these lines or figures are totally different from the *aṅkuśa* and sceptre or staff clearly seen on the obverse of some of these coins.

It has been opined that only kingdoms on the banks of rivers issued coins featuring the river.[9] This contention is not convincing because the river was a very common device or motif on coins throughout India, from very early times. Many ancient kingdoms were deliberately located close to rivers for economic reasons. Further, India has a vast network of rivers and, hence, any kingdom or chiefdom may be expected to have one or more rivers within its territory.

Legends

A few Malaiyamān coins bear legends in the Tamil language and Tamil Brāhmī script. The legends convey the dynastic name (Malaiyamān or Malaiyan) or the king's name (Example: Kāri). They read from left to right.

The legends always occur on the obverse of the horse type coins. On all these coins, the horse stands to the right. These coins do not display any subsidiary symbol or device on the obverse. The placement of the legends is of three types:

1. The legend is spread behind, above and in front of the horse.
2. The legend begins from above the horse and ends in front of it usually below the mouth of the animal.
3. In the case of short legends like *Kāri*, the entire legend is placed in front of the horse.

Sometimes one of the letters forming the legend is partially or totally out of the flan. The legends do not display any specific ornamental flourishes.

NOTES AND REFERENCES

1. For a general survey of the history of the Malaiyamāns, see R. Krishnamurthy, *Sangakāla Malaiyamān Nāṇayangal* (Tamil) (Madras, 1990), pp. 10-15; idem, *Sangam Age Tamil Coins* (Madras, 1997), pp. 131-2. Also see R. Krishnamurthy, 'Sangam Period "Malayaman" Coins', *JNSI* XLIX 1&2 (1987), pp. 41-3.
2. Like the Sangam Chera and Sangam Pāṇḍya coins, Malaiyamān coins, too, are not very common in museum collections. I saw one coin in the collection of the National Museum, New Delhi. A large number of Malaiyamān coins, however, exist in private collections such as those of A. Sitaraman (Tanjavur) and S. Raman (Madras).
3. Some scholars believe that the 143 lead coins of the Aṇḍippaṭṭi hoard (Tamil Nadu) are the issues of another Sangam age chieftain named Chendan who ruled the Chengam area in northern Tamil Nadu around the first century AD. For more details of these coins, refer to Appendix II of this book.
4. R. Krishnamurthy 1990 (supra n. 1), p. 58.
5. For a discussion on this subject and the Tamil literary references, see R. Krishnamurthy 1997 (supra n. 1), pp. 132, 147-8.
6. The reverse of many Roman coins found in south India, including the Malaiyamān territory, bear the oak-wreath motif. Such coins have been found at Veeravasaramu (Andhra), Karur (Tamil Nadu) and Valuvally (Kerala).
7. For more details about the archaeological excavations at Tirukoilur, see Natana. Kasinathan and A. Abdul Majeed, *Thirukkoyilur Excavation* (Madras, 1996); M. Rajesh and T. Arun Raj, 'Some Observations on Seṅgamēdu: A Hinterland Trade Centre of Arikamedu, Tamil Nadu, India', *Circle of Inner Asian Art, SOAS Newsletter* 17 (2003), pp. 17-22.
8. For a brief discussion on this subject, see R. Krishnamurthy, 1997 (supra n. 1), p. 148.
9. This is the opinion of R. Krishnamurthy. See R. Krishnamurthy, 1997 (supra n. 1), p. 148.

CHAPTER 7

Coins of the Sātavāhanas

The Sātavāhanas, as is well known, ruled over a very large empire that included parts of central India, the Deccan and further south, from around 230 BC to the mid-third century AD. The important Sātavāhana rulers included Śrīmukha Sātavāhana (late third century-early second century BC), Sātakarṇi I (189-179 BC), Gautamīputra Sātakarṇi (AD 54-88), Vāsiṣṭhiputra Pulumāvi (AD 88-116), Śivasiri Pulumāvi (AD 145-52) and Śrī Rudra Sātakarṇi (third century AD). The precise dates and genealogy of these rulers have been hotly debated by scholars and is unclear.[1]

Not astoundingly, the Sātavāhanas, during their long reign, issued huge quantities of coins in various metals and their alloys, in varied sizes and shapes, from different mints. Sātavāhana coins have been discovered in scores of sites from Awra in central India and Amreli in Gujarat down to Kanchipuram, Cuddalore and, very recently, Karur and Madurai in Tamil Nadu. The largest number of finds comes from the coastal districts of Andhra Pradesh. The coins occur in hoards, stratified contexts, as ritualistic offerings within Buddhist shrines, and as stray occurrences, mostly on the surface.[2]

PHYSICAL FEATURES AND PRODUCTION METHOD

The Sātavāhanas produced coins in lead, copper, potin, brass, bronze and silver. The earliest and the majority of Sātavāhana coins are made of lead. It is believed that the choice of the large-scale use of lead for currency was mainly due to its low melting point (327 °C), and its softness and malleability for casting coins of varied shapes and sizes. Besides, lead was less expensive than copper and many other metals. The Sātavāhanas had many lead mines within their territory. These included the mines at Kurnool and Agnigundala in Andhra. With the conquest of the kingdom of Kalinga (Orissa), the Sātavāhanas would have had access to the Sarigipalli-Dhumohalli high-grade lead deposits in Orissa. They also obtained lead from the ores in Baraula in Kashmir, Almora in the Uttar Pradesh region and Zawar in Rajasthan. As indicated in the *Periplus*, lead (Spanish lead?) was also imported from the Roman empire, mainly through the port of Barygaza in Gujarat.[3]

The Sātavāhanas used copper not only for making coins but also for icons and jewels. Besides the imports from Rome, they would have extracted copper from the mines at Calliana near Bombay in Maharashtra, and Guntupalaiyam, Kurnool, Venkatagiri, Kalahasti and Ongole in Andhra.

The Sātavāhanas, from very early times, also produced coins in brass (an alloy of copper and zinc), and bronze (an alloy of copper, tin and, sometimes other elements), mainly for circulation in the northern Deccan. Zinc was available in Rajasthan, Gujarat and Andhra. With regard to tin, the Sātavāhana bronze coins contain a very high percentage, sometimes 23 per cent or even more.[4] Hence, the limited ores within India—mainly the deposits in Rajasthan—would not have been adequate for them. They may have imported tin from places like Thailand, and of course, Rome.

Potin is an alloy of copper, zinc, lead and tin. The Sātavāhanas mostly obtained it as a by-product in their mints when thousands of old and broken Sātavāhana copper, lead and other coins were melted for making new ones.[5]

As regards silver coins, the early Sātavāhana rulers did not mint any. From the time of Gautamīputra Sātakarṇi, however, silver coins began to be minted. However, their quantity was less than the copper, lead and potin coins. A plausible explanation for this is that the silver punch-marked coins and the Roman denarii would have, to a large extent, served the purposes of silver specie in the Sātavāhana territory. Even some Western Kṣatrapa silver coins appear to have served as currency in the Sātavāhana territory, prior to the reign of Gautamīputra Sātakarṇi. The Sātavāhanas would have melted the earlier silver coins, including the *kārṣāpaṇas*, Western Kṣatrapa coins and the Roman denarii, for producing silver coins. Besides, they would have also obtained this metal from the few silver deposits in Gujarat and Andhra.

Most of the copper, lead and potin coins are either rectangular, square or circular in shape. A limited number of Sātavāhana lead coins are oval-shaped. The edges of these oval coins are usually, unlike many other Sātavāhana issues, neat and even, without any protrusions or cracks. Hence, they are aesthetically more attractive. The brass and bronze coins are either rectangular or square in shape.

All these coins also display wide variations in size and weight. The sides of many of these quadrangular coins, the diameter of the circular ones, and the length and width of the oval coins normally measure anywhere between 1.2 to 2.8 cm. The rectangular copper coins weigh between 0.75 and 10 grams. The rectangular potin coins weigh between 1.2 and 6.75 grams. The weight of the rectangular lead coins ranges between 4 and 9.5 grams. The square copper coins weigh between 1 and 7.5 grams. The weight of the square potin coins ranges from 1.5 to 12 grams and that of the square lead ones from 1.2 to 10.5 grams.

The circular copper coins weigh between 1.2 and 23 grams while the circular potin ones weigh between 1.5 and 14.5 grams. The circular lead coins weigh between 0.8 and 40.5 grams. The weight of the brass and bronze coins ranges from around 1 gram to over 10 grams.

The silver coins are invariably circular in shape. Among them, the average weight of the royal portrait coins is around 2.7 grams while the average weight of the non-portrait coins is about 1.95 grams. A few silver portrait coins of low weight (around 1.1 grams) have also been found.[6] The diameter of the silver coins is usually between 1 and 2 cm.

As to the technique by which these coins were manufactured, we have cast, die-struck and punch-marked coins among the Sātavāhana issues. Coins displaying a combination of casting and die-striking processes, the casting and punch-marking processes, or all three techniques are also known.

In many cases, the coin blanks were cast wholly and the devices and legends were later punch-marked or die-struck on them. To cite an example of the use of all these three techniques, certain coins of the Sātavāhana king, Satisiri (179-161 BC) depict cast, punch-marked and die-struck symbols on the same flan.

The punch-marked Sātavāhana coins are concentrated in the Malwa region. Some of the earliest coins seem to have been produced here. Perhaps this technique was not meant to be adopted on a mass scale in other parts of the empire. The punch-marked Sātavāhana coins exhibit a higher degree of technical refinement compared to the *kārṣāpaṇas*. While the *kārṣāpaṇas* mostly exhibit various symbols punched in a haphazard manner, the Sātavāhana coins have symbols punched in a methodical and orderly fashion.

Compared to the punch-marking process, the casting technique was more widespread during the Sātavāhana age. In fact, many of the Sātavāhana bust coins appear to have been cast in double moulds. The negative impression of the devices and legends was 'cut' in the mould with a sharp pointer, and a V-shaped notch was provided in the mould for the entry of molten metal into the coin socket. Terracotta moulds used for the production of Sātavāhana coins have been reported from a number of sites.[7] In Maharashtra, Paithan (ancient Pratisthana), the first capital of the Sātavāhanas and a major mint town, has yielded circular clay-mould pieces, depicting the bust of Gautamīputra Yajña Sātakarṇi (AD 165-94) in his youth, middle age and old age respectively. Obviously, each of these mould pieces represents the obverse of his portrait coins issued during different periods of his life. A well-burnt circular mould displaying the reverse of the silver portrait coins of Vāsiṣṭhiputra Pulumāvi was unearthed during archaeological digs at the famous site of Nagarjunakonda in Andhra.

Sātavāhana coin moulds have been reported from Kondapur, Peddabankur, Dhulikatta and Amaravati in Andhra. They have also been discovered from as far south as Kanchi in Tamil Nadu. Five clay moulds were recovered from this site from stratified deposits, within a trench (KCM-5) laid at the Gollachatram complex near the Kāmākṣī Amman temple of the city. Significantly, all the Kanchi moulds seem to have been found close to one another in the same layer. Three of these moulds are of the coins of Vāsiṣṭhiputra Pulumāvi and the other two of Vāsiṣṭhiputra Sātakarṇi (AD 116-45). Except one of the moulds of the former, all the others are of the double mould type. All of them seem to be of the usual elephant *Ujjain* symbol coin-type.

Incidentally, Kanchipuram has also yielded eight Sātavāhana coins—three of lead and five of copper—in a stratified context and some more as stray finds. A few more lead and copper coins have been recovered from stratified layers at the site. These coins have not been cleaned and, hence, are not decipherable. They may also be of the Sātavāhana dynasty.

A rare discovery, again from Paithan, is a square burnt clay piece exhibiting the reverse of the silver portrait issues of Vāsiṣṭhiputra Pulumāvi.[8] Since the legend on this piece is not in the negative and as the devices, too, are in relief, the specimen could not have been used as a mould. Hence, it could have been a 'proof-piece' or a 'model' deposited in the imperial mint. Alternatively, the specimen may have been used as a matrix for the production of dies. There has even been a suggestion that the piece may be a modern forgery, intended for manufacturing a metal-die of the relevant coin-type.[9] Interestingly, another such baked terracotta 'proof piece', featuring the reverse of the silver portrait coins of Śivasiri Pulumāvi, has been recovered from Kondapur.[10]

The contention that most of the Sātavāhana coins are die-struck and that all the clay moulds of this coin series, including the ones recovered from a stratified context, may be the equipment of ancient forgers[11] is not convincing. Hundreds of cast coins of different Sātavāhana rulers have been reported from surface collections, hoards as well as stratified finds from every part of their vast empire and the neighbouring regions. It is not possible to accept that a group of forgers could, for centuries, manage to produce such a huge quantity of imitations, distributed over such a wide geographical area. Moreover, it has now been established that even *kārṣāpaṇas* were sometimes manufactured by the casting process instead of the usual punch-marking method. It is well known that the Sātavāhanas adopted many symbols, motifs and other features of the *kārṣāpaṇas* on their coins. Thus, the Sātavāhana cast coins may also have been directly inspired by the cast *kārṣāpaṇas*, some of which have been recovered in places like Amaravati (Andhra) in the heart of Sātavāhana territory.

Sātavāhana die-struck coins are also fairly widespread. It has been observed that often the die was not the same size or shape as the coin blank on which the designs were impressed from it. Sometimes a circular coin was produced with a square die and vice versa. These faulty mint processes caused certain parts of the legends and devices to be out of the flan. Sometimes the die was struck so hard that it resulted in the overlapping of some devices on the flan.

When the die was struck too hard, especially on a soft metal like lead, the coin blank lost its original shape and began to appear like a small, concave saucer or cup.

Besides producing their own coins, the Sātavāhanas, during the reign of Gautamīputra Sātakarṇi, restruck or countermarked many silver coins and some copper coins of their vanquished foe, Śaka Nāhapāṇa (first century AD), mainly for use in the territories acquired from the Śakas. This was probably because the people in those regions would be familiar with and prefer these old coins. The Sātavāhanas countermarked these coins by die-striking symbols such as the three-peaked hill and the *Ujjain* symbol on them. Such coins have been found at Jogalthambi in Maharashtra, in Goa and at a few other places. One may remember that around the same time, the Sangam Cheras, too, counterstruck Roman denarii and *kārṣāpaṇas* for use as currency in their territory. Even Nāhapāṇa counterstruck some Sātavāhana coins for use in his territory.

Although we do not know the exact location of mints for many early Indian dynasties, in the case of the Sātavāhanas, archaeology has provided us some knowledge of the precise location and functioning of some of their mints.[12] As per the latest evidence, the Sātavāhanas had major mints at Mallar, Tripuri (Madhya Pradesh region) Paithan, Junnar or Min-nagar (Maharashtra), Kondapur, Nagarjunakonda (Andhra) and many other sites. At Nagarjunakonda, a well-designed colony of goldsmiths and mint masters was unearthed east of the citadel.[13] The spot has yielded coins in various stages of production.

As Sātavāhana coins were produced in several mints spread throughout their far-flung empire, certain mints had a special preference for particular techniques and art motifs. This accounts for the concentration of certain types or varieties of Sātavāhana coins produced by certain methods in specific sites and localities. Yet all the mints were bound by some general regulations with regard to the metal, size, shape and weight of the coin, the devices and motifs and, to an extent, the positioning of these devices on the flan.

ART AND SYMBOLOGY

It is strange that many early scholars like V.A. Smith and Altekar summarily dismissed the Sātavāhana coins as of no artistic merit or originality. Later discoveries and studies have proved beyond doubt that these coins display distinct artistic innovations and flourishes.[14]

The Sātavāhana coins display an extremely wide variety of symbols and devices in different combinations. Many of these are either reproductions or modifications of symbols on the *kārṣāpaṇas* that was the main currency in the Sātavāhana region, immediately prior to the coming of the Sātavāhanas. The Sātavāhanas also seemed to have continuously lent and borrowed certain coin symbols and devices to and from their neighbouring kingdoms, chiefdoms and feudatories such as the Mahārathis in the Andhra-Karnataka region. Thus, stylistically and typologically, the coins of these small, little-known chiefdoms and kingdoms are similar to the Sātavāhana coins. Some of these seem to have been used in many areas of the Sātavāhana empire, often along with the usual Sātavāhana coins.

Obverse Devices

Elephant

The elephant is the commonest obverse device (Plates 14, 15). It sometimes occurs on the reverse, too. According to some scholars, the adoption of this device by the Sātavāhanas was to symbolize their victory over neighbouring Kalinga (Orissa), a kingdom traditionally associated with the elephant.[15]

The elephant is portrayed in varied poses on different Sātavāhana coins. The creature is mostly stout and gigantic. On a large number of coins, the animal is in relief and displays a high degree of plasticity. The elephant mostly stands to the right and sometimes to the left. The trunk of the animal either hangs downwards or is raised. If raised, it is sometimes turned or curved towards the back of the animal. On some coins, the trunk curls twice and appears like the letter S. On a large number of coins, the trunk is cut or partially out of the flan. Rarely, even the thin creases or folds on the skin of the trunk are visible. Occasionally, the animal appears to be walking swiftly. On some coins, the tusker is caparisoned or adorned with exquisite jewellery such as neck-bands or a string of pearls around the neck. A flag is sometimes seen above the animal. A rare copper issue of Gautamīputra Yajñaśrī Sātakarṇi displays a warrior (king) riding on the elephant and probably holding an *aṅkuśa.*[16]

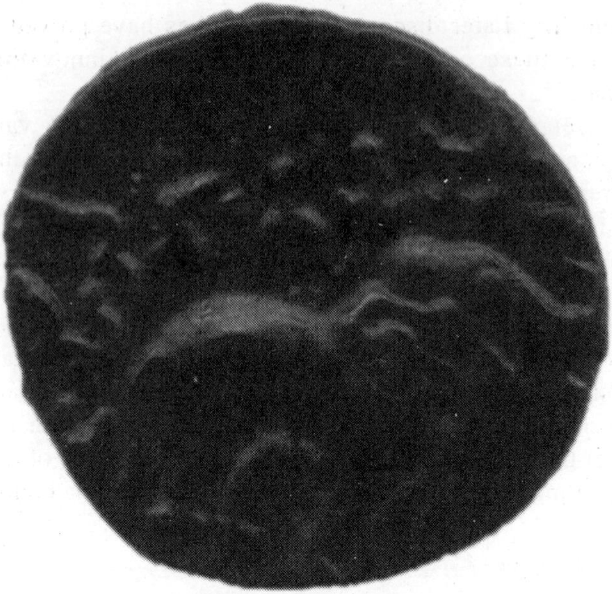

Plate 14: Sātavāhana coin—elephant obverse.

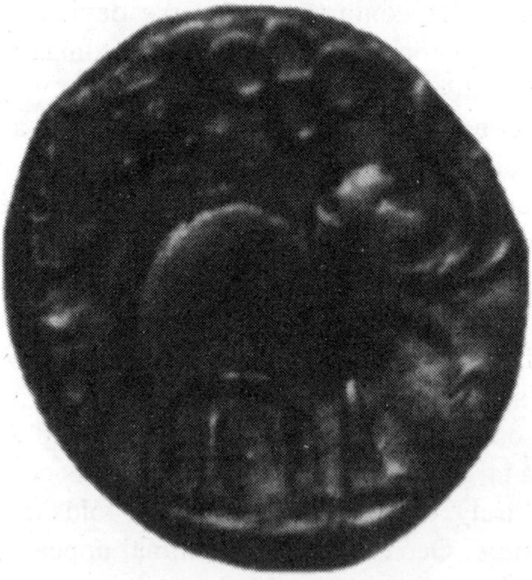

Plate 15: Sātavāhana coin—elephant obverse.
(Photo: Department of Coins and Medals,
The British Museum, London)

On a few coins, the elephant appears to be playfully sprinkling water with its upraised trunk on a lily plant. In some instances, a lotus pond is seen in front of the elephant. Alternatively, the animal appears to be crossing or walking on a pond or river. This was probably to indicate that the animal loved to play in the pond (*gajendralīlā*). On many coins, the elephant appears to carry a circular or quadrangular object, or a group of objects on its back. According to some scholars, these objects may merely be religious symbols.

A circular copper elephant obverse type coin of Kochhiputa Sātakarṇi (second century AD), a newly identified Sātavāhana ruler who is not mentioned in the Purāṇas, has now come to light.[17] The peculiar feature of this coin is that behind the animal is a pot with a lid. It has been pointed out that this particular coin was issued to commemorate the flourishing inland trade and maritime commerce of the Sātavāhanas and, hence, the elephant and the pot or vase—the twin Hindu symbols of prosperity—were appropriately chosen to be shown on the coin. Another Sātavāhana coin features the vase in front of the elephant. The vase on this coin has been interpreted as influenced by the Roman amphora jars that reached the Sātavāhana empire by the process of trade. Interestingly, these elephant-vase obverse coins are found in places such as Nasik and Junnar (in Maharashtra), which were busy trade centres throughout the Sātavāhana period. Junnar has also yielded fragments of imported amphorae.

Bull

The bull is the main device seen on the earliest Sātavāhana coins. The later Sātavāhana rulers, too, adopted this important device. On these coins, the bull mostly stands to the right. The hump is quite prominent. Sometimes the horns are absent or else only a single horn is seen. They are straight or distinctly curved to look like a crescent. The tail is either long and hairy or abnormally short. The crescent moon is often featured close to the animal, sometimes above the head or between the hind legs and the forelegs. The taurine symbol—closely connected with the bull—appears on the reverse of some of these bull coins. This is a good example of the subtle link between the obverse and reverse symbols and devices.

Horse

The horse is not as common as the elephant or bull on Sātavāhana coins. Most coins feature a single horse but a very rare coin depicts two horses to the right. On most of the horse type coins, including the extremely rare silver issues, the animal is realistically portrayed to the right or left. The horse often appears to be in a galloping posture. In most instances, the mane and bushy tail are clear.

Many of the horse type coins are likely to be of the *aśvamedha* type, issued to commemorate the Sātavāhana king's performance of this sacrificial ritual. Significantly, on some of these coins, a sacrificial post (*yūpastambha*) and a circular fire altar (*yajñakuṇḍa*) are clearly seen in front of the horse.

The significance of the horse on Sātavāhana coins may also be linked to the little-known fact that the very name 'Sātavāhana' is believed to have been derived from the Sanskrit name *Saptivāhana* (horse vehicle), one of the names of Sūrya, the sun god. The famous Naneghat inscription of the Sātavāhanas begins with salutations to the sun and moon besides various other gods.

In this connection, one may note that the Sātavāhanas even produced clay seals featuring the *aśvamedha* horse standing on a platform with the sacrificial post in front. These seals also feature the name of the king.[18] They were produced in Paithan and other Sātavāhana mint-towns. Such seals may have been issued, along with the *aśvamedha* coins, to commemorate the performance of this sacrifice. Alternatively, these seals may have served as models for the coins.

Lion

The lion appears as the main obverse device on several Sātavāhana coins. The animal is mostly seen to the right and is featured jumping, walking, standing or seated. The jumping lion coins are the rarest. On some coins, the rich and fluffy mane is beautifully delineated. The long and bushy tail of the animal is usually raised and curled in the form of an inverted S. Stylistically, the representation of the animal on these coins is akin to the stone figures of the lion in the middle phase of the Amaravati school of art (first century AD). On a few coins, a sacrificial post is seen in front of the lion. A large number of the lion type coins have been recovered from the Saurashtra region, famous for its Asian lions. Plausibly, a mint in this area specialized in featuring the neighbourhood lions on coins.

One may recall that, apart from the Sātavāhanas, the Sangam Cheras, too, issued a few lion type coins. On some Sangam Chera coins, the lion appears on the obverse while on the Goddess obverse Chera coins, the lion occurs on the reverse.

Tiger

The tiger rarely appears on Sātavāhana coins. The animal mostly stands to the right or left and has a twisted tail. Its legs appear short and stiff. The animal, with its gaping mouth and wide-open eyes, is portrayed in a ferocious mood.

Camel

Like the tiger, the camel, too, is rare on Sātavāhana coins. The obverse of a unique circular lead coin portrays a camel facing right; the reverse of this coin depicts the *Ujjain* symbol within a square. The long slender neck and the tiny eyes of the animal have been neatly portrayed. There is a vessel or bowl next to it. This coin was excavated from the well-known site of Kondapur (Andhra).

The camel is unknown on the coins of any other early south Indian dynasty, and is hardly seen on ancient south Indian paintings and stone sculptures. On punch-marked coins too, the camel is not very common. A sole *kārṣāpaṇa* exhibiting this animal has been discovered in Andhra. It is possible that both the *kārṣāpaṇa* and the Sātavāhana coin bearing the camel device were manufactured almost around the same time at a single mint in Andhra.

Arched Hill

Various forms of the three-arched, six-arched and ten-arched hills appear not only on the obverse but also on the reverse of many Sātavāhana coins. The portrayal of the ten-arched hill is less common than that of the three-arched and six-arched hills. These arched hills appear both as a main device and also as a subsidiary one along with various other devices and symbols.

The arches are generally semi-circular or conical in shape. Sometimes the interior of the arch seems to be completely filled up and, hence, it appears solid. They are either empty or have a pellet inside. The arches normally touch each other but occasionally appear separate or disjointed with small gaps between each of them.

A crescent is frequently featured above the topmost arch. The ends of the crescent invariably point upwards. A dot or the letters of the Brāhmī word reading *Raño* (meaning 'of the king') are placed within it. A wavy or zig-zag line frequently appears below the hill.

One may recall that the depiction of the arched hill surmounted by the crescent dates back to the days of rock paintings (before 1000 BC) and the early *kārṣāpaṇas* (600 BC?). The Mauryas (fourth-second centuries BC) extensively used this symbol on many of their artefacts. Perhaps they even adopted this symbol as their royal emblem. Except for the Sātavāhanas, though, no other early dynasty gave high prominence to this symbol on their coins. According to a recent study, the early Sātavāhanas deliberately used this Mauryan symbol to announce their victory over Mauryan governors in the Asika-Asmaka-Mulaka regions.[19] One may also infer that the repeated large-scale use of this symbol, along with other typical Sātavāhana symbols and legends on coins, was to continuously reinforce Sātavāhana control over large areas that had hitherto been ruled by the Mauryas. On Sātavāhana coins, the placement of this symbol with certain other symbols and devices on the obverse, or else on the reverse of portrait coins, is also believed to have immense religio-political significance. In India, traditionally, fame has been regarded as milk-white in colour and is repeatedly compared to the spotless white moon. On the Sātavāhana coin, the crescent moon atop the hill is the embodiment of royal fame, and the legend *Raño* within or just above the crescent would appropriately indicate 'the fame of the king'. The coin, thus, represents the Sātavāhana king's fame and glory soaring heavenwards, far higher than the highest peaks of the land. On some coins, however, the arched hill is surmounted by a triangle-headed standard instead of the crescent. The standard is, again, a symbol of royal might and definitely denotes the Sātavāhana king's supreme power and glory.

The hills are also believed to represent the various regions or parts of the vast empire of the Sātavāhanas.[20] The three-arched hill denotes the three territories of Asika, Asmaka and Mulaka surrounded by three hill ranges—the Vindhya-Rikshavat (the eastern Vindhyas and the Vindhyas north of the river Narmada), Pariyatra (the Aravalli and Western Vindhyas) and Sahya (Western Ghats). Likewise, the six-arched hill indicates six territories that include these three, along with the regions of Vidarbha, Akara and Avanti with the Krishnagiri-Macha-Siritana hills. The ten-arched hill represents these six territories besides the regions of Aparanta-Anupa, Saurashtra and Kachcha with the Chakora, Saṭagiri, Malaya and Mahindra hills. Significantly, Sātavāhana coins featuring the arched-hills have been discovered in all these regions.

The zig-zag line below the hill may symbolize the low-lying ocean. In that case, this coin may also indicate that the Sātavāhana empire was bounded by the sea on the east and the west, and the hills (Vindhya mountains) on the north. The zig-zag line has also been interpreted as a snake lying on its back with the hood to the right, raised towards the sky. As the snake mostly resides below the earth, this device may indicate Sātavāhana control over the underworld (*pātāḷaloka*). Alternatively, the device may convey the Sātavāhana victory over the Nāga kingdom in south India. The snake may allude to the Nāga origin of the Sātavāhanas. In fact, the snakes featured on a unique Kṣatrapa coin, probably an issue of Nāhapāṇa, has even been interpreted as representing a Sātavāhana king defeated by the Kṣatrapas.[21]

Ship

A limited number of circular lead coins feature the ship of both the single and double mast types. All the coins clearly exhibit the sturdy body of the ship, slightly curved at both ends. On some coins, the wavy line below the ship may indicate its journey on the high seas. Often, the ship is surrounded by symbols of plenty and prosperity like the *padma* (lotus), *śaṅkha* (conch) and the *svastika*. These symbols allude to the enviable naval strength of the Sātavāhanas, and their prosperous maritime trade with Sri Lanka, South-East Asia and Rome. Appropriately, most of the ship type coins have been discovered in coastal Andhra which was, in those days, studded with a series of trading ports and harbours. A local mint probably chose to feature the ship on coins because it played a big role in the economy of the region.

Apart from the ship coins, certain other Sātavāhana coins feature devices and motifs that indicate the maritime power of this dynasty. For instance, certain lead circular coins feature an anchor-like object above the elephant on the obverse. Such coins mainly occur in the Andhra region.

Wheel

One group of Sātavāhana coins feature various forms of the wheel or *cakra* as the main obverse device. These coins are mostly in copper, lead or potin. The wheel usually has six, eight, twelve or, rarely, thirteen spokes. Most of them have a conspicuous central hub. Sometimes the spokes terminate in arrowheads beyond the rim of the wheel or are capped by solid crescents, again beyond the rim. Occasionally, the wheel is surrounded by a circle of tiny solid balls. Sometimes the wheel is shown revolving, by featuring each spoke slightly slanted or tilted towards the left. On many coins, the wheel is in high relief.

Some scholars have suggested that the wheel on Sātavāhana coins is linked to the Buddhist faith.[22] Yet one should remember that although these rulers encouraged Buddhism, they were essentially Hindus with a special devotion to Viṣṇu. The religious literature of the period indicates that the Kṛṣṇa cult was very popular in the Sātavāhana empire. Kṛṣṇa was known by various other names such as Madhumathana and Gopāla. Many Sātavāhana kings bore names of the gods of the Vaiṣṇava pantheon. There has even been an opinion that the entire Sātavāhana coin symbolism surrounds the Vāsudeva-Kṛṣṇa cult.[23] In these circumstances, the wheel on these coins may be linked to the worship of Viṣṇu, one of whose chief attributes it is.

Bow and Arrow

The bow and arrow is one of the significant devices on Sātavāhana coins. The device is mostly seen on lead coins. On the obverse of these coins, it occurs both as a main device and a subsidiary one, along with other devices such as the bull. On some coins where the bow and arrow occurs as the main device, tiny pellets or the *triratna* symbol surmounted by a crescent are featured close to it. On most coins, the bow and arrow have been realistically portrayed. The former exhibits elasticity and the latter is thin but sharp.

One of the most famous Sātavāhana coins featuring the bow and arrow as the sole obverse device is a circular lead coin of Gautamīputra Sātakarṇi. Here, the bow is fitted with an arrow pointing upwards. This device may denote the military prowess of this ruler whose heroic qualities have been graphically described in the famous Nasik inscription of his mother, Bālāsirī. The inscription pointedly refers to Gautamīputra Sātakarṇi as *Ekadhanudharasa* (the only bow-man), implying that he had no rival bow-man on earth. On some Sātavāhana rectangular lead coins, the bow and arrow occurs just above the bull on the obverse. Here, too, the bow is fitted with the arrow pointing upwards.

One may recall that apart from the Sātavāhanas, the Kuras, who ruled over parts of Maharashtra-Karnataka around this time, also issued coins prominently featuring the bow and arrow. The Sātavāhanas may have issued the bow and arrow coins after their conquest of the Kura territory, mainly for circulation in that region as the people there would have been familiar with this device.[24]

In an earlier chapter, we observed that the Sangam Cheras, one of the southern neighbours of the Sātavāhanas, issued the largest number of coins with the bow and arrow, mostly on the reverse and sometimes, on the obverse. The bow and arrow on some of the Sangam Chera coins is highly stylized compared to the Sātavāhana coins.

Royal Portrait

Like the Sangam Cheras, the Sātavāhanas also issued two varieties of royal portrait coins:

1. Coins showing the full figure of a standing king.
2. Coins portraying the royal bust.

Compared to other types of Sātavāhana coins, the royal portrait coins, whether of the standing king variety or the bust variety, are few in number. Perhaps these coins were commemorative issues, minted to celebrate special occasions such as the coronation or military success of the king. Hence, a limited number of coins were minted under strict royal supervision. This may also partially account for their extraordinary artistic value.

Coins featuring the standing king have been recovered mainly in the northernmost part of the Sātavāhana empire, particularly in the Tripuri-Vidisa region. Many of these coins are made of lead and are circular in shape. On the obverse, the king appears standing to the front, almost at the centre or slightly nearer the left margin of the flan. He is sturdy, robust and muscular. The *Ujjain* symbol, often seen below his right hand, may indicate his territorial conquests in all four cardinal directions. The crescent above the *Ujjain* symbol may further suggest his heavenly powers or divinity. The glorification of the king on the obverse is reinforced by the reverse, which often shows, among other symbols, an enclosure made of wavy lines or curves and, within it, footprints suggestive of the descent of god as the king on earth.

Regarding the Sātavāhana royal bust coins, it seems that these kings commenced the minting of these coins due to certain peculiar politico-economic compulsions. When the Sātavāhanas conquered Nasik and adjoining regions in western India, they realized that the people, especially the traders, had long been accustomed to the bust type silver specie of their erstwhile ruler, Kṣatrapa Nāhapāṇa, and were in no mood to accept or use the non-portrait Sātavāhana coins. Hence, the Sātavāhanas were compelled to issue bust coins modelled on the Kṣatrapa portrait coins.

Until recently, Sātavāhana bust coins were believed to have been minted exclusively in silver. In recent decades, though, lead and even potin bust coins have come to light, mainly at Adam (Maharashtra) where a large number of such coins have been unearthed in a stratified context.[25] The lead bust coins are generally smaller in size and lower in weight than their silver counterparts. A few are exactly half the size and weight of some of the silver bust coins. Bust coins of silver heavily debased with copper have also been reported. These are almost of the same size and weight as many of the pure silver bust coins. Stylistically, there are no major differences between the busts of pure silver and the debased silver and base metal coins.

As several Sātavāhana rulers issued bust type coins, different coins show wide variations not merely in facial features but also in hairstyle and jewellery. On some coins, the bust is in high relief. On most coins, it is turned to the right and displays a prominent forehead, chubby bulbous cheeks, large ears, eyes gazing upwards, long nose and thin elongated lips. The nose is either sharp like a bird's beak or round with conspicuous nostrils. Sometimes the ears are so long and distended that they touch the shoulder probably due to the weight of the heavy rings on them. Many of the busts sport a moustache, which is either thin, short and trimmed or thick, bushy and long, sometimes so long and twisted as to extend far below the lower lip.

As regards the head or the hairstyle of the bust, this could be categorized into three types:

1. Bust having a large crop of hair, mostly neatly combed and arranged in tiny curls or frizzles.
2. The head is partially tonsured and sports a prominent tuft that ends in a loop knot at the back. Often, such heads also sport sidelocks (*kākapakṣa*), close to the ears and almost falling on the corners of the forehead (Figure 3). It is said that such sidelocks were a special characteristic of the mode of hair-dressing for princes and young kings in ancient India. In the great epic *Rāmāyaṇa* (600 BC), Rāma, the divine hero, has been described as adorned with such sidelocks. Again, Kārttikeya, the youthful Hindu god of war, is sometimes shown with these sidelocks. There are ample references to them in ancient Sanskrit literature too.[26] It is believed that such sidelocks and tufts are typical of persons performing Vedic sacrifices and rituals. Significantly, many Sātavāhana rulers, including those who issued bust type coins, performed sacrifices such as the horse sacrifice (*aśvamedha yajña*).
3. The head is covered by a crown. These are of varied types and sizes. In many cases, the crown is like a huge helmet or cap, fully covered with gemstones. Sometimes a conspicuous sunflower or lotus-shaped gemstone or jewel (crest jewel?), again frequently studded with tiny precious stones, is seen fitted on this crown just above the forehead, mostly above the centre of the forehead. Sometimes the crown is plain and not dotted with gemstones. Instead,

it bears two crescent-shaped bands. Rarely, the crown appears to be made of flowers or else is merely flower-shaped.

On many bust coins, especially those not featuring the crown, an ornamented head-band or diadem is seen tied tightly at the back of the head. The long and often distended ears are mostly adorned with ear-rings or studs of varied shapes and sizes. Frequently, the ear-rings are round, oval or leaf-shaped. A pendant or bead often hangs down from the ring. Sometimes the bottom of the pendant gently touches the shoulder. Generally, the pendant is cup-shaped or anchor-shaped.

A unique jewel is a beaded chain extending from the head or the crown down to the upper neck or chin. This round chain tightly fits the neck and has been noted on a sole silver bust coin of a little-known Sātavāhana ruler named Kumbha Sātakarṇi (first century AD), unknown in the Purāṇic lists of Sātavāhana rulers.[27]

Like the Sangam Cheras and Sangam Pāṇḍyas, the Sātavāhana rulers, too, issued bust coins on different occasions and, hence, the different bust coins of any single Sātavāhana king depicts him in different stages of his life—youth, middle age and old age. Probably each of these Sātavāhana kings issued the first bust coins during or soon after his coronation. Naturally, this coin featured the king at his youthful best. Later on in his reign, the king issued bust coins, plausibly to commemorate the birth of a prince or a victory over a powerful neighbouring kingdom. The busts on these coins clearly exhibit his advancing age—wrinkled forehead, slightly sagging cheeks and, in one instance, the lower lip bent forward probably due to the falling of some teeth of both the upper and lower jaws.

At this juncture, one may note that unlike the kings of any of the other major ancient south Indian dynasties, the Sātavāhana kings have even been portrayed in stone sculptures. Archaeological excavations at Kaganahalli near Sannati in Karnataka have revealed portrait sculptures of Sātavāhana rulers, along with the only known portrait sculpture of the Mauryan emperor, Aśoka (272-235 BC) and his queen.[28] Extant specimens of Sātavāhana royal portraits in stone are, however, very few. Although one can trace indisputable stylistic similarities between the Sātavāhana coin portraits and stone portraits, none of the kings on the coins have been unequivocally identified among the stone portraits so far.

Goddess Lakṣmī

Sātavāhana coins featuring Goddess Lakṣmī on the obverse often occur in copper, potin and bronze. These coins are circular, rectangular or square in shape. Many of them have been discovered in the Madhya Pradesh-Maharashtra region. The tall and majestic goddess stands to the front on these coins. Often, there is a full-bloomed or half-bloomed lotus below her feet. Occasionally, she appears within an ornamental frame. The breasts of the goddess have been prominently delineated. Her hands hold various objects such as the *pūrṇakumbha*, staff, lotus and water-lily stalks. Sometimes she wears big ear ornaments. Various auspicious symbols such as the *svastika* and the *Ujjain*-symbol are seen around her.

Besides these Lakṣmī coins, Paithan (Maharashtra), the first capital of the Sātavāhanas, has yielded at least two circular lead coins featuring, on the obverse, the goddess in another form—the form of Gajalakṣmī or Abhiṣeka Lakṣmī—the deity bathed by elephants.[29] Here, the goddess is seen standing on a lotus with two elephants watering her with uplifted trunks. The reverse feature a tree-in-railing. These coins were probably issued by Sātakarṇi II (161-145 BC) after his conquest of the Avanti-Akara region and bear the legend *Siri Sātakaṇisa.*

Initially, some scholars felt that the female figure on various coins may not be a goddess but a Sātavāhana queen.[30] However, the portrayal of the figure in association with the lotus, *pūrṇakumbha,* and other auspicious objects and symbols has made most scholars now accept the figure as Lakṣmī.

The Lakṣmī coins bear testimony to the great reverence of early Sātavāhanas for goddess Lakṣmī or Śrī, the consort of Viṣṇu, one of their favourite deities. All the rulers of this dynasty had the honorific 'Siri' or 'Śrī', meaning 'Lakṣmī' or 'prosperity', prefixed to their names while many Sātavāhana queens suffixed the same honorific to their names. Indeed, the honorific 'Śrī' has been regarded as a Sātavāhana legacy.

Apart from the Sātavāhana coins, Lakṣmī, more particularly Gajalakṣmī, appears to have been portrayed on many other coins and objects of the early historical period, both within and outside the Sātavāhana empire.[31] Within the empire, a figure of Gajalakṣmī, very similar to the one on Sātavāhana coins, is stamped on a potsherd obtained from the Sātavāhana layers at excavations at Yellesvaram (Andhra). Lakṣmī appears on the Mitra coins of Mathura, the coins of Ujjain, Kausambi and Ayodhya *janapadas*, and also, repeatedly, on the Buddhist railings at Bharhut, Bodh-Gaya and Sanchi (Uttar Pradesh-Madhya Pradesh regions), all datable to the first few centuries BC.

Lakṣmī also appears to have been a popular deity even among the ancient Sri Lankans, with whom the Sātavāhanas maintained intimate commercial and cultural relations. Several early historical sites of Sri Lanka have yielded oblong copper-lead plaques, both cast and die-struck, used as coins during the pre-Christian era.[32] The obverse of these plaques portrays Lakṣmī standing on a large lotus. Each of her hands grasps a stalk of the lotus plant, usually springing from either side of the lotus flower below her. These two stalks terminate at the level of her shoulders in a small blossom, upon each of which stands a miniature elephant. Each elephant holds a round water pitcher in its upturned trunk. The trunks form a beautiful arch over the head of the goddess who is adorned with heavy jewellery. The reverse of these plaques portrays the *svastika*, sometimes in association with other symbols such as the *nandīpāda*. Several forms of Lakṣmī occur on many other specimens of early Sri Lankan art. The various names of the goddess such as Śrī, Lacī, Padmā and Tiru are mentioned in the Sri Lankan Brāhmī inscriptions of the pre-Christian era.[33]

Reverting to the Gajalakṣmī coins of the Sātavāhanas, one can safely conclude that the figure of the goddess is artistically superior to that on the Sri Lankan plaques and on many other ancient art objects of the island. It may be conjectured that these coins were the prototype for the beautiful Gajalakṣmī type coins issued by the imperial Guptas in later centuries.

Other Obverse Devices and Symbols

The obverse of the Sātavāhana coins feature many other devices and symbols, mostly in association with one or more of the principal devices such as the elephant, bull, etc. The former category of devices and symbols include the river with fishes, crabs or tortoises, the banyan tree, fruit-bearing tree-in-railing, triangle-headed standard, plan of a Buddhist *stūpa*, conch, *Ujjain* symbol, moon, *śrīvatsa*, *svastika* and *nandīpāda*. Many of these also occur in Sātavāhana stone art.[34]

The *śrīvatsa*, besides its association with Viṣṇu, the god of the Sātavāhanas, was also the royal insignia of the dynasty. Thus, the portrayal of this Sātavāhana emblem at the very commencement of the famous Hathikumbha inscription of Kharavela, the ruler of Kalinga (Orissa), is inferred as proudly proclaiming his victory over the Sātavāhanas. The Sātavāhanas soon retaliated by defeating the king of Kalinga and adopting the elephant, the emblem of Kalinga, as the main obverse device on their coins. The *śrīvatsa* is seen on innumerable Sātavāhana coins from a very early period of their history. There are slight variations in the exact shape of this symbol on the coins of different Sātavāhana rulers. On many coins, it appears as a vertical line, flanked on either side by S-like curves. The *śrīvatsa* occurs either at the beginning or the end of several Sātavāhana stone inscriptions. It is also frequently seen on Sātavāhana sculptures in Andhra and elsewhere.

The Sātavāhanas accorded great importance to the *svastika* symbol too. Besides occurring as a subsidiary symbol, it also appears as the sole obverse motif on some of their coins, mostly in lead and copper. The Sātavāhanas were the earliest kings to portray the *svastika* as the sole obverse symbol on coins. On many Sātavāhana coins, the lines forming the *svastika*, are thick and bold, and this often gives a three-dimensional appearance to the symbol. The symbol is sometimes surmounted by a tiny crescent. Like the *śrīvatsa*, the *svastika*, too, is frequently seen in Sātavāhana art. The Sātavāhanas mostly featured the right-handed *svastika*, on coins or stone. Perhaps, the left-handed *svastika* slowly began to be considered inauspicious.

The triangle-headed standard was often featured along with the bull or the elephant on the obverse. This standard was considered a symbol of royal might and power. Its placement in front of the elephant with its upraised trunk may signify that this mighty animal was paying obeisance to the Sātavāhana king. The triangle-headed standard is also featured on certain Sātavāhana inscriptions, as, for example, at the end of an inscription in Nasik (Maharashtra).

A unique coin features a tree-in-railing with round fruits dropping from its branches. This tree is taken to symbolize the *kalpavṛkṣa.*

Among the rarer and little-known auxiliary devices is the ground plan of a Buddhist *stūpa*. From a distance, this symbol appears to be a wheel or *cakra*. It consists of two concentric circles. Small lines radiate from the outer circle. Seven flower bud-like motifs are seen in between these lines. The inner circle has four arms radiating from its centre, marked by a prominent dot. The outer circle has an opening that leads into a circular passage. The inner circle may represent a *stūpa* enclosing a relic casket. The circular passage around the inner circle may be the circumambulatory passage for devotees. The outer circle and the projections radiating from it may then denote the railings around the *stūpa.* This is, thus, one of the earliest and rarest representations of an architectural ground plan on a coin.

Reverse Devices

Ujjain Symbol

Also called the *Ujjaini* symbol, it consists of a cross, with a ball or circle at the four ends of the lines forming the cross. The symbol derives its name from the fact that it was first observed on the early coins of Ujjaini or the Ujjain state in central India.

Unlike certain other symbols, the *Ujjain* symbol has been extensively studied and interpreted in myriad ways.[35] Many scholars believe that the symbol denotes the four cardinal directions—west, north, east and south. It may also denote the four corners of the earth or universe. In recent decades, the symbol has been intensively analysed from the viewpoint of astronomy. It has been taken to represent the exact location of Ujjain at the intersection of the Tropic of Cancer and the *madhyamarekhā* (the 0 meridian or central meridian, as per traditional Hindu astronomy). Significantly, due to its strategic geographical location, Ujjain was a centre of astronomical studies from ancient times. The symbol is also believed to signify the complex movement of the various planets around the sun.

On Sātavāhana coins, the *Ujjain* symbol first appears not on the reverse but on the obverse. Here, it is shown as four disjointed circles with no cross-bar, on the back of a bull. However, the complete symbol is more commonly seen on the reverse of Sātavāhana coins. In fact, it is the main reverse motif on an overwhelming majority of these coins (Plate 16). One notices significant differences in the size and shape of the balls, and the cross linking the balls on different coins. On some, the balls or circles of the symbol appear plain and hollow. On others, each circle either contains a pellet or dots or else seems to be completely filled up to appear like a solid ball. The symbol is often represented along with other sacred symbols such as the *svastika* and *śrīvatsa*. Sometimes these appear within the circles or balls. In some instances, the *Ujjain* symbol is surmounted by the *triratna* symbol and, rarely, the latter replaces each of the four circles of the former. On a rare silver coin, a spear-like object with two projections on its shaft and a lathe-worked grip is seen next to the *Ujjain* symbol. On the reverse of silver portrait coins, the symbol is most beautifully delineated with a pretty crescent above the top orb.

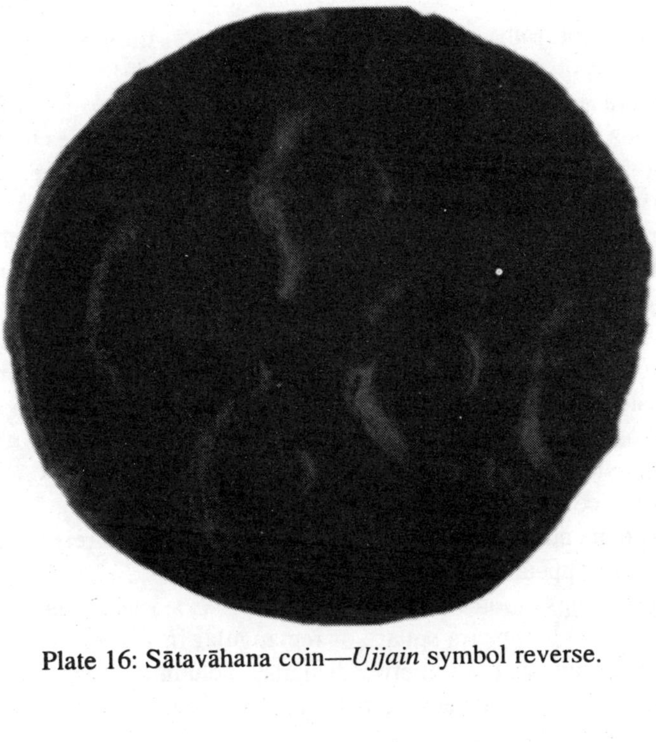

Plate 16: Sātavāhana coin—*Ujjain* symbol reverse.

It has been surmised that the adoption of the *Ujjain* symbol on Sātavāhana coinage signified the conquest of Ujjain by a Sātavāhana ruler who, thereafter, performed the *aśvamedha* sacrifice.[36] While this may be true, one should also remember that this symbol, along with many others, was extremely popular in almost every part of the Indian subcontinent and was exhibited on their coins by many kings, including the Sangam Cheras who were very far from Ujjain and had never seen or conquered this place. Ancient kings may have chosen to feature the *Ujjain* symbol on their coins merely to signify their extensive territorial conquests, plausibly in all the four directions.

Tree-in-railing

Next to the *Ujjain* symbol, the tree-in-railing is the commonest reverse motif on Sātavāhana coins. It occurs both as a main device and as an auxiliary one, in association with other devices and motifs.

Unlike the rather stiff and stylized trees on the coins of many other early Indian dynasties, the trees on most of the Sātavāhana coins are realistically portrayed. Hence, one is able to identify, on the basis of the shape of the tree and its leaves, the species to which it belongs. Thus, we see mango, palm, coconut and teak trees on the reverse of Sātavāhana coins.

On a rare lead circular elephant obverse coin of Gautamīputra Sātakarṇi, a standing goddess appears along with two trees-in-railing on the reverse. The goddess appears to be holding or clinging to the trees-in-railing and may be the goddess of the forest (*Vanadevatā*).

In order to create variety, the imaginative die-cutter or coin maker has featured the various types of trees in myriad ways. While some are shown with thick trunks and multiple branches, others appear tall and slender. Occasionally, the tree is shown growing on a hill, as on the coins of the Sangam Pāṇḍyas (first century BC). On some Sātavāhana coins, the leaves are dotted or spotted. Rarely, a few of the leaves appear torn or withered.

The railings around the trees also exhibit wide variations. Usually the low railing appears square or rectangular in shape. Sometimes it exhibits intricate geometric designs, including 'criss-cross' or check and woven basket patterns (Plate 17). Many of these railings,

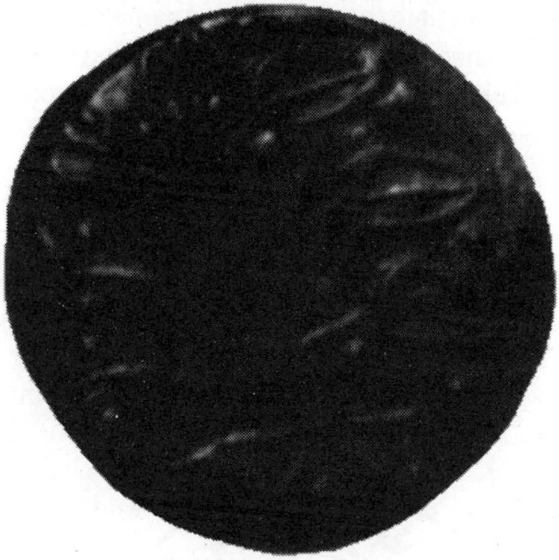

Plate 17: Sātavāhana coin—tree-in-railing reverse.
(Photo: Department of Coins and Medals,
The British Museum, London)

appear to have been reproductions of bamboo railings, which would have been very common in south India those days.

Other Reverse Devices and Symbols

Among other reverse symbols and devices are the river or lake with various aquatic creatures, the bull, the six-arched hill, ten-arched hill, sun, crescent moon, *śrīvatsa* and *svastika*. Among these reverse devices, the bull (calf?) on a potin rectangular coin is unique. Here, the bull's bushy tail appears to be tied to a column. A thick string links the column with the animal's neck. The precise significance of this device is not clear.

The rivers on the coins have been interpreted as denoting either the Ganga, the most sacred river of India, or any one of the smaller rivers flowing in the Sātavāhana territory. To cite an instance, the river on some of the Sātavāhana bronze coins found in the Bhilsa and Tripuri regions (central India) might denote the river Betwa.

The sun symbol is most beautifully featured on the reverse of the silver portrait coins. Here, it appears as a perfect circle with a dot in its centre. Small rays radiate from the circle. The Sātavāhanas had a special attachment to the sun god and some of their inscriptions include prayers to this deity.[37] One may recall that the very name of the dynasty was derived from the name Saptivāhana, one of the many names of the sun god.

Legends

On most Sātavāhana coins, the legend is confined to the obverse. It is in the Prakrit language and Brāhmī script, and conveys the name of the ruler. The silver portrait coins, however, bear legends on both sides (Figures 3, 4). The obverse legend is in the Brāhmī

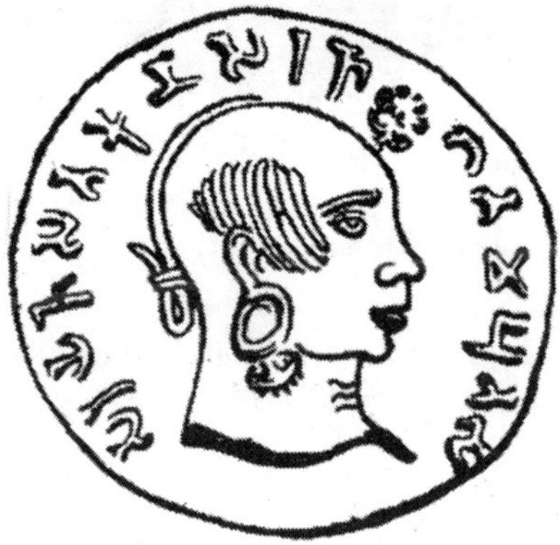

Figure 3: Sātavāhana bust type coin—obverse.

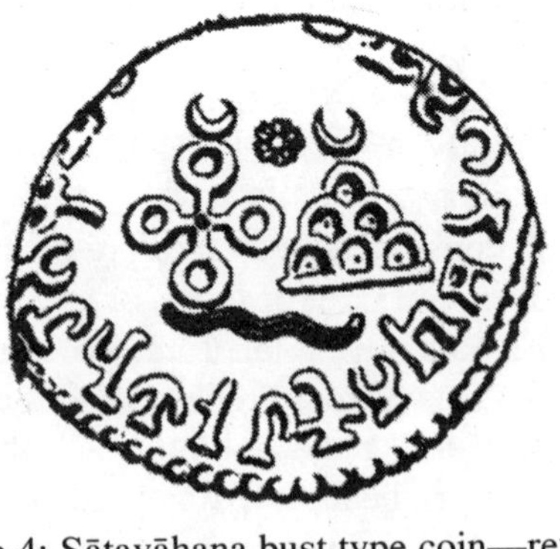

Figure 4: Sātavāhana bust type coin—reverse.

script and Prakrit language, but there is no unanimity amongst numismatists as regards the precise script and language of the reverse legend. The obverse and reverse legends are, however, identical in import, and mention the issuer together with his 'matrynomic' (name of the mother or *ṛṣipatnī*), regal title (*rājan*) and the honorific (*Siri*). According to tradition, the mothers of the Sātavāhana kings fervently prayed to the seven *ṛṣipatnīs* and it was believed that these noble kings were born by the grace of the latter.

We have already noted that the Sātavāhana portrait coins were modelled on the Kṣatrapa portrait coins. Since the latter had legends on the obverse and reverse, the Sātavāhanas, too, followed this practice. The contention that the very introduction of legends on Sātavāhana coins was inspired by Indo-Greek coins,[38] is, however, no longer accepted because indigenous coins bearing names of rulers and kingdoms, and pre-dating Indo-Greek issues, have now been discovered in many places in India.

As regards the script and language of the Sātavāhana coin reverse legends, D.C. Sircar was the first to point out that these are in a Dravidian script, resembling Tamil more than Telugu.[39] In the same vein, Ajay Mitra Shastri has argued that the language is Dravidian or proto-Dravidian from which both Tamil and Telugu later evolved.[40] Another group of scholars feel that these legends are in the usual Brāhmī script and Telugu language. I.K. Sarma, who has made an in-depth study of the legends, describes them as Telugu poetical compositions in the *Ragaḍa* metre.[41] Scholars like Somasundara Rao vehemently refute Sarma's contention by arguing that Telugu evolved as a distinct, full-fledged language only from the eleventh century AD and the earliest poetical inscriptions in archaic Telugu can be dated to the ninth century AD.[42] Moreover, these coin legends merely furnish the names of the kings and do not describe any of their qualities or achievements. Thus, they hardly qualify as specimens of poetry. Indeed, some of the earliest and finest metrical compositions on coins can be seen on issues minted by the imperial Guptas, who ruled large areas of north India after the decline of the Sātavāhanas in the third century AD.

R. Nagaswamy and, more recently, I. Mahadevan have stated that the Sātavāhana coin reverse legends are in the Tamil language and Tamil Brāhmī script.[43] Mahadevan has categorically enumerated certain Tamil Brāhmī letters such as *ca*, *ma* and *ḷu* which occur in these legends. The same Tamil Brāhmī letters are frequently seen in the Tamil Brāhmī cave inscriptions of the first-second centuries AD in Tamil Nadu. The occurrence of the *puḷḷi* (dot) in these legends further confirms that the language is Tamil because the *puḷḷi* is exclusive to Tamil writing. However, the Sātavāhana coin maker or scribe seems not to have been very fluent in Tamil grammar and, hence, he mechanically translated the Prakrit terms into Tamil, resulting in legends that convey a meaning but are not in idiomatic or correct Tamil.

The reasons which prompted the Sātavāhanas to incorporate Tamil legends on their coins can be traced to the fact that Prakrit and Tamil were the major languages used for political and administrative purposes in south India in that period. By incorporating Tamil legends, the Sātavāhanas ensured that the Tamil-speaking people in their empire could read and understand them. These people mostly lived in the southern fringes of the empire—mainly in the Tirupati region or the southernmost areas of the present-day state of Andhra Pradesh. Further, silver coins would have circulated extensively among high-level traders of varied kingdoms, while the base metal coins would have mainly served as day-to-day currency among the common people and occasionally carried to other kingdoms during the process of trade. In this context, it is well known that the Sātavāhanas maintained intimate commercial and cultural ties with the Tamil-speaking Sangam Chera, Sangam Cōḷa and Sangam Pāṇḍya kingdoms. Thus, the Tamil legends on Sātavāhana silver coins would have helped the kings and traders of these Tamil kingdoms to understand them. As silver was scarce in Tamiḷakam, these kingdoms would have especially welcomed the Sātavāhana silver coins. Some of the Tamil kings like the Sangam Cheras and Sangam Pāṇḍyas would have melted these coins for producing their own silver specie. This would, incidentally, account for the absence of Sātavāhana silver coins in any site in Tamiḷakam.

On Sātavāhana coins, the legends usually read from left to right. Generally they are placed along the margin or border of the flan. Particularly on the circular coins, including the portrait coins, the legends appear as a well-proportioned arch or canopy around the main device. On some coins, however, the legend is a little away from the border and is placed just above the main device like the elephant. On such coins, the legend-line sometimes amusingly twists and turns in accordance with the bodily contours of the elephant. On many quadrangular coins, the legend is placed as a straight line on the top. On the standing king type coins, it sometimes starts just above the head of the king and, thus, appears as a neat label for the portrait.

The coin makers do not seem to have carefully planned the placement of the legends on the die or the mould. Hence, some of the letters, especially towards the end of the longer legends, are crammed and distorted for want of sufficient space. Besides, due to the carelessness and haste of the coin makers and defects in the minting processes, portions of the legend are often out of the flan.

NOTES AND REFERENCES

1. For a broad history of the ancient Andhra region, with special reference to the Sātavāhanas, see K. Gopalachari, *Early History of the Andhra Country* (Madras, 1976), pp. 1-129; K.A. Nilakanta Sastri, *A History of South India: From Prehistoric Times to the Fall of Vijayanagara* (New Delhi, 2002), pp. 83-103.
2. Sātavāhana coins are seen in numerous museums and private collections in India and abroad. In south India, the Andhra Pradesh State Archaeological Museum, Hyderabad, and the Government Museum, Egmore, Chennai, have very large collections of Sātavāhana coins. The former has over 50,000 coins, including many of the recent finds. The latter houses over 6,000 coins, including several little-known nineteenth-century and early twentieth-century finds. The majority of the coins in both the museums remain unpublished. In the Madras Museum, many of the coins are not even labelled or correctly identified. Among private collections in Tamil Nadu, the most important is that of S. Raman (Madras).

   There are two important catalogues of Sātavāhana coins: M. Rama Rao, *Select Sātavāhana Coins in the Government Museum, Madras* (Madras, 1959, rpt. 2000); idem, *Sātavāhana Coins in the Andhra Pradesh Govt. Museum* (Hyderabad, 1961). Unlike the latter, the former is not very widely known, and is not consulted or cited by many scholars.

   Some of the stratified finds of Sātavāhana coins have been systematically catalogued in S.C. Ray, *Stratigraphic Evidence of Coins in Indian Excavations and Some Allied Issues* (Varanasi, 1959), pp. 35-8. Research papers and monographs focusing on specific types and aspects of Sātavāhana coins are numerous. For the most exhaustive bibliography of Sātavāhana coins, see D. Raja Reddy and P. Suryanarayana Reddy, 'Andhra Coins: A Bibliography', *SSIC* XIII (2003), pp. 91-125.

The most well-known and widely-consulted study of Sātavāhana coins is I.K. Sarma, *Coinage of the Sātavāhana Empire* (Delhi, 1980).

3. The *Periplus* 56 lists copper, tin and lead as exports from Rome to India.
4. This has been proved by archaeo-chemical studies on a few Sātavāhana bronze coins in Hyderabad and Chennai. Also see I.K. Sarma, 'An Appraisal of Recent Discoveries of South Indian Coins', *SSIC* V (1995), pp. 9-27.
5. I had a discussion on this technical point with A.N. Lahiri in 1989 in New Delhi. See I.K. Sarma 1980 (supra n. 2), p. 56.
6. Many of these coins are in private collections. See Shashikant G. Dhopate, 'Half Denomination Silver Portrait Coin of Yajna Satakarni', *SSIC* XIII, (2003), pp. 20-2. Here, the author discusses the significance of the low weight of these coins.
7. Information regarding these mounds is scattered in a number of publications. See. I.K. Sarma 1980 (supra n. 2), p. 58; idem, 'Sātavāhana Coins From Paithan and Connected Problems', *SSIC* I (1991), pp. 33-43; K.V. Raman and P. Shanmugam, 'Terracotta Coin Moulds From Kanchipuram', *SSIC* I (1991), pp. 23-9.
8. The find was first reported by A.M. Shastri. For a lively discussion about the significance and genuineness of the find, see I.K. Sarma 1991 (supra n. 7), pp. 33-43; A.M. Shastri, 'Sātavāhana Silver Coinage', *SSIC* I (1991), pp. 45-60; idem, 'Kondapur: A Sātavāhana Silver Coins Mint', *SSIC* III (1993), pp. 81-5. I discussed this find with A.M. Shastri at Hyderabad in 1998.
9. I.K. Sarma 1991 (supra n. 7), pp. 33-43.
10. A.M. Shastri 1993 (supra n. 8), pp. 81-5.
11. A.M. Shastri 1991 (supra n. 8), pp. 45-60; idem 1993 (supra n. 8), pp. 81-5.
12. I.K. Sarma 1980 (supra n. 2), p. 58; A.M. Shastri 1993 (supra n. 8), pp. 81-5; idem, 'Three Sātavāhana Mint-Towns', *SSIC* IV (1994), pp. 57-62.
13. I.K. Sarma 1980 (supra n. 2), p. 58.
14. For an interesting discussion on this subject, see I.K. Sarma 1980 (supra n. 2), p. 63.
15. I.K. Sarma 1980 (supra n. 2), p. 64.
16. The find was first reported by Shobhana Gokhale. I.K. Sarma, however, does not agree with Gokhale's identification of the king or rider on the elephant. See I.K. Sarma 1991 (supra n. 7), pp. 33-43.
17. Shobhana Gokhale, 'Elephant and Vase Type Coin of Kochhiputa Satakarni', *SSIC* II (1992), pp. 107-10. Also see Shobhana Gokhale, 'Junnar in Trade During Satavahana Period', in Amal Kumar Jha, ed., *Coinage Trade And Economy* (Nashik, 1991), pp. 55-7.
18. Such seals are not widely-known. One such seal has been published by S.J. Mangalam. See S.J. Mangalam, 'Satavahana Terracottas From Paithan', in P. Sitapati and V.V. Krishna Sastry, eds., *Satavahana Seminar Souvenir*

(Hyderabad, 1981), p. 53. For the intimate link between the Sātavāhanas and the horse, see I.K. Sarma 1980 (supra n. 2), pp. 3, 72. Also see I.K. Sarma, 'A Critical Assessment of the Coinage of the Sātavāhanas: Sequence and Dating', *SSIC* XI (2001), pp. 18-27.

19. D. Jithendra Das, 'Sātavāhana Coins From the *Maha Stupa* Excavation at Kanganhalli in Karnataka', *SSIC* XI (2001), pp. 36-48.
20. I.K. Sarma 1980 (supra n. 2), pp. 65-6. Also see C. Sivaramamurti, *Numismatic Parallels of Kālidāsa* (New Delhi, 1983), pp. 11-13.
21. A.M. Shastri, 'On an Enigmatic Khaharata Coin', *SSIC* VI (1996), pp. 19-23.
22. Scholars like A.M. Shastri and A.K. Narain felt that the wheel on some of the Sātavāhana coins may represent the wheel of Buddha. See I.K. Sarma 1980 (supra n. 2), p. 68.
23. For a brief survey of the Hindu religious literature of the Sātavāhanas, see K. Gopalachari 1976 (supra n. 1), pp. 127-9. Also see I.K. Sarma 1980 (supra n. 2), pp. 3-5.
24. R. Krishnamurthy and Mohd. Safiullah, 'A Satavahana Lead Coin With Bow and Arrow Symbol', *SSIC* XV (2005), pp. 35-8.
25. I am grateful to A.M. Shastri for bringing the non-silver portrait coins to my notice. See B.K. Sahay, 'Portrait Coins of Sātavāhanas: A Reappraisal', *JNSI* LIII 1&2 (1991), pp. 30-1.
26. For details regarding these references in Sanskrit works, including Kālidāsa's poems, see C. Sivaramamurti 1983 (supra n. 20), pp. 9-11.
27. Shashikant G. Dhopate, 'Silver Portrait Coin of (Gautamiputra) Kumbha Satakarni', *SSIC* XIV (2004), pp. 41-3. For details about some interesting and rare sub-varieties of Sātavāhana portrait coins, see Laxmikant B. Varma, 'Rare Portrait Coins of Skanda Satakarni', *ND* XVII (1993), pp. 25-7.
28. D. Jithendra Das 2001 (supra n. 19), pp. 36-48. A gallery of portrait sculptures featuring the members of the Sātavāhana royal family existed at Junnar in Maharashtra. Only the feet of these sculptures with the label inscriptions have survived.
29. I.K. Sarma 1991 (supra n. 7), pp. 33-43.
30. Many scholars like I. Mahadevan initially considered the figure to be a Sātavāhana queen.
31. I.K. Sarma 1991 (supra n. 7), pp. 33-43.
32. H.W. Codrington, *Ceylon Coins and Currency, Memoirs of the Colombo Museum,* Series A, No. 3 (Colombo, 1924, rpt. 1975), pp. 26-31; S.K. Sitrampalam, 'A Note on the Lakshmi Plaques of Śrī Lanka', *SSIC* II (1992), pp. 151-8. Also see Osmund Bopearachchi and Rajah M. Wickremesinhe, *Ruhuna—An Ancient Civilisation Re-visited: Numismatic and Archaeological Evidence on Inland and Maritime Trade* (Colombo?,1999), pp. 28-9, 91-7. Such plaques bearing the figure of Lakṣmī rarely occur in south India, too. See R. Krishnamurthy, 'Oblong Copper Coin With "Mother

Goddess" Symbol From Karur, Tamil Nadu', *JNSI* LIII 1&2 (1991), pp. 59-61.

33. For more details of these epigraphical references, see S.K. Sitrampalam, 1992 (supra n. 32), pp. 151-8.
34. For some of these symbols and devices in Sātavāhana art and other features of their art, see O.C. Gangoly, *Andhra Sculptures* (Hyderabad, 1973); H. Sarkar and S.P. Nainar, *Amaravati* (New Delhi, 1972); I.K. Sarma, *Religion in Art, and Historical Archaeology of South India: Contacts and Correlations* (Madras, 1987).
35. One of the latest and most interesting studies on the *Ujjain* symbol is Haripriya Rangarajan, 'The Significance of Ujjaini Symbol', *SSIC* IX (1999), pp. 14-22. Also see I.K. Sarma 1980 (supra n. 2), p. 69; Savita Sharma, *Early Indian Symbols: Numismatic Evidence* (Delhi, 1990), pp. 135-8.
36. The portrayal of the *Ujjain* symbol on the coins of any dynasty is often taken to mean the conquest of Ujjain by that dynasty. See I.K. Sarma 1980 (supra n. 2), p. 69.
37. For instance, the famous Naneghat inscription commences with salutations to the sun god and various other gods.
38. Scholars like A.M. Shastri hold this opinion. See A.M. Shastri 1991 (supra n. 8), pp. 45-60. Also see I.K. Sarma 1980 (supra n. 2), pp. 61-2.
39. D.C. Sircar, 'Silver Coin of Vasishthi-putra Satakarni', *Epigraphica Indica* 35 (1963-4), pp. 247-52.
40. A.M. Shastri 1991 (supra n. 8), pp. 45-60.
41. I.K. Sarma 1980 (supra n. 2), pp. 113-22.
42. C. Somasundara Rao, 'A Note on Bilingual Legends on Sātavāhana Coins', *SSIC* VII (1997), pp. 17-21.
43. I. Mahadevan, *Early Tamil Epigraphy: From the Earliest Times to the Sixth Century* AD (Madras, 2003), pp. 199-205.

CHAPTER 8

Coins of the Ikṣvākus

Around the third century AD, the disintegration of the mighty Sātavāhana empire resulted in the rise of several dynasties such as the Ikṣvākus, the Śālaṅkāyanas or Vaingēyakas, the Kāndāras or Ānandas and the Viṣṇukuṇḍins in the Andhra country, and the Pallavas on the south-eastern coast.

The word 'Ikṣvāku' literally means 'gourd' in Sanskrit. It is traditionally believed that the remote ancestors of the Ikṣvāku dynasty emerged from a gourd. The Ikṣvākus originally lived in north India and later migrated to the south in search of power.

In the Andhra region, the Ikṣvākus were initially the feudatories and later the successors of the Sātavāhanas. The important Ikṣvāku rulers were Vāsiṣṭhiputra Śrī Chāmtamūla or Chāmtamūla I (AD 227-50), Māthariputra Śrī Vīrapurīṣadatta (AD 250-70), Vāsiṣṭhiputra Śrī Ehavala Chāmtamūla or Ehavala Śrī or Chāmtamūla II (AD 270-95) and Rudrapurīṣadatta (AD 295-306). It is said that the early Pallava king, Shivaskandavarman, defeated Rudrapurīṣadatta and captured his territories. From Andhra, the Pallavas slowly but steadily expanded their kingdom and soon emerged as the most powerful kingdom in south India. Nagarjunakonda or Śrīparvata Vijayapuri was the capital of the Ikṣvākus. The kings of this dynasty were great patrons of art and literature.[1]

Finds of Ikṣvāku coins are not many and they have not been reported from any site outside the Ikṣvāku territory.[2] Archaeological excavations at Nagarjunakonda in Andhra have revealed scores of Ikṣvāku coins in a stratified context. Amaravati, also in Andhra, has revealed at least 8 Ikṣvāku coins in a stratified context. A hoard of 277 Ikṣvāku coins was reported from the Ongole region of Andhra. A batch of coins, probably the remnants of a hoard, was discovered at a place called Pamarru in the Krishna district of Andhra. A little-known rare horse type coin of Chāmtamūla I was reported from Kesanapalli in Guntur district in Andhra.

PHYSICAL FEATURES AND PRODUCTION METHOD

In the fields of administration, art and coinage, the Ikṣvākus mostly imitated their erstwhile overlords, the Sātavāhanas. Thus, many coins of the Ikṣvākus and the Sātavāhanas bear striking similarities with regard to the metal, minting process, fabric, size, and obverse and reverse symbols and devices.

The Ikṣvāku coins are mostly in lead and sometimes in potin. As for the source of the metals, the Ikṣvākus would have tapped copper, lead and zinc deposits in the Andhra region. Further, copper, tin and lead was imported from the Roman empire. The Ikṣvākus also had easy access to the old Sātavāhana lead and potin coins, which they would have melted to produce new coins.

The weight of Ikṣvāku coins range, on an average, between 1 and 6 grams; many of the published specimens weigh around 3 to 4 grams. Some Ikṣvāku coins with an abnormally heavy weight, ranging from 29 to 43 grams, have also been reported. The lighter coins seem to have lost weight during the long years when they were used as money. In fact, several Ikṣvāku coins show traces of having been in circulation for a considerable period of time. The soft nature of lead, the main metal used in these coins, may have also contributed to their worn-out condition.

Almost all the known Ikṣvāku coins in their present worn-out condition, appear to be irregular in shape but, originally, many of them may have been round with a diameter of 1 to 1.8 cm. It is equally plausible that at least a few of these circular coins may have been, soon after their manufacture, irregularly cut or clipped at a corner to ensure their correct weight. A small number of Ikṣvāku coins are oval or egg-shaped. A few others appear slightly oblong with a prominent, pointed projection at one end.

All the Ikṣvāku coins were cast probably using terracotta moulds. Extant specimens of such moulds are, however, not available.[3] The Ikṣvākus did not take adequate care to properly couple the obverse and reverse moulds and, hence, the representation of the obverse and reverse devices are not in any specific, fixed orientation. Often, the devices are partially out of the flan and there are quite a few instances of the overlapping of one symbol or device with another. At the Ikṣvāku capital of Nagarjunakonda, the remnants of an Ikṣvāku mint have been discovered.[4] The mint area has yielded a large cluster of hundreds of coins. Probably all the Ikṣvāku coins were issued from this mint.

Ancient forgeries of Ikṣvāku coins are not unknown. These were also made by the casting technique. A notable example which has, as per its legend, been assigned to Vīrapurīṣadatta (AD 250-70), portrays the elephant both on the obverse and reverse.[5] Another rare Ikṣvāku coin bears the *Ujjain* symbol on the obverse and reverse. This coin, too, may be an ancient forgery or a mint freak. As the elephant type forged coin occurs in a hoard along with hundreds of genuine Ikṣvāku coins, one may surmise that these forgeries, too, were produced around the same time as the genuine coins, and both categories circulated together in the Ikṣvāku territory.

ART AND SYMBOLOGY

Compared to the coins of many early south Indian dynasties, including the Sātavāhanas, Sangam Cheras and Sangam Pāṇḍyas, the Ikṣvāku coins display a very limited number of devices and motifs. The reasons for this could be traced to several factors. First, the rule of the Ikṣvākus was, comparatively, of a short duration of barely a century and a quarter. Further, their territory was not very large. They had to fight many wars, leaving them with little time to think of innovations in coinage. Also, by the time of the Ikṣvākus, the circulation of *kārṣāpaṇas* had considerably decreased and, hence, they would have hardly known or seen those coins to reproduce the *kārṣāpaṇa* symbols on their coins. Hence, these rulers merely continued with some of the most common and popular coin types of the Sātavāhanas.

OBVERSE DEVICES

Elephant

The elephant, the royal emblem of the Ikṣvākus, is the most common obverse device on their coins (Plate 18). Over 99.9 per cent of Ikṣvāku coins display this animal. The elephant is shown standing or walking mostly to the right and, very rarely, to the left. The trunk

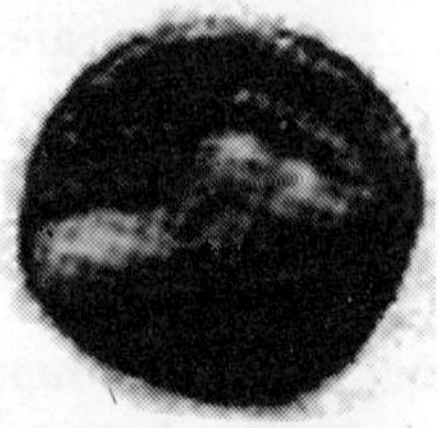

Plate 18: Ikṣvāku coin—elephant obverse.

is mostly uplifted and, rarely, dangling downwards. In a majority of specimens, the tusks are absent. A long, thin, plain rope, sometimes twisted or rolled, is occasionally seen hanging from the neck of the elephant. Rarely, the animal is enclosed within a circle.

On many coins, a part of the elephant is out of the flan. For instance, in several cases, the head facing right and the beautifully upturned trunk alone are seen on the extreme left, as though the elephant is just entering the flan from there! Similarly, on some other coins, only the back of the elephant is seen on the extreme right, as though the animal is leaving or walking out of the flan!! In most cases, the trunk is altogether absent or else appears cut or mutilated. Occasionally, the legs of the animal are out of the flan.

It is obvious that the Ikṣvākus copied the elephant device from the Sātavāhana coins. In fact, it has been accepted that the elephant on the coins of Chāmtamūla I, the founder of the Ikṣvāku dynasty, bear close resemblance to that on the issues of Gautamīputra Śrī Yajña Sātakarṇi (AD 165-94).[6] The elephant on the coins of the Ikṣvāku ruler, Chāmtamūla II (AD 270-95), is also strikingly similar to the elephants on many Sātavāhana potin coins found in Nagarjunakonda, the Ikṣvāku capital, and in central India.

However, unlike the almost lifelike elephants on Sātavāhana coins, the Ikṣvāku coin elephant is often very crudely and disproportionately delineated, except on a few coins of Chāmtamūla II where the animal is slightly better executed. On many Ikṣvāku coins, the elephant is shown as merely three dumpy, circular or elliptical lumps—one denoting the head and neck portion, the second signifying the stomach or the mid-portion of the body, and the third, the back and tail of the creature. The coin makers never cared to portray the finer anatomical details, including the natural folds in the skin and the hair on the tail.

The extremely poor artistic merit of the elephant on Ikṣvāku coins becomes all the more astonishing in the context of the fact that the age of the Ikṣvākus saw the zenith of perfection of the plastic art of Āndhradeśa.[7] The sinuous animal and human figures occurring in the Ikṣvāku stone sculptures of Nagarjunakonda reveal the sculptor's keen sense of observation of even the minutest details, his sound knowledge of human and animal anatomy, and, above all, his unique skill of effectively creating an illusion of life and movement in each of the figures. The elephant, the favourite animal of the Ikṣvākus, has been exceedingly well-executed in stone. To mention but one instance, it is sculpted on one of the lower panels of the famous *Chāyā-stambha* (memorial pillar) erected in honour of Chāmtamūla I by his sisters and wives at Nagarjunakonda. Here, the king is shown riding the elephant, with a parasol held by an attendant seated next to him. This elephant appears majestic, realistic and well-proportioned. Even the natural folds in the skin of the animal have been skilfully brought out by the artist.

Horse

The obverse of a few Ikṣvāku coins feature the horse instead of the elephant. Unlike the latter, the horse appears lifelike. It stands to the right or left. The animal is well-fed and well-built, with a sheath of muscles rippling under the skin. The slight bends in the legs create an illusion of movement. The eyes of the animal are turned downwards and appear to gaze at the ground. On some coins featuring the horse to the right, a column or post (*yūpastambha*) is seen in front of it. On a few specimens, a part of the legend (*Siri*) *Cāta* is seen. The legend indicates that the issuer of this unique coin is Chāmtamūla I. The presence of the horse with the sacrificial post suggests that this coin was minted to mark the *aśvamedha* sacrifice performed by this ruler. An important inscription of Chāmtamūla I's son and successor, Vīrapurīṣadatta, from Nagarjunakonda, categorically states that the former performed several sacrifices including the *aśvamedha*. The epigraphs also reveal that Chāmtamūla I bore many high-sounding titles, the most well-known among which is *aśvamedhayājin*. He is believed to have performed the horse sacrifice twice.

The extreme paucity of Ikṣvāku horse type coins may be because a very limited number were issued on the occasion of the two horse sacrifices performed by Chāmtamūla I. He never issued this coin type later. Also, there is no concrete evidence to show that any of the other Ikṣvāku rulers ever performed the *aśvamedha* sacrifice or issued horse type coins. Being a commemorative issue associated with a rare royal achievement, it is not surprising to note that the delineation of the figure on the horse coin is more perfect and lifelike than the figures on other Ikṣvāku coins.

Reverse Devices

Ujjain Symbol

Like the Sātavahana coins, most of the Ikṣvāku coins also bear the *Ujjain* symbol on the reverse (Plate 19). The size of the symbol varies from coin to coin. Rarely, the symbol is small with a well-defined margin on all sides. However, in most instances, the symbol occupies the entire flan with portions often outside it. Sometimes the four orbs of the symbol are not perfect circles but triangles with curved ends. In a few instances, the orbs are not linked by the 'central' cross—either the cross was not delineated at all, or else has worn out. The mid-point of this symbol is rarely shown as a prominent circle or pellet. Sometimes the fillet within each of the orbs is prominently exhibited. No other symbol or design occurs along with the *Ujjain* symbol on any coin.

Plate 19: Ikṣvāku coin—
Ujjain symbol reverse.

Six-petalled Flower?

On a limited number of coins, the reverse does not feature the *Ujjain* symbol. Instead, there are six circles surrounding a central one. All are equal in size. This device appears to be a six-petalled flower. On most coins, the flower occupies the entire flan, with parts of the petals often lying outside it. One may recall that such six-petalled flowers of a slightly different shape are seen as subsidiary devices on a few coins of the Sangam Cheras, who ruled over Kerala region from around 300 BC to AD 300.

Legends

Many of the Ikṣvāku coins bear legends on the obverse in the Brāhmī script and Prakrit language. The legend denotes the name of the king who issued the coin.

The Ikṣvākus followed the matriarchal system and the kings often prefixed the names of their mothers or other senior female members of their clan or extended family to their names. Unlike the Sātavāhanas, the Ikṣvākus did not incorporate the 'matrynomic' in their coin legends. The legends merely state the name of the king with the honorific 'Śiri' or 'Śrī'.

The letters forming the legend are never written in a straight line. They are engraved along the rim of the coin immediately above the animal device, usually commencing from the tail portion and proceeding in a clockwise direction. No part of the legend is ever seen in front of or below the animal. On all known Ikṣvāku coins, only a portion of the legend appears within the flan. Interestingly, on most coins of Ehavala, the letter *ha* in the name appears to be deliberately engraved above the head of the elephant. It may be pointed out that exigencies of space often affected the form of some of the letters, causing variations in size and, occasionally, even the precise shape of the alphabet on different coins of the Ikṣvākus.

A comparison between the stone inscriptions of the Ikṣvākus and the legends on their coins reveals that the execution of the latter is not artistic and is devoid of the ornamental flourishes for which Ikṣvāku Brāhmī epigraphs in stone are widely known. In the stone inscriptions, the letters are of the typical cursive style where the elongated *mātrā* strokes are generally straight and terminate in a beautiful curve or loop. On the coins, however, the *mātrā* strokes, partially due to lack of space, are very short and are also not straight but sloping or slanting. On one coin, the bottom loop or bend of the letter *ra* is turned towards the right while, on another coin, the *ha* in the name 'Ehavala' has been accorded a *U-mātrā* and, hence, one can read it as Ehuvala.

Slash Marks and Countermarks

A sole Ikṣvāku coin bears a prominent, oblique chisel mark or slash mark on the trunk of the elephant that is depicted on the obverse.[8] No legend is seen and, hence, the precise issuer and date of this coin are not known. It is part of a large hoard of 277 Ikṣvāku lead coins found in the Ongole area of Andhra. The chisel mark on the coin is identical in size, depth and manner of execution to the slash marks seen on a number of Roman gold and silver coins found in south India, especially in the Krishna Valley of Andhra, which was, significantly, within the Ikṣvāku kingdom.[9] The slashing or defacing of the coins of a political rival was a common practice in ancient Africa and some other regions. In India, though, except for these Roman coins, the sole Ikṣvāku coin and a few Indo-Greek coins, there is no record of any other ancient coin bearing such slash marks. As regards the slash marks on the Roman coins, there have been several theories and opinions with regard to their purpose or significance. Many scholars have argued that these marks were intended to obliterate the denominational value of the foreign coins and validate them as local currency in India. The precise significance of the mark on the Ikṣvāku coin and the Indo-Greek coins is, however, uncertain.

At least two Ikṣvāku coins bear minute countermarks of tiny circles on the reverse. These belong to the Ongole hoard. The precise date and significance of these marks are not clear. One may recall that similar countermarks are sometimes seen on Roman coins found in Andhra and certain other places in south India.[10]

NOTES AND REFERENCES

1. For a broad history of the ancient Andhra region, with special reference to the Ikṣvākus, see K. Gopalachari, *Early History of the Andhra Country* (Madras, 1976), pp. 130-55; K.A. Nilakanta Sastri, *A History of South India: From Prehistoric Times to the Fall of Vijayanagara* (New Delhi, 2002), pp. 83-103.
2. The Andhra Pradesh State Archaeological Museum, Hyderabad, is the only museum with a good collection of Ikṣvāku coins. These coins are so rare that they are unknown in private collections in Tamil Nadu. The sole published catalogue pertaining to the Ikṣvāku coins is R. Subrahmanyam, *A Catalogue of the Ikshvaku Coins in the Andhra Pradesh Government Museum* (Hyderabad,

1979). This documents 274 of the 277 Ikṣvāku coins in the Ongole hoard (Andhra). The other publications pertaining to Ikṣvāku coins include Brajadulal Chattopadhyaya, *Coins and Currency Systems in South India c.* AD *225-1300* (New Delhi, 1977), pp. 7-9, 189-90; I.K. Sarma, 'A Critical Study of the Numismatic Evidences From Nagarjunakonda Excavations', *SSIC* IV (1994), pp. 63-78; idem, 'An Appraisal of Recent Discoveries of South Indian Coins', *SSIC* V (1995), pp. 9-27; idem, 'Coins From Amaravati Excavations', *SSIC* VIII (1998), pp. 44-57; T.S. Ravishankar, 'A Note on Three Ikshvaku Coins', *SSIC* X (2000), pp. 32-6; K. Munirathnam, 'A Lead Coin From Andhra Pradesh', *SSIC* XII (2002), p. 16; D. Raja Reddy, 'An Overview of Andhra Region Coins', *SSIC* XV (2005), pp. 7-29. Most of these recent publications refer to Ikṣvāku coins in passing and are not in-depth studies of this coin series.

3. R. Subrahmanyam 1979 (supra n. 2), p. 2, fn. 1 mentions a terracotta mould from Nagarjunakonda. Yet this is a Sātavāhana coin mould. Subrahmanyam is silent about the dynastic affiliations of this mould but his account wrongly seems to imply that the mould is of the Ikṣvākus.
4. I.K. Sarma 1995 (supra n. 2), pp. 9-27.
5. This coin belongs to the Ongole hoard. R. Subrahmanyam 1979 (supra n. 2), p. 25, coin no. 48.
6. R. Subrahmanyam 1979 (supra n. 2), p. 3, fn. 1.
7. The bibliography for Ikṣvāku art is vast. See R. Subrahmanyam 1979 (supra n. 2), pp. 3, 8. Also see O.C. Gangoly, *Andhra Sculptures* (Hyderabad, 1973); H. Sarkar and B.N. Misra, *Nagarjunakonda* (New Delhi, 1980), which has a useful bibliography on Nagarjunakonda.
8. This coin belongs to the Ongole hoard. R. Subrahmanyam 1979 (supra n. 2), p. 38, coin no. 204.
9. For an analysis of the nature and significance of slash marks on ancient coins, mainly Roman coins in India, see S. Suresh, *Symbols of Trade: Roman and Pseudo-Roman Objects Found in India* (New Delhi, 2004), pp. 40-52. Also see P.J. Turner, *Roman Coins From India* (London, 1989), pp. 29-36.
10. Such marks are sometimes also seen on the Sātavāhana and Western Kṣatrapa coins. For more details about these marks, refer to Chapter 2 of this book.

CHAPTER 9

Coins of the Viṣṇukuṇḍins

The Viṣṇukuṇḍins or Viṣṇukuṇḍis ruled over Andhra and large parts of Maharashtra from around the fifth century AD to at least the beginning of the seventh century. Among the best-known Viṣṇukuṇḍin kings are Govindavarman I (AD 419-56) and Madhavavarman (AD 553-93). The other important rulers of this dynasty include Indrabhattārakavarman (AD 529-56) and Vikramendravarman II (AD 556-70). The precise dates and chronology of the various Viṣṇukuṇḍin rulers are still uncertain.[1] The place name Vinukonda in Andhra is believed to have been derived from the name 'Viṣṇukuṇḍin'. Vinukonda has a hill fort and many scholars believe that it was the capital of the Viṣṇukuṇḍins.

Viṣṇukuṇḍin coins have been found at many places such as Amaravati, Dharanikota, Gopalapatnam, Gurzala, Keesarigutta, Nagarjunakonda, Nelakondapalli, Peddavegi, Tangadupalli, Tangutur, Telkunta, Warangal and Yellesvaram in Andhra, and Brahmapuri (Kolhapur), Nagar, Nagpur, Nasik, Nevasa and Paunar in Maharashtra. Incidentally, Paunar has yielded one of the largest hoards of Viṣṇukuṇḍin coins in Maharashtra.[2] It consists of over 200 coins, packed in a copper pot. Stray finds of Viṣṇukuṇḍin coins continue to be found in the Paunar region. Recently, Viṣṇukuṇḍin coins have been found at Tirukoilur in Tamil Nadu.[3] This is the first ever discovery of Viṣṇukuṇḍin coins south of Andhra.

PHYSICAL FEATURES AND PRODUCTION METHOD

For many years, scholars believed that the majority, if not all, of the Viṣṇukuṇḍin coins were made of copper. However, it has now been discovered that many of these so-called copper coins are actually made of iron, with a thin coating of copper. Occasionally, the iron core is found to be alloyed with copper and tin. Sometimes the coating is not of pure copper but an alloy of copper, tin and, perhaps, silver too (ternary alloy or bronze). In rare instances, the coating is reported to be a thin foil of pure silver or even gold.

Coins made wholly of iron without any coating have also been found, mainly in Andhra. It has been reported that the iron in the Viṣṇukuṇḍin coins is of a very high quality, almost like steel. Despite its high quality, the iron coins have rusted because they have been buried in the soil for hundreds of years. Due to excessive rusting of the iron core, many of these, newly-discovered coins appear swollen and heavy. It is difficult to determine the original, correct weight and size of these coins. The Viṣṇukuṇḍin iron coins, whether plated with other metals or not, could be safely identified with the *Loha māśakas* mentioned in ancient literature.[4] The Viṣṇukuṇḍins were, thus, the first Indian dynasty to use iron for making coins.

The Viṣṇukuṇḍins minted potin coins, many of which were discovered in the Maharashtra region. Base silver coins of this dynasty have also been reported but it has recently been proved that these specimens are actually made of a perfect alloy of copper, tin, zinc and lead (potin), which accounts for their silvery appearance and hardness. The metallic composition of these coins has also been confirmed by specific gravity tests and chemical analysis.

As to the source of metals for Viṣṇukuṇḍin coins, copper, lead and zinc deposits in Andhra would have been tapped. Iron, too, was available in south India. They would also have melted the old Sātavāhana copper, lead, potin and silver coins for manufacturing new ones. Gold, used for plating a few of the iron coins, may have been obtained by melting the old Roman gold coins available to the Viṣṇukuṇḍins. In this connection, one may note that by the time the Viṣṇukuṇḍins came to power, trade between south India and the Mediterranean regions was on the decline. Yet, as detailed in the following section on 'Art and Symbology', many old Roman coins, mainly the gold ones, continued to circulate in south India, at least during the early period of Viṣṇukuṇḍin rule.

Due to the slow decline of Indo-Mediterranean trade, the Viṣṇukuṇḍins, unlike their predecessors, did not import metals like copper, lead and tin from Rome. The resultant paucity of these metals would have prompted them to seek an alternate one for their coins. This was iron which was easily available and less expensive than other metals.

By now, the circular shape began to be considered the most convenient and ideal for coins. Thus, the Viṣṇukuṇḍins and many later dynasties invariably adopted it for their coins. The Viṣṇukuṇḍin circular coins have a diameter usually ranging between 1.4 to 2.5 cm. On an average, Viṣṇukuṇḍin coins weigh between 4 to 7 grams but exceptionally light coins weighing 0.5 gram and unusually heavy coins weighing 10.5 grams have also come to light. In general, Viṣṇukuṇḍin coins appear to be heavier, thicker and stronger than the issues of many other ancient dynasties of south India. Some of them exhibit a slight protrusion or bulge towards the centre of the flan, both on the obverse and reverse.

As for the technique by which these coins were made, in most cases, the circular coin-flan was first prepared by the casting process and the symbols and devices were later executed by the method of die-striking. The anvil-die was used for the reverse symbols and the punching die for the obverse ones.

Viṣṇukuṇḍin coins appear to have been minted from several mints located in Andhra and Maharashtra. This may, to an extent, account for the marked differences in the weight, fabric and style of the different coins. Significantly, coins bearing certain symbols and devices, as also those of a particular weight and fabric, are concentrated in specific sites or areas of the vast Viṣṇukuṇḍin territory.

ART AND SYMBOLOGY

Apart from using the symbols and devices of their predecessors, the Viṣṇukuṇḍins introduced several new and innovative motifs on their coins.

Obverse Devices

Bull

The bull is the earliest obverse device on Viṣṇukuṇḍin coins and is either seated or standing. In the case of the standing bull, the hump is prominently delineated. The bull is mostly well-built and sturdy. The tail is sometimes lifted up and has a conspicuous twist or curl, almost forming a loop, towards the end. Occasionally, a floral design is seen in front of the animal.

One may recall that the Sātavāhanas, too, issued bull type coins. In fact, the bull was a very popular device on the coins of the early Sātavāhanas. Yet Sātavāhana coins mostly feature the animal standing and not seated. In any case, these Sātavāhana bull coins do not seem to have served as the prototype for the Viṣṇukuṇḍin bull coins. The latter seem to have been inspired by the bull type coins of the Śālaṅkāyanas, the little-known, immediate predecessors of the Viṣṇukuṇḍins in Andhra. Indeed, the dynastic name 'Śālaṅkāyana' literally means *nandī* (the bull of Śiva). Not inappropriately, the couchant bull, which was the dynastic crest of the Śālaṅkāyanas, is seen on the seals of their copper plates. The majority of the published Śālaṅkāyana coins portray the same bull on the obverse.[5] In addition, Chandavarman (AD 395-420) of this dynasty is also believed to have minted a few coins of another type with the 'standing humped bull' on the obverse. Interestingly, Viṣṇukuṇḍin coins display both these types without any change whatsoever in the stylistic features.

Like the Śālaṅkāyana coins, the Viṣṇukuṇḍin bull coins may also represent Śiva whose mount was the bull. At Nagarjunakonda and many other places, the Viṣṇukuṇḍins built temples in honour of Śiva and his son, Kārttikeya.[6] In fact, Nagarjunakonda was one of the leading religious and political centres during the early period of Viṣṇukuṇḍin rule.

Lion

The lion is the commonest obverse device on issues of the Viṣṇukuṇḍins. On most coins, the creature is highly stylized. Usually it is standing to the right or left. The animal generally exhibits a gaping mouth, upraised left paw, and uplifted and curved tail. The fluffy bunch of bristles at the end of the tail are beautifully delineated. On many coins, the mane is clearly seen. Slight variations in the delineation of various anatomical features of this animal are discernible on different specimens of this type. On some coins, the lion is wearing a beaded chain round the neck. Sometimes the animal is decorated with some sort of spiked or beaded chain, or shawl on its back. On the basis of subtle differences in the lion device, over twelve different sub-varieties of the lion type coins have been identified. Often, a crescent is shown above the lion and, rarely, below the raised leg. Occasionally, the *śrīvatsa* symbol is depicted near the mouth of the animal. Sometimes intricate floral designs appear below the forelegs.

The lion is the dynastic emblem of the Viṣṇukuṇḍins and also appears on their copper-plate seals like the Tummalagudam plates (first set) of Govindavarman I and the Chikkula plates of Vikramendravarman II. Interestingly, the lion on the seal of the Chikkula plates has an abnormally long tail that is twisted thrice and, hence, it appears to have a double tail. The lion motif frequently features in Viṣṇukuṇḍin sculptures, especially at the base of the pillars. The animal is portrayed on the Velpuru pillar inscription of the dynasty.

On Viṣṇukuṇḍin coins, the depiction of the crescent and *śrīvatsa* symbols close to the royal emblem—the lion—appears to have immense political significance. The crescent, appropriately placed mostly above the lion, may indicate the king's power and glory soaring heavenwards (*āchandra tārārkā*). Likewise, the *śrīvatsa* symbol may indicate that the Viṣṇukuṇḍins were the most worthy and powerful successors of the Sātavāhanas, whose royal insignia was the same symbol. To take this interpretation a step further, the placement of the *śrīvatsa* symbol in front of the mouth of the lion may indicate that the Viṣṇukuṇḍins were so powerful that they could swallow or crush even a mighty empire like the Sātavāhanas.

Horse

The horse is not very common on Viṣṇukuṇḍin coins. An unusual copper coin depicts, on the obverse, a caparisoned horse to the right. The animal's left foreleg is raised. A bearded warrior is riding the horse and wears a big cap, coat and trousers, besides prominent earrings. The *śrīvatsa* symbol appears between the forelegs of the animal. The entire device is enclosed by a linear circle, which, in turn, is surrounded by a circle of conspicuous dots. This coin has been reported from the Vidarbha region of Maharashtra.

It may be recalled that horse-type coins were issued by a number of earlier dynasties, including the Sangam Cheras, Sangam Pāṇḍyas, Malaiyamāns, Sātavāhanas and Ikṣvākus. Artistically, the lifelike horse on the Viṣṇukuṇḍin coin is far superior to the representation of the animal on the coins of any other dynasty. Moreover, the

Viṣṇukuṇḍins were the first south Indian dynasty to portray a warrior (king?) riding a horse on their coins. It is plausible that the warrior on the horseback type Roman gold coins could have inspired them to produce coins with the same device. This argument may also be supported by the fact that the dress, including the cap and trousers, worn by the warrior on the Viṣṇukuṇḍin coin, is typically Roman. Significantly, Roman coins, including the warrior on horseback types, have been recovered in large numbers in and around Vinukonda in the heart of the Viṣṇukuṇḍin territory.[7] Although many of these Roman coins reached India between the first and third centuries AD, there is enough evidence to show that these foreign coins, especially the gold ones, did continue to circulate in south India even during the early years of Viṣṇukuṇḍin rule.[8] In fact, gold imitation coins, portraying a combination of motifs on the Roman aurei of the first century AD and later, were produced in the Andhra region even during the fifth century AD when the Viṣṇukuṇḍins rose to power. Some of these also display the warrior on horseback. At least a few of these imitations would have been produced with the metal obtained by melting genuine Roman aurei.

Like many of their predecessors, including the Śālaṅkāyanas, the Viṣṇukuṇḍins, too, performed the *aśvamedha* sacrifice. Unlike the other kings, though, they do not seem to have issued special coins to commemorate this great event. The above Viṣṇukuṇḍin horse coin without the *yūpastambha* and *agnikuṇḍa* can hardly be called an *aśvamedha* type coin. It may have been issued by any one of the powerful Viṣṇukuṇḍin kings who wanted to portray himself with his favourite war horse.

Kalaśa

Many Viṣṇukuṇḍin coins feature the *kalaśa* on the reverse but a few feature the motif on the obverse as well. On the obverse, the *kalaśa* or pot is profusely decorated on the exterior (Figure 5). It is round in shape, and has a narrow neck and thick, prominent lip or rim. The pot rests on two slanting supports. Small circular objects—coins or flowers—coming out of the mouth of the pot are shown all round it. The *kalaśa*, similar to the ones depicted on coins, is also seen in Viṣṇukuṇḍin sculptures in Mogalrajapuram and other places in Andhra Pradesh.

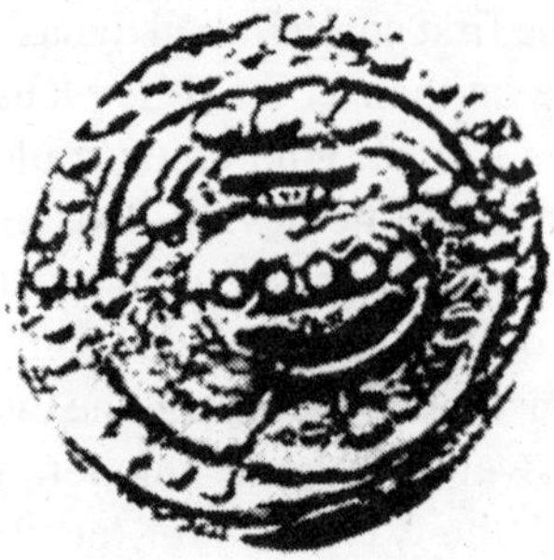

Figure 5: Viṣṇukuṇḍin coin—*kalaśa* obverse.

Subsidiary or Smaller Obverse Devices and Symbols

The obverse of some Viṣṇukuṇḍin coins feature subsidiary or smaller symbols and devices close to the main device. These are mostly of religious significance and include the *śrīvatsa* and crescent. These symbols and devices frequently occur along with the lion.

Reverse Devices

Kalaśa

The *kalaśa* is the most common reverse device on Viṣṇukuṇḍin coins. There are significant variations in the precise size, shape and decorative features of the pot on different coins. It is mostly spherical or ovoid in shape. Sometimes the pot is decorated with concentric bands on the exterior. It often rests on an arch-based column or pedestal. It is flanked by two lamps or lamp-stands, one on either side.

The *kalaśa* on the reverse can be classified into two broad varieties, the first being more common than the second:

1. Pot surmounted by horizontal objects or flames.
2. Vase overflowing with flowers or coins.

It has been opined that the former represents a fire altar or fire-pot from which the remote ancestors of the Viṣṇukuṇḍins are believed to have emerged.[9] The latter representation undoubtedly signifies a *pūrṇakumbha*—the sacred vase signifying abundance and joy. Representations of the latter variety of the pot with foliage and flowers also appear on a few other ancient Indian coins such as an early, non-legend, rectangular cast copper coin (second century BC), and the vase-type copper issues of Chandragupta II (AD 380-412).

Temple

It has recently been pointed out that on some Viṣṇukuṇḍin coins, the reverse device that looks like a *kalaśa* is actually the plan or layout of a temple in linear perspective.[10] The temple consists of three components, one behind the other in a straight line. In front, there is a porch behind which is a rectangular *maṇḍapa* with an inverted, boat-like roof. At the far end, one can see the tall *vimāna,* which may be *ekatala* (single-tiered) or *dvitala* (double-tiered), and is surmounted by one or more *kalaśa* finials. Interestingly, brick temples with the same layout or ground plan have been unearthed at Nagarjunakonda. These have images of Śiva and Kārttikeya.

On the coins, the temple is flanked by a ploughshare (*hala*) on each side. The ploughshares exhibit short, horizontal rods to fasten the rope and yoke the animal. These ploughshares may represent the Hindu god, Kārttikeya, whose *lāñchana* (emblem) it was. The temple on the coin may have been dedicated to this god. Alternatively, the ploughshares may merely be the emblem of a guild such as the Chitrameḷis who were given the right to mint these coins.

Lotus

A few rare Viṣṇukuṇḍin coins feature a full-bloomed lotus occupying the centre of the reverse side (Figure 6). The pointed ends of the petals are skilfully indicated by thin, tiny strokes.

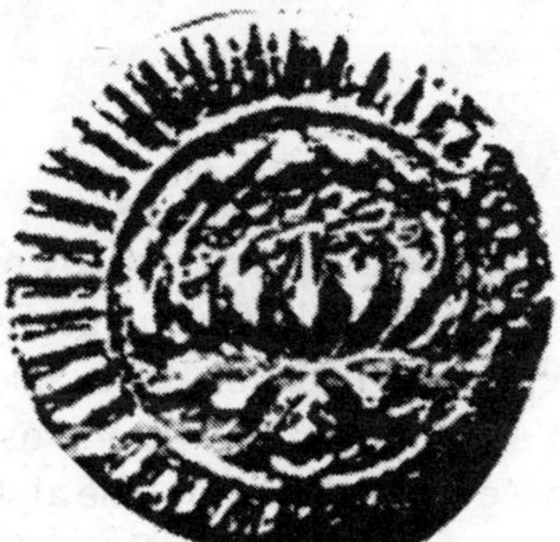

Figure 6: Viṣṇukuṇḍin coin—lotus reverse.

Conch

On some coins, a bulbous conch is prominently featured in the centre of the flan. It is flanked by a lamp on either side.

Other Reverse Devices and Symbols

The other reverse devices and symbols include the *Ujjain* symbol surmounted by a crescent, the crescent, a crescent with a dot in each of its four corners, the sun with long rays, *śrīvatsa*, taurine, trident, sword, axle of a wheel, and the wheel. These are featured in various combinations and positions on different coins. Among these, the taurine is most important. On many coins, it is flanked by a ploughshare on either side.

Some coins feature the revolving wheel (*sudarśana cakra?)* very similar to the ones on Sātavāhana coins. On many Viṣṇukuṇḍin coins, this wheel is flanked by two upright ploughshares, one on either side. Sometimes the wheel occurs along with the conch.

On most Viṣṇukuṇḍin coins, the reverse device is enclosed by a circle with rays emanating outwards from its circumference and terminating along the edge of the coin. This rayed circle border was not a Viṣṇukuṇḍin innovation but dates back to the coins of the Śālaṅkāyanas. On Viṣṇukuṇḍin coins, this border has been interpreted in various ways.[11] Some scholars believe that it is merely a decorative device. Others feel that it denotes the sun. Another group of scholars opine that it represents the fire or the fire altar with which the Viṣṇukuṇḍins are traditionally associated. A few others feel that the rayed circle may be a wheel. One may recall that even when the main reverse device is the wheel, it is enclosed by the rayed circle.

LEGENDS

Many Viṣṇukuṇḍin coins bear legends, mostly on the obverse. They are in the Brāhmī script and Sanskrit language. By this time, Sanskrit had almost totally replaced Prakrit on coins, and stone and copper-plate inscriptions in south India. The legend usually occurs above the main obverse device such as the bull. The alphabets are generally devoid of any ornamental or decorative flourishes. The legends are short and portions of it are often out of the flan. Hence, many of them have not been satisfactorily deciphered. Legends such as *Śrī Raṇamitra*, *Vikrama*, *Budharāja* and *Harirāja* have been reported. These may denote the names or titles of either the Viṣṇukuṇḍin kings, or their subordinates and feudatories who were authorized to mint coins.

V.V. Mirashi published a Viṣṇukuṇḍin coin bearing a legend which he read as *Śrī Bhadram.*[12] He interpreted it is denoting Śrī Bhadra, the presiding deity of the great temple at Bhadrachalam in Andhra. S.J. Mangalam has vehemently disputed this interpretation on the grounds that the present temple at Bhadrachalam cannot be traced back to the period of the Viṣṇukuṇḍins. Further, the coin does not bear the figure of the deity. Legends signifying the name of a deity without his figure are generally unknown in the Indian numismatic tradition.

NOTES AND REFERENCES

1. For a general survey of the history of the Viṣṇukuṇḍins, see K. Gopalachari, *Early History of the Andhra Country* (Madras, 1976), pp. 205-13; K.A. Nilakanta Sastri, *A History of South India: From Prehistoric Times to the Fall of Vijayanagara* (New Delhi, 2002), pp. 83-103.
2. The most important collection of Viṣṇukuṇḍin coins exists in the Andhra Pradesh State Archaeological Museum, Hyderabad. Some coins are also seen in various private collections such as those of A. Sitaraman (Tanjavur). Viṣṇukuṇḍin coins are not very common but are not as scarce as Ikṣvāku coins. The main reason for this is that the Viṣṇukuṇḍin territory included parts of present-day Maharashtra and, thus, was bigger than the Ikṣvāku kingdom. Viṣṇukuṇḍin coins have been found in large numbers in Maharashtra and these coins are scattered over various collections within that state.

   The most comprehensive catalogue of Viṣṇukuṇḍin coins is M. Rama Rao, *Viṣṇukuṇḍin Coins in the Andhra Pradesh Government Museum, Hyderabad* (Hyderabad, 1963).

   More recent publications on Viṣṇukuṇḍin coins include Brajadulal Chattopadhyaya, *Coins and Currency Systems in South India c.* AD *225-1300* (New Delhi, 1977), pp. 11-15, 191-5; S.J. Mangalam, 'A Unique Inscribed Viṣṇukuṇḍin Coin From Vidarbha', *SSIC* I (1991), pp. 81-6; I.K. Sarma, 'A Critical Study of the Numismatic Evidences From Nagarjunakonda Excavations', *SSIC* IV (1994), pp. 63-78; idem, 'An Appraisal of Recent Discoveries of South Indian Coins', *SSIC* V (1995), pp. 9-27; idem, 'Coins From Peddavegi Excavations (1985-87)', *SSIC* VI (1996), pp. 49-65; idem, 'Coins From Amaravati Excavations', *SSIC* VIII (1998), pp. 44-57.

For an exhaustive bibliography of Viṣṇukuṇḍin coins, see D. Raja Reddy and P. Suryanarayana Reddy, 'Andhra Coins: A Bibliography', *SSIC* XIII (2003), pp. 91-125.

3. These coins are unpublished and are in the collection of A. Sitaraman (Tanjavur).
4. For a more detailed discussion on this subject, see I.K. Sarma 1996 (supra n. 2), pp. 49-65.
5. See Brajadulal Chattopadhyaya 1977 (supra n. 2), pp. 9-11.
6. I.K. Sarma 1994 (supra n. 2), pp. 63-78.
7. Vinukonda itself has yielded a hoard of 15 Roman aurei. Many places in the neighbourhood have revealed Roman gold coins. The reverse of some of these coins display the warrior on horseback. For more details about these finds, see S. Suresh, *Symbols of Trade*: *Roman and Pseudo-Roman Objects Found in India* (New Delhi, 2004), pp. 26-88, 165-70.
8. For a discussion about these evidences, see S. Suresh 2004 (supra n. 7), pp. 26-88.
9. S.J. Mangalam,'New Discoveries of Viṣṇukuṇḍin Coins From Maharashtra', Paper presented at the colloquium on South Indian Archaeology (Hyderabad, 1990).
10. I.K. Sarma 1994 (supra n. 2), pp. 63-78; idem 1998 (supra n. 2), pp. 44-57. Also see I.K. Sarma, 'Viṣṇukuṇḍin Coins From Peddavegi Excavations and Related Issues', *ND* XVI (1992), pp. 95-111.
11. I had a discussion on this subject with A.M. Shastri in 1998 and, more recently, with I. Mahadevan and R. Krishnamurthy. Mahadevan feels that the rayed circle border represents the sun while A.M. Shastri feels that this type of border connotes a flame or fire, closely associated with the Viṣṇukuṇḍins who are believed to have emerged from the fire-pot.
12. For an interesting discussion on this legend and its interpretation, see S.J. Mangalam 1991 (supra n. 2), pp. 81-6.

CHAPTER 10

Coins of the Pallavas

The Pallavas were a famous dynasty that ruled over parts of Tamil Nadu and southern Andhra Pradesh from around the third to the ninth centuries AD.[1] Their main capital was Kanchipuram, while the secondary capital and chief port was Mahabalipuram or Mamallapuram in Tamil Nadu. It is believed that the first members of the Pallava dynasty served as chieftains and governors under the Sātavāhana kings. With the fall of the Sātavāhanas, the Pallava chieftains slowly became autonomous rulers. There is very little information about these early Pallava rulers, the best-known among them were Shivaskandavarman and Vishnugopa who ruled the region around Kanchipuram in the fourth century AD. Interestingly, the Allahabad Pillar Inscription of the Gupta ruler, Samudragupta (AD 335-80), mentions that he defeated twelve kings in the Deccan and south India, including Vishnugopa of Kanchi.

Simhavarman (AD 550-70) and his son and successor, Simhavishnu (AD 570-80) were the two great Pallava rulers who extended the kingdom, and laid the foundation for a powerful dynastic rule in southern India. The genealogy and history of the Pallavas are quite clear to us from the time of Simhavarman.

Simhavishnu was succeeded by his son, Mahendravarman I (AD 580-630). Mahendra suffered a defeat at the hands of Pulakesin II (AD 609-42), the renowned ruler of the western Chalukya kingdom that comprised large parts of present-day Karnataka.

Mahendra's son, Narasimhavarman I or Māmalla (AD 630-68), was the next Pallava ruler. He avenged his father's defeat by crushing the Chalukyas at Manimangalam near Kanchipuram (Tamil Nadu). He subsequently pursued the retreating Chalukya army, crossed the river Tungabhadra, triumphantly entered Pulakesin's capital, Vātāpī (Karnataka), and planted a *jayastambha* (pillar of victory) there. After this grand victory, Māmalla assumed the title *Vātāpikoṇḍān* (the conqueror of Vātāpī). The next important Pallava ruler was

Narasimhavarman II or Rājasimha (AD 700-28). He was succeeded by his son, Parameshvaravarman II (AD 728-31).

Parameshvaravarman's death led to utter confusion in the Pallava kingdom since he did not leave behind any heir. Consequently, Nandivarman II Pallavamalla (AD 731-96), son of Hiranyavarman Mahārāja, who belonged to the junior or collateral branch of the *Kāḍava Kula* (Kāḍava family) of Bhīmavarman, brother of Simhavishnu, was selected king by a group of officials of the Pallava kingdom.

Nandivarman was barely twelve years old when he ascended the Pallava throne. During his long reign, he fought fierce battles with many south Indian kingdoms such as the Chalukyas, Gangas and Pāṇḍyas. The Chalukya ruler, Vikramāditya II, drove Nandivarman away from Kanchipuram and occupied the city for some years. Later, Nandivarman married Revā, the daughter of the Rashtrakuta king, Dantidurga, who helped him defeat the Chalukyas.

Nandivarman was succeeded by his son, Dantivarman (AD 796-847). Dantivarman was defeated by the Pāṇḍyas and had to surrender large territories to them. His son, Nandivarman III (AD 846-69), was the next Pallava ruler. The battle fought between Nandivarman III and the Pāṇḍya king, Śrīmāra Śrīvallabha, at Teḷḷāru in northern Tamil Nadu, is vividly described in a quasi-historical poem called *Nandikkalambakam* by an anonymous author. Nandivarman's victory in this battle earned him the title *Teḷḷāru Erinda* (destroyer of Teḷḷāru).

Nandivarman III was succeeded by his son, Nripatunga (AD 859?-899). After his death, the Pallava rulers were too weak to control the kingdom and it broke up into smaller divisions controlled by feudal chiefs. By the end of the ninth century AD, the Cōḷas under Vijayālaya and his successors had occupied most parts of Pallava territory.

CONTRIBUTION TO LITERATURE AND ART

The Pallavas fostered literature, music, dance, architecture and the visual arts, including numismatic art.[2] Bhāravi, the renowned Sanskrit poet, lived in the court of Simhavishnu. His well-known poem *Kirātārjunīyam* describes the achievements of Arjuna, the hero of the epic *Mahābhārata.* Mahendravarman I was himself a poet and a dramatist. He wrote two Sanskrit plays, the *Bhagavata Gujjam* and the *Matta Vilāsa Prahāsana.* Dandin, the reputed Sanskrit scholar, lived in the Pallava court during the reign of Rājasimha. He was the author of *Kāvya Darśana*, *Daśakumāracharita* and *Avantī-sundarīkathāsāra.*

Pallava architecture and sculpture can be broadly divided into four distinct phases or styles:

1. *Mahendra style*: The reign of Mahendravarman I heralded a renaissance in religion, literature and art. Mahendra was not merely a scholar but also a musician and painter. His four-line Sanskrit inscription at the Mandagapattu rock-cut temple describes him as an 'inventive minded' king who discarded perishable materials like brick, timber, metal and mortar for constructing temples and who, instead, began to scoop shrines out of the living rock. We have no extant examples of masonry temples of the reign of Mahendravarman, but only rock-cut ones. The pillars of the rock-cut temples are massive and are divided into three parts: the upper and lower parts are square in section, while the middle part is octagonal. The bracket above the pillar is cut away obliquely at 45 degrees or is rounded, and normally has a wavy ornament on either side of a smooth central band.

   The *caitya*-window or *kūḍu* is simple, with a human head looking out, and has a finial like a spade-head. The doorkeepers (*dvārapālas*) are often seen on either side of the doorway of the sanctum. They are huge and hefty, carry a heavy club, are sometimes horned and sport the sacred thread (*yajñopavīta*) running over the right arm. Yet these figures are not fierce-looking and unlike their later counterparts, have only one pair of arms. The sculptures of human beings display well-formed, rounded limbs, a rather elongated face, a double chin, a not too conspicuous nose and thick lips.
2. *Māmalla style*: During the reign of Māmalla, cave-temples continued to be erected. Simultaneously, free-standing, monolithic temples also come into existence. The pillars are more slender and ornamented, and are supported by squatting lions. The *kūḍu* continues to be simple and has the spade-head finial. The *dvārapālas*, too, are much the same as in the earlier period.
3. *Rājasimha style*: During the reign of Rājasimha, the practice of erecting rock-cut temples ceased. All the extant temples are of

the masonry type. The pillars are slender and are supported by rampant or prancing lions.

A new feature is that the central *vimāna* or sanctum tower is given greater prominence. It is quite large compared to the tiny *gopura* or entrance tower, which is no larger than the small cells arranged in a row all around the main shrine. The *kūḍu* continues to have the spade-head finial but is more decorated. The *dvārapālas*, too, are more ornamented. Little-known forms of Śiva such as Rāvaṇānugrahamūrti and Dakṣiṇāmūrti are now seen in large numbers.

4. *Post-Rājasimha style*: Numerically, Pallava temples post-dating Rājasimha are few. All of them are of the masonry type. Historically and iconographically, the Vaikunṭa Perumāḷ temple at Kanchi, built by Nandivarman II Pallavamalla, is the most important among them. Many of these temples follow the Rājasimha style with some variations and innovations.

General features: The Pallavas built temples dedicated to various Hindu gods such as Śiva, Viṣṇu and Brahmā. Most Śiva temples of all phases of Pallava art feature the Somāskanda (Śiva with Pārvatī and baby Skanda) on the wall behind the *Śivaliṅga* in the sanctum. The *liṅga* is generally prismatic or fluted in form.

COINS

Like the Sātavāhanas, the Pallavas issued coins of different varieties and types. Stray finds of Pallava coins have been reported from many places such as Guntur and Nellore in Andhra, Tiruvanmiyur (within Madras city), Mahabalipuram, Kanchipuram, Arani, Tirukoilur, Kumbakonam, Tiruchirappalli, Karur, Pudukkottai. Madurai and Dharmapuri in Tamil Nadu. Archaeological excavations at Kanchipuram have yielded eight Pallava lead coins in a stratified context.[3]

Pallava coins have been found in Sri Lanka. A little-known specimen has been reported from a stratified context at the Buddhist site of Anuradhapura in the northern part of the island.[4] A Pallava coin has also been discovered at Khuan Luk Pat, an ancient port on the west coast of Thailand.[5]

Physical Features and Production Method

The Pallavas minted coins in a variety of metals and alloys such as silver, electrum (an alloy of gold and silver), copper, lead, bronze and potin. The majority are of copper or bronze. Apparently, the Pallavas, to a large extent, followed the footsteps of the Sātavāhanas in the choice of metals and alloys for coinage.

An archaeo-chemical study of a Pallava lead coin has, surprisingly, revealed that the lead content is not more than 42.1 per cent; substantial quantities of tin (23.9 per cent) and copper (18 per cent) were deliberately added to the lead to make the coin more resistant to wear and tear. This coin also contains small quantities of iron, zinc, calcium and silver.[6] Technical studies have revealed that many of the Pallava bronze coins, too, contain a high percentage—sometimes as high as 43.7 per cent—of tin.[7]

As for the source of various metals, the trade between India and the Mediterranean regions had declined by the time the Pallavas began to mint coins. Hence, they could not have imported metals like copper, lead and tin from Europe.

The Pallavas would have obtained copper from some of the mines in Andhra. As noted above, certain areas in Andhra were part of the Pallava kingdom, as for example, the copper-rich Nellore region. Besides, the Pallavas would have imported copper and silver from the Viṣṇukuṇḍins and other kingdoms further north. They would have imported tin from China, Thailand and some other South-East Asian countries. The close cultural and commercial contacts between these foreign kingdoms and the Pallavas is now well-established. In this context, the find of a Pallava copper coin from Thailand, as noted above, is not surprising.

The Pallavas would have definitely melted the coins of their predecessors, such as the Sangam Cōḷas, Malaiyamāns and Sātavāhanas, to obtain metal for minting new coins. This may partially explain the paucity of the coins of the latter three dynasties in Pallava territory.

The melting of Sātavāhana lead coins by the Pallavas is now scientifically proved.[8] Archaeo-chemical analyses of select Sātavāhana and Pallava lead coins has revealed that they all were made from a particular variety of lead, generally known from certain ores in Europe. This variety does not contain chromium but has vanadium as a trace element. Since the Pallavas could not have imported European lead, they would have melted the Sātavāhana lead coins produced with the European lead, imported mainly through the port of Barygaza in Gujarat.

Pallava coins are generally circular in shape with a diameter normally varying between 1.1 to 2.2 cm. Recently, a few bigger bronze bull: conch type coins, with a diameter ranging from 2.3 to 2.9 cm, have been published.[9] Like some of the Ikṣvāku coins, a few Pallava circular coins have a small, pointed projection at one end. A very limited number of Pallava bronze coins are rectangular or square in shape. The average length of each side of these quadrangular coins is around 2 to 4 cm. These coins appear to be the earliest issues of this dynasty. They represent a 'link' or 'transition' between the quadrangular coins of the Sangam Cheras, Sangam Cōḷas, Sangam Pāṇḍyas and Malaiyamāns, and the usual circular coins of the Pallavas.

The thickness of Pallava coins ranges from 0.08 to 0.4 cm, and the weight from less than 1 gram to about 8 grams, although, in recent times, unusually heavy lead coins weighing 9.8 grams have come to light. It is clear that many of the low-weight coins lost weight due to long years of circulation before being lost or buried.

As to the minting technique, the Pallavas, like the Sātavāhanas, utilized the die-striking, casting and, rarely, the punch-marking processes for making coins. Among the silver and copper coins, die-struck, cast and punch-marked specimens are known. Among potin and lead coins, die-struck and cast specimens are known. The bronze coins are mostly die-struck. The electrum coins, that are comparatively fewer in number, are also invariably die-struck.

Four broken, circular, terracotta moulds of Pallava coins have been recovered in a stratified context in the Pallava capital of Kanchipuram. Three of these exhibit the bull device with certain small symbols. The fourth mould exhibits a rectangular matrice with an indistinct floral design. According to R. Krishnamurthy, these moulds are ancient forgers' equipment meant to produce fake coins because well-produced, die-struck coins, bearing the same symbols and devices appearing on the first three mounds, have been discovered in large numbers.[10] Yet one should remember that Pallava cast coins, bearing these symbols and devices as also other motifs, have been found in large numbers at different sites. Moreover, archaeo-chemical studies of certain genuine Pallava coins have conclusively established that they were produced by the casting process.[11]

Besides producing various types of coins in the mints located at Kanchipuram, Tirukoilur and certain other places, the Pallavas also seem to have restruck, with a good die, some of their own old, worn-out coins to revalidate them as currency. Often, the new design or device on these restruck coins was the same as the old or original one. Tirukoilur has yielded a bronze lion obverse and *svastika* reverse type coin, restruck with the same obverse and reverse motifs, respectively.

ART AND SYMBOLOGY

The symbols and devices on Pallava coins are many and varied. No correlation or pattern is discernible between them *vis-à-vis* the metal of the coin and the technique of its manufacture. Many of the symbols and motifs occur in different metals and alloys.

Obverse Devices

Lion

Some of the earliest Pallava coins feature the lion. The animal is mostly standing to the right or left. The mouth is wide open and, in many cases, the mane is clearly delineated. The tail is unusually long and slender, and curls or bends at two or three points, sometimes terminating in a big loop. On an enigmatic specimen, the animal's tongue is stretching out of the mouth and the penis is prominently shown. Occasionally, a beaded chain and/or a perforated belt are seen on the lower portion of the neck of the animal. Sometimes a part of these jewels extends to the animal's back. In some instances, objects like the sword appear in front of the beast. On a rare coin, a trident is seen above the lion.

Coins featuring a bow and arrow along with the lion may be commemorative coins issued to mark the Pallava victory over the Chera kings whose symbol was the bow. Another group of coins feature a lion encircled by the *śrīvatsa* symbol on the top, the bow in the front, the tiger below and the fish at the back. These, too, may be commemorative issues minted to announce the Pallava victory over the Cheras whose emblem was the bow, the Cōḷas whose emblem was the tiger, and the Pāṇḍyas whose symbol was the fish. Plausibly, such coins were issued by the Pallava ruler, Simhavishnu, who bore the title *Avanisimha* (lion of the earth), and who subjugated the Cheras, Cōḷas, Pāṇḍyas and many other kingdoms of south India.

Yet another rare lion type coin features a boar below and a fish behind the lion. The boar was the emblem of the Western Chalukyas and the fish, the Pāṇḍyas. Hence, this coin is tentatively identified as an issue of Narasimhavarman I or Māmalla, who defeated both the Chalukyas and the Pāṇḍyas. The placement of the boar below the lion may have further significance if we consider the fact that the Chalukyas posed a greater threat than the Pāṇḍyas to the Pallavas. We have already noted that Māmalla's father, Mahendra, was defeated by the Chalukyas. Hence, Māmalla's war against the Chalukyas was mainly to restore the prestige of the Pallava royal family. Thus, to Māmalla, his resounding victory in this war was a specially cherished achievement, publicized by deliberately portraying the Chalukya boar below the lion, which was his favourite animal that was featured on several of his monuments.

Initially, the dynastic crest of the Pallavas was the lion. The names of many of the early Pallava kings began with the word *simha*, meaning 'lion' in Sanskrit, like Simhavarman and Simhavishnu. The lion is portrayed on the seals of some of the Pallava copper-plate inscriptions. This may be the result of their contact with the Viṣṇu-kuṇḍins of Andhra whose emblem, too, as noted in the earlier chapter, was the lion. This line of argument is further corroborated by the fact that the early Pallavas are believed to have hailed from Andhra and some of the earliest copper-plate charters of the dynasty are from this region. It has also been opined that the Sātavāhana lion: *Ujjain* symbol coin type, circulating in the Andhra region, served as the prototype for the Pallava lion coins.[12] The Śālaṅkāyanas, who ruled parts of Andhra immediately prior to the Pallavas, also minted coins with the lion device. There are stylistic affinities between the lions on the Pallava coins and those on the Sātavāhana and Śālaṅkāyana coins.

As indicated above, the lion is frequently seen in Pallava art. At the Vaikunṭa Perumāḷ temple at Kanchi, stone sculptures portray various types of Pallava thrones adorned with the figures of lion and, sometimes, the crocodile too. At the Pallava palace site at Mahabalipuram, the stone-built throne is actually in the form of an exquisitely carved couchant lion whose back is slightly flat (Plate 20). The animal is also often carved at the base of pillars at several Pallava temples. The recent tsunami (December 2004) has uncovered a huge, free-standing boulder close to the sea at Mahabalipuram. It bears many sculptures, including a lion with its forepaws raised and mouth open. This lion is stylistically similar to the lions seen on many Pallava coins.

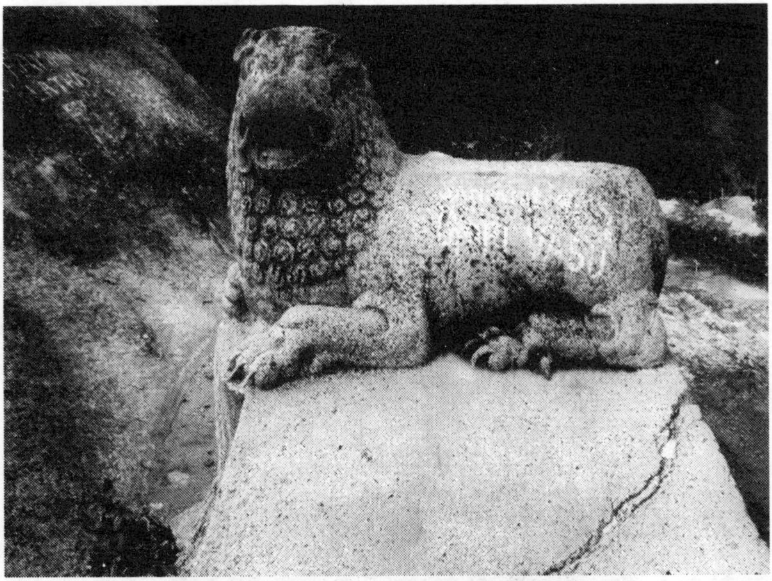

Plate 20: Pallava lion-shaped throne, Mahabalipuram.

Bull

Among the issues of the Pallavas, the bull type coins are the most numerous. Bulls of varied breeds are seen on the different coins of this type. The bull is mostly standing and rarely appears seated. The animal generally faces right and, occasionally, the left. On some rare specimens, the face of the animal is turned towards its back. The creature is usually endowed with short horns, an elongated face and a well-formed hump. The form of the bull is quite plastic, with the heavy, undulating dew-lap sometimes stretching well below the middle of the forelegs. The animal has a long tail which is either hanging down or twisted upwards, such that the tip almost touches the hump. Sometimes a chain or garland adorns the neck of the animal. On some specimens, a chain of smooth, round beads or pearls is seen just behind the hump. On an unusual coin, the animal stands on a pedestal or a platform. Auspicious symbols and devices, such as the conch, *śrīvatsa*, sheath of corn, snake-like symbol, crescent moon and sun, are frequently depicted above the bull (Plate 21).

One may note that the bull type coins of the Sātavāhanas, Śālaṅkāyanas and Viṣṇukuṇḍins were in circulation in certain specified pockets of the Pallava territory during the pre-Pallava and early Pallava periods. These coins would have prompted the Pallavas to depict the bull device on their own coins. Significantly, all the Pallava coins recovered from stratified contexts at the Pallava capital of Kanchi are of the bull type.

In addition to the lion, the bull also served as the family crest of the Pallavas, especially during the sixth-seventh centuries AD, which

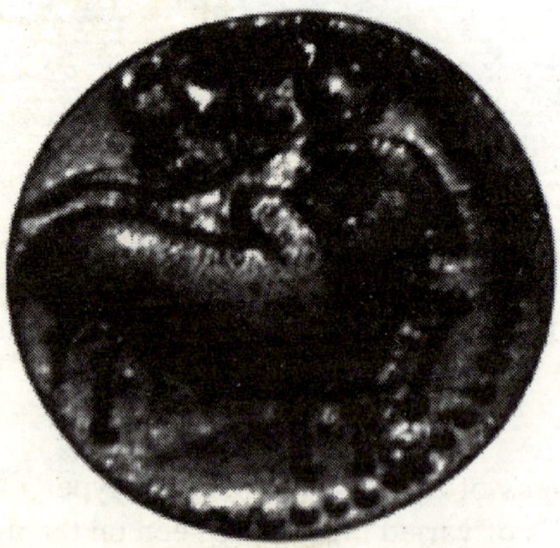

Plate 21: Pallava coin—bull obverse.
(Photo: A. Sitaraman, Tanjavur)

saw the height of their power. The bull features on the seals attached to Pallava copper-plate charters from a very early period of their history. Interestingly, the bull on many coins is identical—in size, shape, style and other features—to the figure of the animal on many Pallava copper-plate seals. Many of these seals, such as the one discovered at Vilavetti (in Andhra), also portray symbols and devices like the conch, *śrīvatsa*, crescent and snake above the bull.

There could be other reasons, too, for the association of the bull with the Pallavas. The Pallavas were initially pastoral people and, hence, their attachment to this animal is understandable. Moreover, they were ardent worshippers of Śiva whose *vāhana* (mount) is the *nandī* (bull). Many of the Pallava temples, including the rock-cut cave shrines spread throughout Tamil Nadu, are dedicated to Śiva.

The Pallava bull coins are artistically superior to the bull type coins of all the earlier dynasties of south India and amply reflect the marked advancement in the art of the period. These are undoubtedly among the finest and most beautiful of the different coin types issued by this dynasty. The elegance and delicacy of form of the bull indicates a very high standard of refinement in plastic art. On many coins, the bull appears like a perfect three-dimensional stone or metal sculpture. In fact, the style agrees admirably with that found on Pallava stone sculptures at Mahabalipuram and Kanchipuram. For example, the seated bull seen on a few Pallava coins is stylistically akin to the seated bull sculptures surrounding the Shore Temple at Mahabalipuram.

Horse

The horse is very rare on Pallava coins. The obverse of certain rare specimens depicts this animal, mostly standing or galloping to the right. It is well-built with eyes gazing downwards. The animal wears a chain or garland of flowers round the neck. An intricately carved *yūpastambha* (sacrificial post) is seen to the front of the animal, indicating that the coin was issued to commemorate an *aśvamedha* sacrifice performed by a Pallava king.

According to R. Krishnamurthy, this horse type coin was issued by an early Pallava king named Simhavarman II who ruled in the fifth century AD.[13] However, there is no epigraphical or other evidence to show that this king ever performed the sacrifice. According to the inscriptions, Śivaskandavarman and Kumāraviṣṇu, both of the fourth century AD, were among the early Pallava kings who performed this sacrifice.[14] Further, the Vaikunṭa Perumāḷ temple of Kanchi has a sculpture panel showing the preparations for an *aśvamedha* sacrifice during the reign of Nandivarman I (AD 490-510). This panel is among the series of sculptures of historical events portrayed on the walls of the cloister surrounding the main shrine. The sculpture shows a brahmin next to a horse. There is no specific evidence to show that any of the other Pallava rulers performed the horse sacrifice, although the successors of Mahendravarman I, especially Mahāmalla, won innumerable battles and were capable of performing it. In these circumstances, it is not possible to attribute the horse coin to any particular Pallava ruler.

As regards Pallava stone sculptures of the *aśvamedha* sacrifice, in addition to the above sculpture, there is one more in the same series of historical sculptures within the Vaikunṭa Perumāḷ temple. Here, we see two armed foot-soldiers and another man seated on the ground, attempting to gain control over a ferocious horse that is richly decorated. The horse is tied to a pillar or *yūpastambha*. This sculpture may signify the *aśvamedha* sacrifice performed by either Śiva-skandavarman or Kumāraviṣṇu, most probably the latter.

One should remember that the Pallavas were contemporaries of the imperial Guptas, who ruled vast regions in north India and were especially known for their grand *aśvamedha* sacrifices, *aśvamedha* sculptures and *aśvamedha* type coins. The Pallavas maintained close commercial and cultural relations with the Guptas. Kumāraviṣṇu is believed to have performed the *aśvamedha* sacrifice after he won back his capital city of Kanchi from the Guptas who, under Samudra-gupta, had captured Kanchi during the reign of Kumāraviṣṇu's father, Vishnugopa.

Besides the *aśvamedha* sculptures, the horse occurs in several other Pallava stone sculptures. In the Vaikunṭa Perumāḷ temple itself, one of the sculptured panels of the east wall of the *dvitala* of the main *vimāna* features a horse. It is standing at one corner of a tall platform. In front of the horse, there are four royal figures, three in *anjali* (hands folded in prayer). Below, there is a kneeling figure in *anjali* (Figure 7). The horse is also seen among the sculptures close to the Shore Temple at Mahabalipuram (Plate 22).

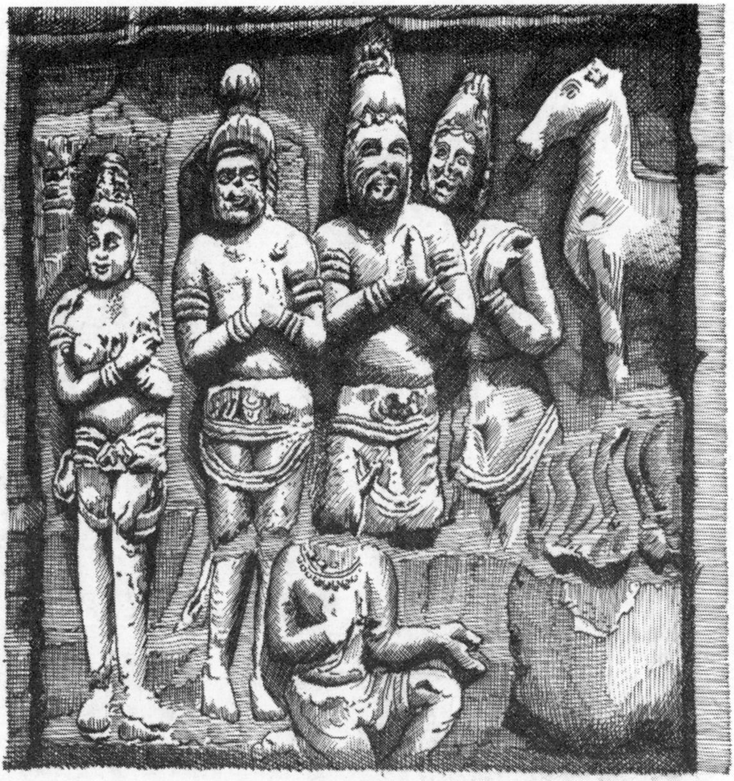

Figure 7: Royal figures worshipping the horse—sculpture on east wall of the *dvitala* of the main *vimāna*, Vaikunṭa Perumāḷ temple, Kanchi.

In recent years, a bust type coin of the Pallava dynasty was reported. It is in a private collection and has not been adequately published. Some senior scholars have even questioned the genuineness of this coin. According to coin collectors, this broken, circular Pallava bronze coin portrays a bust with a huge, ornamented crown in the shape of an elephant's head. The bust is also adorned with necklaces. A parasol or the backrest of a throne is seen behind it. Part of a legend, most probably in the Sanskrit language and Pallava Grantha script, is seen on the right.

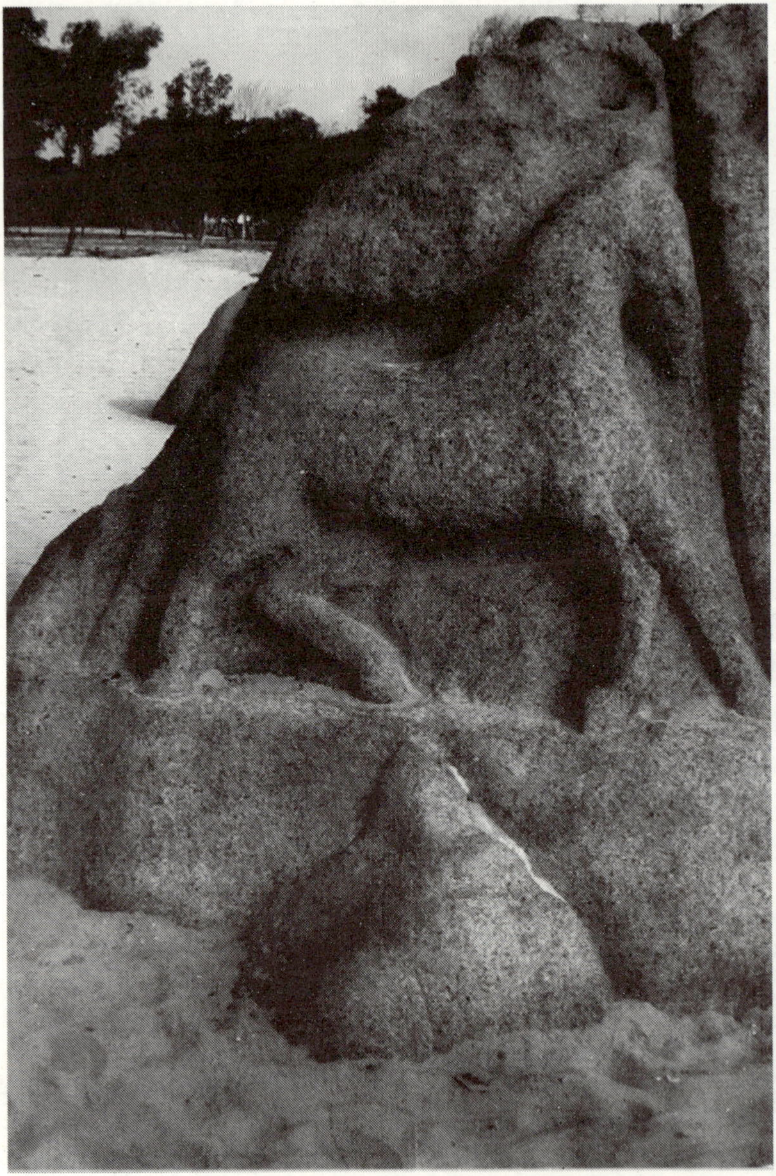

Plate 22: Pallava horse sculpture, Mahabalipuram.

Significantly, a fragmentary inscription in the Vaikuṇṭa Perumāḷ temple of Kanchi refers to an elephant head-shaped crown worn by the Pallava king, Nandivarman Pallavamalla.[15] Such a crown is not featured in any of the stone sculptures of the Pallavas. In this connection, one may recall the elephant scalp crown featured on the royal portrait coins of the famous Indo-Greek ruler, Demetrius I (200-185 BC).[16] On the basis of this similarity, some scholars have even argued that the original homeland of the Pallavas is north-western India—the region ruled by the Indo-Greeks.[17] Even the name 'Pallava' is believed to have been derived from the name 'Pahlava', another name for the Parthians who ruled north-western India around the first century AD, after the Indo-Greeks.

Temple Vimāna

A few rare coins feature the *vimāna* or tower above the sanctum of a temple (Plate 23). The *vimāna* usually has four or five tiers and is strikingly similar to that of many Pallava temples such as the Vaikuṇṭa Perumāḷ temple at Kanchipuram. Incidentally, the *vimāna* of this temple is four-tiered (Figure 8).

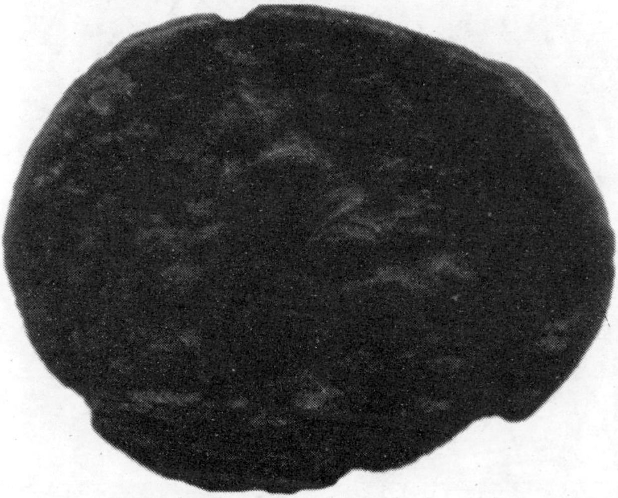

Plate 23: Pallava coin—temple *vimāna* obverse.
(Photo: S. Raman, Madras)

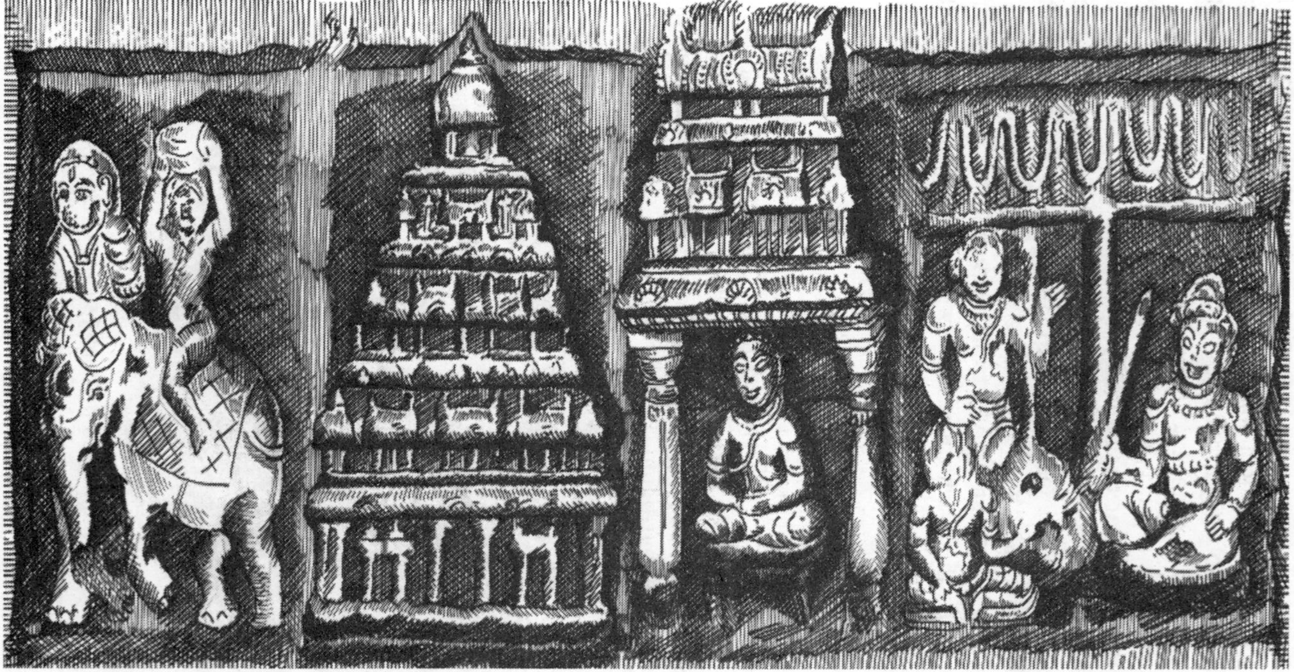

Figure 8: Main *vimāna* of the Vaikuṇṭa Perumāḷ temple, Kanchi—featured among the sculptures of historical events on the walls of the cloister surrounding the main shrine of the temple

Other Obverse Symbols and Devices

The obverse of Pallava coins bear many smaller symbols or devices, mostly occurring in association with the major device, which is usually the lion or the bull. These include the *śrīvatsa*, crescent moon, star, conch, flag, and war weapons like the sword. They often occur in varied combinations above the main device, sometimes in front of it and, occasionally, below or behind it.

Among the smaller symbols and devices, the star is an important one. It invariably occurs above the main device. On many coins, the star is five-pointed, but six-pointed and seven-pointed stars are also sometimes seen. It probably represents the north star, familiar and useful to sea-faring people like the Pallavas. Appropriately, some of the coins bearing this star feature, on the reverse, a boat or ship with a single mast.

Stretching the intimacy between the Pallavas and the sea further, the snake-like figure above the main obverse device is sometimes taken to be a wavy line denoting the river or, more likely, the sea. Some of the symbols above this line have been identified as denoting an anchor tied to a post.

The snake or snake-like figure on Pallava coins may also allude to the Nāga origin of the Pallavas. It is believed that the earliest Pallava king was born to a Nāga princess, whose precise name and identity are uncertain. The snake symbol may even signify Nandivarman I's subjugation of a Nāga king, who has sometimes been identified as Kadamba Krishnavarman II of Triparvata, north of the Pallava territory. Again, the birth of the above-mentioned earliest Pallava ruler and Nandivarman's fight with the Nāga king are prominently sculpted in the Vaikuṇṭa Perumāḷ temple.

A prominent flag is seen above the bull on some coins. It appears to be fluttering rapidly in the breeze. This flag may denote the Pallava royal flag, appropriately placed above the royal emblem—bull. Such flags are sometimes seen above war horses and elephants in the Pallava sculptures of the Vaikuṇṭa Perumāḷ temple.

A general observation is that religious symbols and motifs such as the *śrīvatsa* occur more often along with the bull on the obverse, while war weapons appear generally along with the lion as the main obverse device. A plausible explanation for this is that many of the lion type coins were issued by the early Pallava rulers when the kingdom was fast expanding due to a series of wars and conquests. In such circumstances, the special attachment that these rulers had for various war weapons is understandable. By the time the Pallavas began to issue the bull type coins in large numbers (sixth-seventh centuries AD), the kingdom had, to a large extent, stabilized politically and economically. The *bhakti* movement was now slowly becoming popular. Hindu temples began to be erected in large numbers. Hence, coins, too, began to exhibit more religious symbols along with the bull device.

Reverse Devices

Unlike the coins of all the other early south Indian dynasties, the Pallava coins depict more symbols and devices on the reverse than on the obverse.

Wheel

The wheel is one of the most common reverse devices on Pallava coins (Plate 24). The size varies from coin to coin. Sometimes the wheel is quite small, occupying just the centre of the flan. In other cases, it occupies a major area or even the entire flan. Some wheels have a prominent axle, circle, or a dot within a circle at the centre. The number of spokes varies from seven to eighteen. Some wheels appear to be revolving with all the spokes slanted towards one direction. There are significant variations in the size and shape of the spokes on different coins. The wheels on some Pallava coins, like the wheels on certain Sātavāhana coins, have spokes that

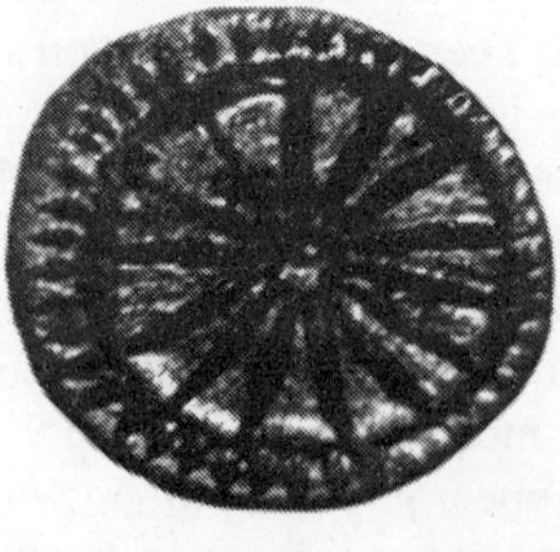

Plate 24: Pallava coin—wheel reverse.
(Photo: A. Sitaraman, Tanjavur)

terminate in an arrow-head. On some others, the spokes are smooth, slender, cylindrical bands. Sometimes they appear like flames emanating from the centre of the wheel. Rarely, the spokes extend beyond the rim of the wheel. Occasionally, a smaller wheel is placed within a bigger wheel.

Sometimes, the exterior of the rim or the circumference of the wheel is laced with a series of tiny semi-circles or arches. On a few specimens, each of these arches contains a pellet, a tiny line or dash. In some instances, instead of these semi-circles or arches, pointed rays emanate from the exterior of the rim or circumference of the wheel. The wheel is occasionally enclosed within a linear circle or a circle of dots. On rare coins, the wheel is enclosed within a linear circle, whose rim is, on the exterior, laced with a series of semi-circles or arches. On some coins, the wheel is flanked by a lamp-stand on either side.

It is plausible that the wheel on some of the Pallava coins is associated with Buddhism because there are evidences to show that at least one early Pallava king named Buddhavarman (AD 335-55) was a Buddhist. A sculpture of this king seated next to a Buddhist *caitya* is seen within the Vaikunṭa Perumāḷ temple of Kanchi. On most coins, though the wheel may allude to Viṣṇu's wheel. In fact, the vast majority of Pallava coins featuring Śiva's *nandī* or bull on the obverse and Viṣṇu's wheel on the reverse are taken to indicate a syncretistic religious movement. In Pallava times, temples for Śiva and Viṣṇu were built next to each other and, often, a single temple had adjoining shrines for both. The Pallava rulers were particularly known for their religious catholicity. The wheel frequently occurs on the walls and pillars of Pallava monuments at Mahabalipuram and Kanchipuram. A few of these wheels are stylistically identical to those on Pallava coins.

Conch

The conch is another common reverse device on Pallava coins (Plate 25). The amazing variety seen on these coins amply reflects the innumerable types of conches available on the southern Coromandel coast that was under the control of the Pallavas. The conch is usually exhibited with its mouth or nozzle pointing downwards in the centre of the flan. On many coins, its spirals have been

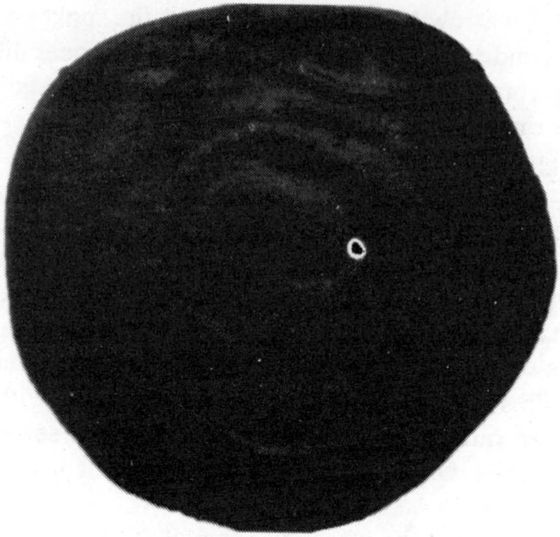

Plate 25: Pallava coin—conch reverse.
(Photo: S. Raman, Madras)

realistically delineated. On a few, the nozzle is unusually long. Sometimes the conch appears bulbous or balloon-shaped and is in high relief. Occasionally, it is flanked by a lamp or lamp-stand on either side.

The conch is generally enclosed by a linear circle. In some instances, the exterior of the rim or circumference of this circle is laced with a series of semi-circles or arches. Sometimes dots or pellets are seen in between or above these arches. Rarely, each arch contains a dot, a tiny line or dash. On a few coins, the conch is enclosed within a rayed circle, similar to the rayed circle border seen on the reverse of many Viṣṇukuṇḍin coins. In fact, Pallava coins featuring this particular design on the reverse and the lion on the obverse are exactly similar to Viṣṇukuṇḍin coins bearing the same obverse and reverse types. Hence, not surprisingly, some of these Viṣṇukuṇḍin coins were initially wrongly attributed to the Pallavas.

Kalaśa and Sprout

The reverse of a sizeable number of Pallava coins feature the *kalaśa* (pot) with a tender sprout or plant. On some specimens, one of these objects—the *kalaśa* or the plant—is absent or worn-out. On some coins, the plant or shoot with tiny leaves, flowers and fruits, appears to be emerging from the mouth of the *kalaśa*. This may be identified as the *pūrṇakumbha* or *pūrṇakalaśa*—the pot of plenty—seen on Viṣṇukuṇḍin coins, too.

On many Pallava coins, however, the *kalaśa* is seen next to the plant or sprout. The pot is mostly round in shape, and has a prominent neck and small mouth. Occasionally, it has a thick, conspicuous lip that appears like a flat band above the neck. Rarely, the bottom of the pot is flat. Some have a rectangular pedestal or base. A few pots look like Roman amphorae without the handles. Sometimes the pot rests on two, small, slanting sticks or supports—exactly like the ones seen on Viṣṇukuṇḍin coins.

The sprout or plant often appears either like a sheath of corn or the branch of a tree. Judging from the shape of the leaves, at least some of these branches are of a mango tree. Occasionally, the plant looks like a dry twig without a single leaf or flower. In some cases, it almost looks like a full-fledged tree with multiple branches and huge bunches of leaves and round fruits.

Although the sprout and *kalaśa* are seen on coins of many ancient Indian dynasties, the Pallava coins alone frequently feature these two devices together. This unique combination may be linked to the origin of the dynasty. It is believed that Drona, one of the remote ancestors of the Pallavas, was born out of a pitcher or *kalaśa*. Again, the very name 'Pallava' means 'sprout', and Drona's grandson named Pallava, the first Pallava king, was born in a litter of sprouts.

The story of the birth of Pallava, the founder of the Pallava dynasty, in a litter of sprouts, and the close association between the Pallava kings and the sprout (*pallava* or *aṅkura*), are attested by many Pallava stone inscriptions and copper-plate charters. The names of many Pallava princes and kings had the suffix *aṅkura*. For instance, an early Pallava queen, Chārudēvī's son (fourth century AD), was called Buddhyāṅkura (sprout of intelligence). Mahendravarman I called himself Laḷitāṅkura (beautiful sprout), while Rājasimha was also known as Nayāṅkura (sprout of polity) and Taruṇāṅkura (young sprout).

Mahendravarman's famous Sanskrit play, *Bhagavati Gujjam*, contains many punning allusions to sprouts or shoots of the *asoka* tree. For these shoots, the play deliberately uses the word *pallava*. The implication is that the Pallavas were an offshoot of the renowned royal family of Aśoka of the Mauryan dynasty (fourth to second centuries BC).

At the Vaikunṭa Perumāḷ temple, a sculpture panel features Drona below whose feet is an ornamented pitcher to indicate that he emerged out of it. Another panel in the same temple shows the newborn baby, Pallava, sleeping in a cradle with a high backrest formed by a litter of sprouts. The baby's proud father, Aśvatthāman (Drona's son), is seen next to the infant (Figure 9). The fragmentary sprout or broken branch of the tree may even signify the popular legend that the Pallavas had to clear large tracts of forests to build and expand their kingdom. Thus, the Pallavas are also called *Kāḍuvetti* (woodcutters) in inscriptions and in literature.

Svastika

Like the Sātavāhanas, the Pallavas, too, gave immense prominence to the *svastika* symbol on their coins. Many Pallava coins feature a single, big *svastika* on the reverse (Plate 26). Again, like the

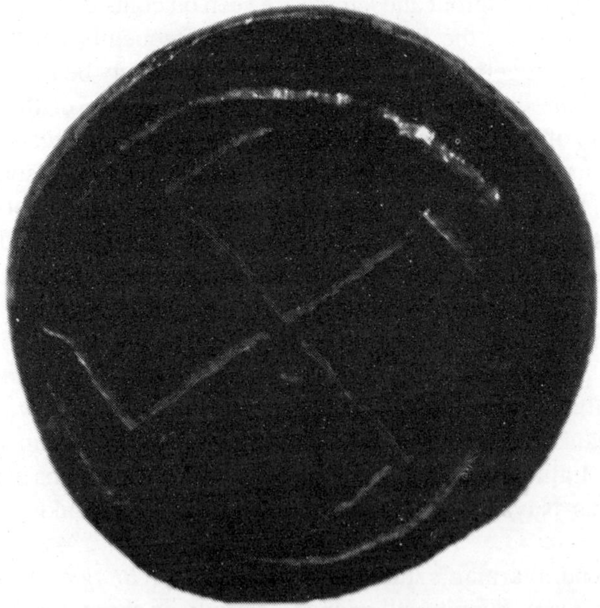

Plate 26: Pallava coin—*svastika* reverse.
(Photo: S. Raman, Madras)

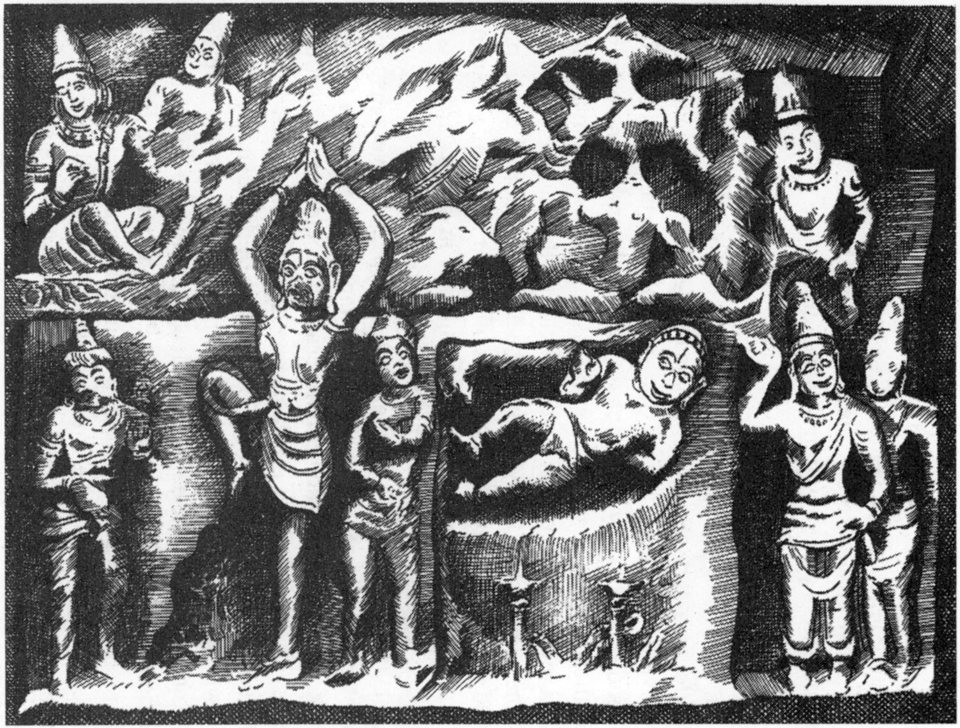

Figure 9: Baby Pallava sleeping in a cradle formed by a litter of sprouts—featured among the sculptures of historical events on the walls of the cloister surrounding the main shrine of the Vaikunṭa Perumāḷ temple, Kanchi.

Sātavāhana coins, most Pallava coins feature the right-handed *svastika* alone. The left-handed *svastika* is not wholly unknown but is very rare on Pallava coins.

On many Pallava coins, the arms of the symbol are straight and thick, and often end in tiny circles or pellets. Such pellets are also sometimes seen at the centre of the symbol and at the points where the arms intersect each other. In rare instances, a few pellets are seen scattered around the symbol. The *svastika* is mostly enclosed within a linear circle. Rarely, the *svastika* is flanked by a lamp on either side and is placed within a rayed circle.

Elephant

Animal devices, though quite common on the obverse, are very rare on the reverse of Pallava coins. Until recently, we believed that the Pallavas did not portray the elephant on the obverse or reverse of any of their coins. However, recent discoveries of Pallava coins include a few specimens bearing this device on the reverse. On these coins, the elephant is fairly well-delineated. The animal has large eyes and short pointed tusks. The folds of the ear are clearly visible. The trunk hangs downwards and terminates in an inward twist. Sometimes a lotus is depicted above the tusker.

It is clear that the Pallava elephant reverse type coins were inspired by the elephant type coins of the Sātavāhanas and Sangam Cōḷas, who ruled the southern Andhra-northern Tamil Nadu region prior to the Pallavas. The Pallava elephant reverse coins includes a rare, rectangular one that is one of the first issues of this dynasty.

It is well known that the elephant mainly features on the obverse of the coins of most of the early dynasties, including the Sātavāhanas and Sangam Cōḷas. Unlike many of these dynasties, the Pallavas strictly reserved the obverse of their coins for symbols and devices connected with royalty—the royal emblem (lion or bull), the *aśvamedha* horse or the royal bust. Hence, even when they chose to portray the elephant on their coins, they relegated the animal to the reverse.

Like their predecessors, the Pallavas, too, maintained a large contingent of war elephants. The elephants also played a ceremonial role within the Pallava palace. They were present during the coronation of the various kings.[18] As noted earlier, these kings even had crowns in the shape of the head of the elephant.

The elephant is repeatedly featured in Pallava stone sculptures. At Mahabalipuram, the finest elephant sculptures are those carved within the Bhagīratha's Penance (or Arjuna's Penance) Panel on the surface of a large rocky cliff (Plate 27). Here, we see two gigantic but well-proportioned elephants, one slowly following the other, with six little calves playing around their legs. In the Vaikuṇṭa Perumāḷ temple, elephants are frequently shown in sculptures portraying wars fought by the Pallavas. In some of these sculptures, the Pallava king is seen riding the elephant. One such war scene sculpture even portrays the Pallava army's capture of the prized elephant named Paṭṭavardhana from the Gangas in the eighth century AD. An enigmatic, unpublished sculpture has recently been noticed on the north wall of the *ardhamaṇḍapa* of the *āditala* of the same temple. This sculpture features an elephant to the right, with two couples riding on it. The legs of the couple in front (near the head of the elephant) are seen hanging down, and, hence, this may be a royal couple—the king and queen. The legs of the couple at the rear

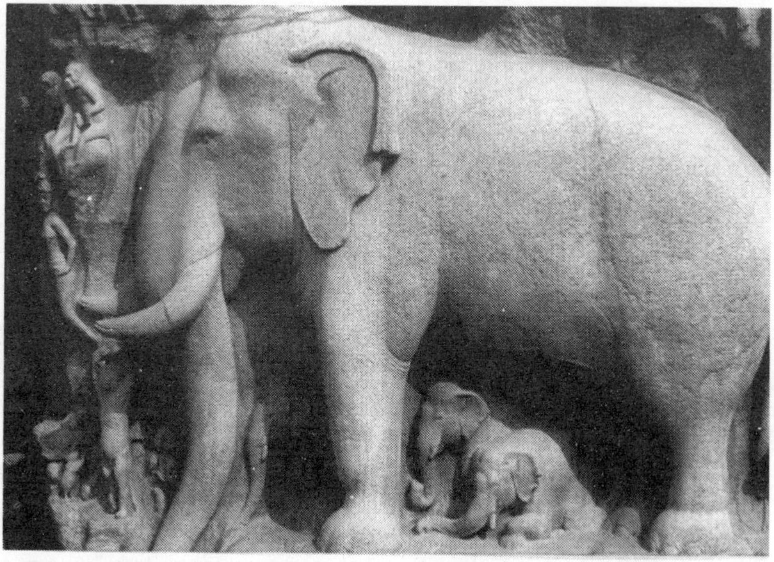

Plate 27: Pallava elephant sculpture, Mahabalipuram.

are not hanging down. Hence, they may be the servants of the king. The latter woman holds a flag. The elephant is adorned with a shawl and anklets. The shawl has four bells hanging along its edge.

Architectural Devices

The reverse of several Pallava coins feature architectural devices such as the ground plan and elevation of various structures or buildings. Some coins feature a building having a rectangular ground plan with a small square projection at one end. Some buildings have curved corners and a domed roof. Those with three cells or chambers appear to denote the triple-celled Pallava temples, such as the Mahiṣāsuramardinī cave temple and the Trimūrti cave temple at Mahabalipuram (Plate 28). Appropriately, the coins feature a lamp flanking the temple on either side. Some coins feature a building with a pyramidal roof (Plate 29) and a row of slender pillars or columns. This structure may also represent a Pallava temple. It has stylistic affinities with the temples seen on some Sangam Pāṇḍya coins (around first century AD).

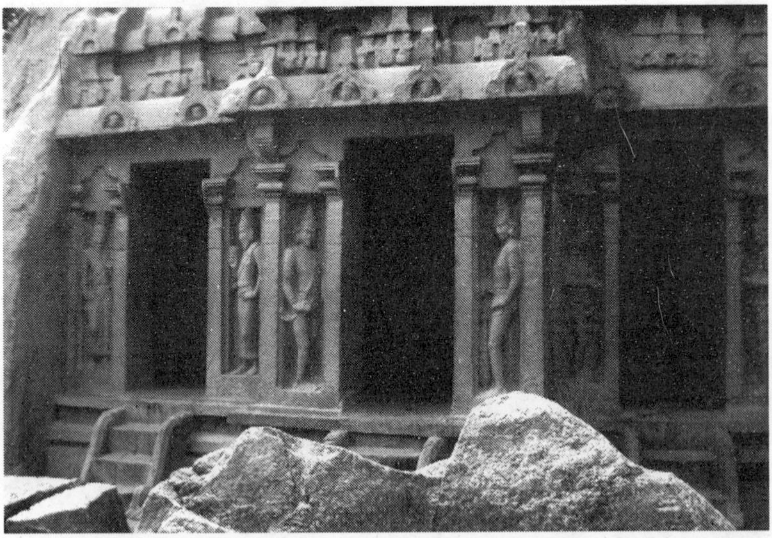

Plate 28: Pallava triple-celled Trimūrti cave temple, Mahabalipuram.

Plate 29: Pallava coin—pyramidal temple reverse.
(Photo: S. Raman, Madras)

On some other coins, the architectural ground plan may represent the famous *ghaṭikā* (university) that flourished in Kanchi even prior to the Pallava occupation. Throughout the Pallava period, it was a leading academic institution that attracted students and scholars from distant kingdoms. The staff members of the *ghaṭikā* were very senior scholars. They wielded great powers, to the extent that when a Pallava king died without a male heir, they could select or nominate a suitable successor. For example, around the year AD 731, when the Pallava king, Parameshvaravarman II, died without a male heir, the *ghaṭikaiyar* (also called *ghaṭakayār*), or members of the *ghaṭikā*, were instrumental in selecting Nandivarman Pallavamalla as the next king.

Some coins portray a simple rectangular basin, which may be a tank. The Pallavas are widely known for their large irrigation tanks, many of which have survived to this day. Mahabalipuram, their secondary capital and chief port, was dotted with several cisterns, tanks and ponds, some of which were linked to one another through long, winding canals.

A rare coin features a unique and complicated architectural device that has been identified as the layout of the harbour at Mahabalipuram (Plate 30). The coin features four, long, parallel walls erected along the shoreline. The wall at the farthest left is the longest. At one end of this, there is a shorter wall such that the angle between

Plate 30: Pallava coin—harbour walls? reverse.
(Photo: S. Raman, Madras)

the two is 90°. The other end of this short wall has a ball attached to it. The wall and ball may be a locking mechanism to control the level of water inside the harbour.

Interestingly, in the vicinity of the Shore temple at Mahabalipuram, archaeologists have uncovered a harbour structure, almost similar to the structure on the coin.[19] It consists of rows of stepped walls that form part of the elaborate stonework foundation and superstructure of a breakwater in the harbour (Plate 31). The latter is made of blocks of reddish laterite, with a stepped system of keyed granite slabs specifically meant to keep the walls from yielding to the force of the sea waves that dash against them. The gaps between the stone blocks are filled with rough lime plaster. Although these groyne walls are now some distance from the shoreline, during the Pallava period, the sea appears to have extended right up to these walls.

Appropriately, the above harbour coin is an issue of Narasimhavarman I or Mahāmalla, who expanded the port-city of Mahabalipuram and embellished it with a series of temples and tanks.

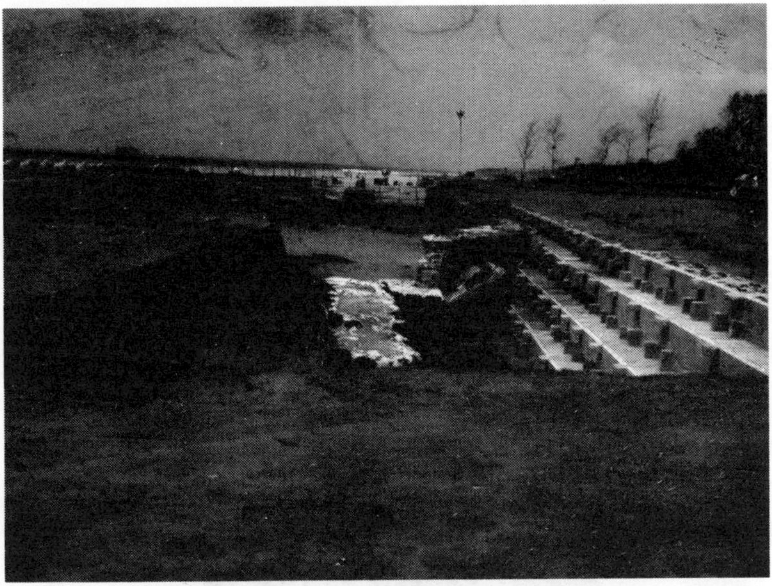

Plate 31: Pallava harbour walls, Mahabalipuram.
(Photo: Usha Kris, Madras)

He also strengthened and expanded the harbour at this place. His contributions were so great that the city, earlier called Mallai, was renamed Mahāmallapuram, after one of his titles *Mahāmalla*, meaning great wrestler. Mahāmallapuram was later shortened to Māmallapuram or Mahabalipuram.

Ship

The ship reverse Pallava coins are not very common (Plate 32). Many of these are made of lead or copper and, rarely, bronze. Ships with single and double masts are seen on the coins. Usually, the body is slightly curved and ornamented at both ends. The ship often has a semi-circular bottom. In one instance, one can clearly see a mast with a folded sail in the middle of the ship. This sail, interestingly, closely resembles the *śrīvatsa* symbol.

The ship type coins reflect the naval strength of the Pallavas. Historians strongly believe that the Pallavas inherited, from the Sātavāhanas, the lucrative maritime commerce with Rome, Sri Lanka, South-East Asia and China.[20] Yet, as indicated earlier, trade with Rome slowly declined during the rule of the early Pallavas, before

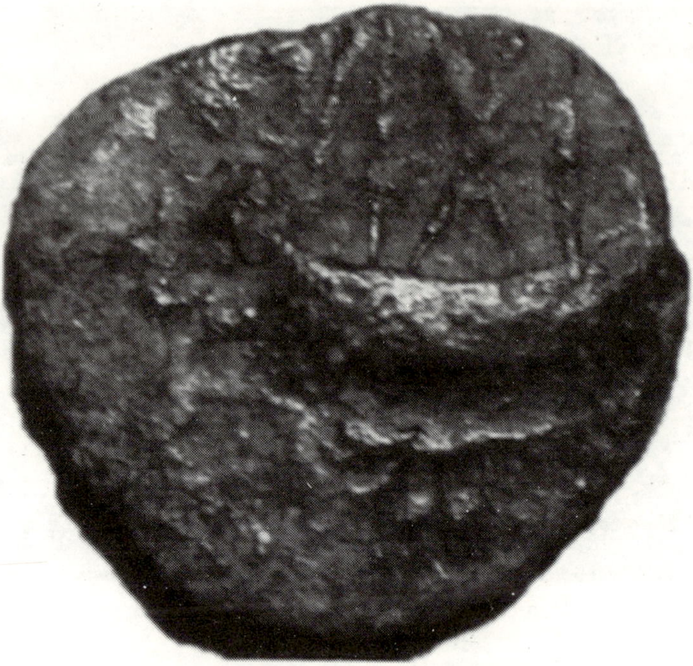

Plate 32: Pallava coin—ship reverse.
(Photo: S. Raman, Madras)

they began minting coins on a large scale. However, the Pallava kings continued to maintain close commercial and cultural contacts with Sri Lanka, South-East Asia and China. As stated earlier, Mahabalipuram was the chief port of the Pallavas. They had many smaller ports such as Mylai or Mylāpore, now a part of the city of Madras.

The Pallavas modelled their ship reverse coins on the ship type coins of the Sātavāhanas and Śālaṅkāyanas. The latter are of lead and so are the earliest Pallava ship coins. While Sātavāhana coins feature the ship on the obverse, the Śālaṅkāyana and Pallava coins depict the device on the reverse.

Other Reverse Symbols and Devices

The other symbols and devices seen on the reverse of Pallava coins include the *Śivaliṅga* on a quadrangular pedestal, *śrīvatsa*, sun, geometric patterns, river or sea, flower with five or eight petals, three-arched hill, *chowrie* (fly whisk), *udukkai* (a musical instrument in the form of a small drum), flag mast, umbrella, bow, tiger, fish, boar, lion, peacock, beetle, turtle or tortoise, and snake.

Among these, the *śrīvatsa* is prominently featured on many coins. Often, the symbol is the sole motif on the reverse. It is usually placed at the centre of the flan. The space between the curved arms of the symbol is frequently filled up and, hence, it appears like a heavy, solid object. Sometimes it is flanked by a lamp on either side and is enclosed within a plain or floriated circle.

Some coins of Mahendravarman I feature an eight-petalled flower with a prominent circle in the middle. The petals are broad and big. The flower may represent the lotus. The fly whisk is a rather rare device on the reverse of Pallava coins. Some coins of Mahendravarman I feature two slanting fly whisks, one over the other, that appear like a cross.

The flag mast, rarely featured on the reverse of certain Pallava coins, is of a unique design (Plate 33). The mast has a triangular

Plate 33: Pallava coin—flag mast reverse.
(Photo: S. Raman, Madras)

head. Four or more thin, narrow ribbons or a thin, striped cloth banner appear attached to the bottom of the triangle. The ribbons or banner appear to be rapidly fluttering to the left, probably due to a violent breeze. The mast stands on an ornamented quadrangular or flower-shaped pedestal. Some coins feature a richly-decorated umbrella laced with beads or semi-precious stones. Rarely, two such umbrellas are shown, one above the other. Probably these represent the royal parasols.

Mahendravarman I issued a series of coins featuring the bow (Chera emblem), tiger (Cōḷa emblem) and fish (Pāṇḍya emblem) on the reverse. He would have issued these to commemorate his victories over the Cheras, Cōḷas and Pāṇḍyas. One may recall that Mahendra's father, Simhavishnu, minted coins with these emblems on the obverse, to proclaim his victory over these three royal families. Mahendra also issued a coin portraying the boar, the Chalukya emblem, on the reverse. This coin announced one of his early victories against the Chalukyas, although much later, he was badly defeated by the Chalukyas. Mahendra's son, Mahāmalla, minted several coins exhibiting one or two fishes (Pāṇḍya emblem) on the reverse to indicate his victory against the Pāṇḍyas. Unlike the fishes on the reverse of many early Pāṇḍya coins, those on Mahāmalla's coins are realistically depicted, with the fluttering fins marked by a series of tiny strokes.

The reverse of a few Pallava coins feature the rayed circle border. One may recall that such a border first appears on the coins of the Śālaṅkāyanas and became very common on the issues of the Viṣṇukuṇḍins. While this border design is confined to the reverse of the latter coins, some Pallava coins have revealed the motif even on the obverse. There is no coin, whether of the Pallavas or any other series, which has revealed the motif both on the obverse and reverse.

Legends

In recent decades, many Pallava coins bearing legends have been discovered. These mostly occur on the obverse. As per the script and language, they can be classified into three categories:

1. *Brāhmī script and Prakrit language legends:* Pallava coins bearing such legends are rare and mostly belong to the early period of

their rule. These coins further substantiate the Andhra origin of the Pallavas. One may recall that the Brāhmī script and Prakrit language were very popular in Andhra during the pre-Pallava period, and the majority of Sātavāhana coins have legends in this script and language. The earliest Pallava copper-plate charters are in this script and language and have been found in Andhra.

2. *Pallava Grantha script and Sanskrit language legends:* During the age of the Pallavas, Sanskrit became very popular in the Tamil Nadu region. Many Pallava copper-plate charters and stone inscriptions are in Sanskrit. Some Pallava kings like Mahendravarman I were Sanskrit scholars. Many of their coins display legends in Sanskrit.
3. *Tamil script and Tamil language legends:* The Pallavas also used the Tamil language and Tamil script for many inscriptions and coin-legends.

The legends mostly occur above the main obverse device. In the case of a quadrangular coin, though, the legend occurs at the extreme left. They are to be read from left to right.

The legends are usually short and, sometimes, portions of them are outside the flan. Most of them represent the name or any of the high-sounding titles (*birudas*) of the king. These titles mainly embody the ruler's divine origin, physical strength, intellectual prowess and artistic abilities.[21] For example, Mahendravarman I had over 130 titles documented in his inscriptions at Chezarla, Pallavaram, Vallam, Mamandur, Kanchipuram, Mahendravadi, Madagapattu, Dalavanur, Siyamangalam and Tiruchirappalli in the Andhra-Tamil Nadu region. Among these, the Pallavaram cave-temple (on the outskirts of Madras city) lists over 100 titles, many of which are also listed in inscriptions at other sites. The names of some of his temples have been derived from some of these titles. The Laḷitāṅkureśvara temple (at Tiruchirappalli), for example, is named after Mahendra's famous title *Laḷitāṅkura* (beautiful sprout).

A study of Pallava lithic records reveals that the kings appear to have had many names and titles. Only a few of these are represented on coins. Of course, sometimes, the coins have revealed new titles, unknown to the stone inscriptions. Further, as some of these titles were borne by more than one Pallava ruler, it is hazardous to attribute any coin to a particular king solely on the basis of the legend.

Some of the titles found on Pallava coins include *Daṇḍikkalla* (mace bearer), *Darppaviṣaḥ* (poison to enemies' pride), *Nihikāmutrikaḥ* (attached neither to the pleasures of this world nor to the heaven), *Pukāpiṭuku* or *Pakāpiṭuku* (indivisible or powerful), *Lakṣitaḥ* (auspicious or distinguished), *Laḷitāṅkura* (beautiful sprout) and *Vidhi* (ruler). A recently-discovered, unpublished coin bears the legend *Māmalla* (great wrestler), one of the titles of Narasimhavarman I.

Unlike the legends on the coins of many other early south Indian dynasties, those on the Pallava coins have generally been artistically engraved. On many coins, the ends of the alphabet are slightly elongated and terminate in a beautiful curve or loop. Thus, these legends exhibit an ornamental cursive style of writing and are excellent specimens of numismatic calligraphy. The same artistic flourishes can be seen on many Pallava copper-plate charters and stone inscriptions, too. A close examination of all the major Pallava inscriptions and coin-legends reveals that for each script, they had two distinct styles of writing—the ornate cursive style and the ordinary style. Both were employed for the stone and copper-plate inscriptions, while the ornate style was preferred for coin-legends. The Pallavas seem to have learnt the ornate cursive style from the Ikṣvākus who employed it for their stone inscriptions but not for coin-legends.

On some coins, the first few letters of the legend appear big and clear, while the last few are small, cramped and distorted. This indicates that the scribe or die-engraver did not plan or measure the space for the legend beforehand so as to accord equal space to each of the letters. Instead, he began engraving the legend from some arbitrary point and, in the middle of the legend, suddenly discovered that the space was too small for the remaining letters. Hence, these letters were engraved in a smaller size and without any ornamentation.

NOTES AND REFERENCES

1. For a general account of the eventful history of the Pallavas, see C. Minakshi, *Administration and Social Life Under the Pallavas* (Madras, 1977); R. Krishnamurthy, *The Pallava Coins* (Madras, 2004), pp. 1-40.
2. For details regarding the art of the Pallavas, see Michael Lockwood, *Māmallapuram: A Guide to the Monuments* (Madras, 1993); Michael Lockwood et al., *Pallava Art* (Madras, 2001); C. Sivaramamurti,

Mahabalipuram (New Delhi, 1978); K.R. Srinivasan, *Cave Temples of the Pallavas* (New Delhi, 1964).

3. Many museums have Pallava coins but not in very large numbers. The museums include the National Museum, New Delhi, and the Government Museum, Egmore, Madras. Some of the Pallava coins from Kanchipuram are in the office of the Chennai Circle of the ASI, Madras. Till date, no museum has published a catalogue of the Pallava coins in its collections. From the days of Walter Elliot (late nineteenth century), many books on Indian numismatics mention Pallava coins in passing. During the last two decades, three important books dealing with Pallava coins have been published. These are K.A. Thirugnanasampandam, *Kanchi Pallava Coins* (Erode, 1989); Arumuga Sitaraman and Sankaran Raman, *Pallavar Kasugal* (Tamil) (Tanjavur, 2002); R. Krishnamurthy 2004 (supra n. 1). Research papers on Pallava coins have, however, appeared in several journals, mainly the *JNSI* and the *SSIC*. See R. Krishnamurthy, 'Two More Pallava Coins With Legends', *JNSI* LIII 1 & 2 (1991), pp. 62-3. For an exhaustive bibliography of Pallava coins, see P. Shanmugam, 'Tamil Nadu Coins: A Bibliography', *SSIC* XIV (2004), pp. 120-59.
4. Some of the Pallava coins found in Sri Lanka are in the collection of the National Museum, Colombo. At least one coin is exhibited in a museum in Anuradhapura.
5. P. Shanmugam, 'Two Coins of Tamil Origin From Thailand', *SSIC* IV (1994), pp. 95-100.
6. V. Jeyaraj, 'A Technical Study on a Pallava Lead Coin', *SSIC* I (1991), pp. 121-3.
7. R. Krishnamurthy 2004 (supra n. 1), pp. 168-71, 174-5.
8. See R. Krishnamurthy 2004 (supra n. 1), pp. 172-4.
9. For example, see R. Krishnamurthy 2004 (supra n. 1), pp. 84 (coin no. 141), 99 (coin no. 201).
10. R. Krishnamurthy 2004 (supra n. 1), pp. 108-10. The mounds are in the collection of the museum of the Department of Ancient History and Archaeology, University of Madras, Madras. Also see K.V. Raman and P. Shanmugam, 'Pallava Coin Moulds From Kanchipuram Excavations', *SSIC* V (1995), pp. 77-80.
11. V. Jeyaraj 1991 (supra n. 6), pp. 121-3.
12. Brajadulal Chattopadhyaya, *Coins and Currency Systems in South India c. AD 225-1300* (New Delhi, 1977), pp. 16-19.
13. R. Krishnamurthy 2004 (supra n. 1), pp. 180-1.
14. For a detailed discussion on Pallava epigraphical references to *aśvamedha* sacrifices, see C. Minakshi, *The Historical Sculptures of the Vaikuṇṭha-perumāḷ Temple, Kāñchi* (Delhi, 1941), pp. 10-11.
15. C. Minakshi 1941 (supra n. 14), pp. 34-5.
16. For a discussion on such coins, see Osmund Bopearachchi, *Indo-Greek, Indo-Scythian and Indo-Parthian Coins in the Smithsonian Institution*

(Washington, D.C., 1993), p. 42; B.N. Mukherjee, *Kushana Coins of the Land of the Five Rivers* (Calcutta, 1978), p. 72.

17. Many scholars like I. Mahadevan strongly believe that the Pallavas originally hailed from north-west India. Many other scholars like R. Krishnamurthy support the 'Andhra origin' of the Pallavas. For more details on this, see R. Krishnamurthy 2004 (supra n. 1), pp. 1-13.
18. A total of 18 'Coronation Scenes' are seen among the Pallava historical sculptures on the walls of the cloister surrounding the main shrine of the Vaikuṇṭa Perumāḷ temple at Kanchipuram. The elephant features in some of the scenes.
19. For more details regarding archaeological digs and discoveries at Mahabalipuram, see Alok Tripathi, 'The Underwater Exploration of Mahabalipuram in Bay of Bengal', *Purātattva: Bulletin of the Indian Archaeological Society* 32 (2001-2), pp. 93-100; K.T. Narasimman, 'Recent Discoveries Made by Chennai Circle During This Decade', in K. Damodaran, ed., *Tamil Nadu: Archaeological Perspectives* (Madras, 1999), pp. 156-62.
20. For more details about the trade activities of the Pallavas, see K.A. Thirugnanasampandam 1989 (supra n. 3), pp. 9-11.
21. For more details regarding the *birudas*, see Michael Lockwood and A. Vishnu Bhat, 'The *Birudas* of Mahēndravarman', Paper presented at the third annual congress of the Epigraphical Society of India (Udupi, 1977).

CHAPTER 11

Epilogue

The present study has attempted to document, highlight and analyse the artistic value of the various coins that circulated in south India up to around the mid-ninth century AD, i.e. till the commencement of the rule of the Imperial Cōḷas or medieval Cōḷas under Vijayalaya and his illustrious successors. Simultaneously, the socio-cultural and religious significance of the symbols and devices on the coins has also been investigated. In the process, some of the physical features and technical aspects of the coins, especially with regard to the size, shape, metal, the extent of its purity, and the minting technique, have also been studied.

Coins, like historical monuments, sculptures and paintings, usually have a symbolic meaning behind the visual form. While the form is clearly visible and lends itself to description and photography, the meaning is often elusive without the context being made intelligible from various perspectives. Thus, the size, shape, and obverse and reverse motifs of a coin, are definitely not products of an accident nor something that slowly evolved at random. On the other hand, it is becoming increasingly clear that all aspects of a coin, mainly the choice of the symbols and devices, were carefully planned and decided in accordance with the complex socio-economic and religious conditions, and the art traditions of those days. Every symbol and device had a specific purpose to serve, a distinct meaning to convey.

In India, the earliest coins and the earliest literary evidence for the use of coins came from the northern part of the subcontinent. As in most ancient civilizations, barter was replaced by various forms of primitive currency long before the introduction of metallic currency in India. These primitive currencies included cowrie shells, cattle and even elephants. The use of cattle as currency seems to have been fairly widespread even outside India. Besides, the Vedas (1500-600 BC?), the *Manusmriti* (1000-600 BC?), the *Avesta* (1500 BC?), and some early Greek and Roman texts (date:?) refer to cattle as a medium of exchange.

The earliest literary reference to metallic currency in India is the description of the gifts of gold pieces offered to priests in the Vedic texts. The size and shape of these gold pieces are not known. They were probably small bits or ornaments and were popularly known as *niṣka*. Archaeology has, so far, been unable to throw any light on the use of cattle or *niṣka* as currency. Textual descriptions are also inadequate to identify the *niṣka* among the limited extant specimens of protohistoric jewels discovered in some places in India, including south India.

By around 600 BC, the use of regular metal currency was known in many parts of north India. Thus, the early punch-marked coins were made and used much before the earliest Iranian and Greek invasions of India. They were not introduced by the Greeks or the Achaemenians nor inspired or modelled on their coins. The choice of silver for the earliest Indian currency may have been because it was not as rare and expensive as gold. Further, silver was available in sufficient quantities in north India.

The *kārṣāpaṇas* slowly spread from north India to south India. In due course, such coins began to be produced in many sites even in the peninsular tip of the subcontinent. Surprisingly, although silver was scarce in the extreme south, the earliest coins produced here were of silver, probably to maintain an uniformity in a currency series that was used in many regions and kingdoms. Copper, too, was sometimes used to produce *kārṣāpaṇas* both in the north and south.

In the third century BC, many powerful dynasties such as the Sātavāhanas and Sangam Cheras rose to power and prominence in south India. Initially, these dynasties used the *kārṣāpaṇas* reaching their territories through pilgrims and traders. Some of the south Indian kings also began to make their own *kārṣāpaṇa*-type coins.

Gradually, the south Indian dynasties began to create new coin types that were produced not merely by the conventional punch-marking technique but also by the more sophisticated casting and die-striking processes. It is interesting to note that the bigger and more powerful dynasties adopted all these three techniques while the smaller kingdoms chose two. For example, the mighty Sātavāhanas and, later, the Pallavas produced coins by all these three methods whereas smaller kingdoms such as the Sangam Cheras and Sangam Pāṇḍyas used the punch-marking and die-striking methods alone. Still smaller kingdoms and chiefdoms such as the Malaiyamāns (Tamil Nadu) and the Ikṣvākus (Andhra) stuck to one technique—the former to the die-striking and the latter to the casting. It is also pertinent to note that, despite the introduction of better techniques, the punch-marking technique never altogether disappeared but survived in certain regions, especially in south India, even in the medieval period.

As more than one authorized mint seemed to have been in operation in each of the early south Indian kingdoms, each may have specialized in minting coins by any one of the three techniques. Thus, one can also see significant stylistic and metallographic differences between different coins of the same type, and sometimes the same ruler, produced in different mints.

Apart from silver and copper, various other metals and their alloys also began to be used for making coins. A number of south Indian dynasties produced lead coins in large numbers. Coins were also made of potin that was obtained initially as a by-product when old copper and lead coins were melted in the mints. The Sātavāhanas and, later, the Viṣṇukuṇḍins and Pallavas issued bronze coins that almost appeared like gold. The use of electrum for coins came much later—the Pallavas and the Western Chalukyas issued electrum coins almost at the same time (seventh century AD). This is not surprising because in the fields of art and coinage, these two dynasties heavily borrowed ideas and features from each other.

None of the ancient south Indian dynasties ever minted gold coins. The report of the discovery of Pallava gold coins from Tiruchi (Tamil Nadu) is not true. The main reason for the absence of gold coins of any of these dynasties is that Roman and Byzantine gold coins circulated as money in large areas of south India from around the first century AD to at least the fifth century AD. Thus, the south Indian kings did not feel the need to mint gold coins. Recent research has indicated that the terms *dīnārī*, *suvarṇa* and *hiraṇya* occurring in ancient south Indian inscriptions and Sanskrit literature refer to the imported gold coins. The first south Indian dynasty to mint gold coins was probably the Western Chalukyas (seventh century AD). Later, other dynasties such as the Eastern Chalukyas and the Pāṇḍyas started making them.

As regards the shape of the coins, most of the early historical south Indian dynastic issues initially followed the *kārṣāpaṇa* tradition, and mostly minted square and rectangular coins in large quantities. Various other shapes were also experimented with from time to time. However, by the second century AD or even slightly earlier, the circular shape was considered the most suitable for coins. After this date, all south Indian coins are mostly round in shape.

The early south Indian dynastic issues mostly followed the *kārṣāpaṇa* weight-standard but there are significant differences in the size of the coins issued by different dynasties/kings. These issues were also greatly influenced by the symbols and devices on punch-marked coins. They were also exposed to influences of the Greek and Roman coins that reached western and southern India by the process of trade.

As for the symbols and devices on coins, the available evidence is not adequate to comment on the precise reasons for the frequent portrayal of some of them in preference to others, and also for the occurrence of specific combinations of symbols on the coins of certain dynasties. The present study has revealed certain interesting trends and patterns in this regard. In most instances, the symbols and devices were meant, either blatantly or subtly, to emphasize the exalted strength, power and achievements of royalty.

Most of these early dynasties, at least during the initial years of their rule, merely followed the coin symbols and devices of their immediate predecessors. This was probably done to give breathing time to the people to accept the new leadership and new types of coins. Besides, links with the preceding dynasty, embodied in the form of common coin devices, accorded the new ruling family a sense of royal legitimacy and credibility in the eyes of the public. Thus, the earliest coins issued by the Pallavas are of the lion type, modelled on the Sātavāhana lion type coins. In the case of the Ikṣvākus, they simply followed the Sātavāhana numismatic traditions and did not introduce any changes during their comparatively short rule of little over a century.

Once a new dynasty consolidated itself politically and economically, it attempted changes and innovations in coin motifs. The rich variety of symbols and devices on the *kārṣāpaṇas* were often reproduced, either in the same form or in a modified version, and in different combinations, on dynastic issues. New symbols and motifs in consonance with local needs and aspirations were also introduced. These slow but steady changes widened the differences between the *kārṣāpaṇas* and the issues of southern dynasties.

Each dynasty adopted a particular symbol or device as the royal emblem (*rājalāñchana*) and featured it extensively on its coins and inscriptions. The size and positioning of the emblem on the coin differed from dynasty to dynasty. To cite examples, the Sangam Cheras, Sangam Cōḷas and Sangam Pāṇḍyas featured their royal emblems—the bow or bow-arrow, tiger and fish, respectively—as the sole device on the reverse of their coins. The *śrīvatsa*—the insignia of the Sātavāhanas—occurs in various forms and sizes both on the obverse and reverse of their coins. On Pallava coins, their dynastic crest—initially the lion and later the bull—occurs on the obverse, mostly in association with auspicious symbols or war weapons.

Often, a king minted coins featuring the emblem of a rival ruler after defeating him in war. There could be two main reasons for such a practice. First, the king wanted to proclaim and publicize his victory over his foe through coins. Second, the people in the conquered areas would be familiar with the coin-types of their erstwhile ruler. Hence, it would be prudent for the victorious king to issue coins of those types, mainly for circulation in the newly-captured territories. Thus, the Sātavāhanas are believed to have issued coins with the bow and arrow—the symbol of the Kura kingdom (Maharashtra-Karnataka region)—soon after their conquest of the Kuras. Again, the Sātavāhanas began to portray the elephant extensively on their coins after their resounding victory over Kharavela of Kalinga (Orissa), whose emblem was the elephant. Sometimes a king minted coins featuring the royal emblems of two or more defeated rulers. For instance, the Pallavas issued coins featuring the bow (Chera emblem), tiger (Cōḷa emblem) and fish (Pāṇḍya emblem).

On some coins, the exact placement or positioning of the enemy's emblem had immense political significance. The Sātavāhanas sometimes placed their insignia—the *śrīvatsa*—above the elephant, to proclaim their supremacy over the Kalinga kingdom whose symbol was the latter. On Viṣṇukuṇḍin coins, the placement of the *śrīvatsa* symbol in front of the mouth of the lion, the Viṣṇukuṇḍin emblem, may indicate that they were so powerful that they could swallow or crush even a mighty empire like the Sātavāhanas.

Certain coin devices and symbols appear to have an intimate link with the place or region in which the coins were minted or used. In this connection, it may be pointed out that the hills and river on many of the Malaiyamān coins have been taken to represent the physical topography of Tirukoilur, the Malaiyamān capital. Similarly, the ship type coins of the Sātavāhanas are mostly seen in coastal Andhra, a region famous for its maritime commerce with ancient Rome, Africa and South-East Asia. Again, the Sātavāhana lion type coins are clustered in the Saurashtra region, well known for its Asian lions. In each of these cases, the king or mint authorities deliberately chose to portray a device closely connected with the place or region on the coins.

As regards religious symbols and devices on coins, it is generally presumed that their portrayal reflected the religious leanings of the king. This is not always the case. There are ample instances where a ruling family belonging to a certain religion issued coins bearing devices connected with another faith. There could be several reasons for this practice. Perhaps the ruler issued such coins as part of a political stratagem, to earn the goodwill and support of people belonging to other religions or faiths, both within and outside his kingdom. Alternatively, the ruler might have followed a liberal and tolerant religious policy and, thus, issued coins with devices connected with many religions. The Sātavāhanas, who were essentially Hindus, issued coins bearing Buddhist motifs. Similarly, the Pallavas issued coins bearing motifs connected with Śaivism and Vaiṣṇavism. Interestingly, there are instances of Pallava coins bearing motifs connected with one faith on the obverse and another on the reverse.

Coming to royal portraiture on coins, ancient south Indian coins of this type are few, despite the series of recent discoveries of portrait coins of the Sātavāhanas, Sangam Cheras and Sangam Pāṇḍyas. Why did these kings, who issued a rich variety of coins and made every attempt to project and strengthen their might, not think of frequently featuring themselves and their names/titles on their coins? One reason for this lies in the very attitude of early Indian kings towards coinage. They did not view coins as an expression of the identity of the issuing authority nor as a means of publicity for the royal family. Consequently, coinage in ancient India did not serve as a symbol of state authority as it generally did in the Greek, Roman and, to an extent, even the Islamic tradition where the king's portrait was taboo but his name found a prominent place on the coins. One may recall that, traditionally, two main events marked the accession of a new Muslim ruler: the *khutba*—the inclusion of his name in public prayers at the mosque each Friday, and *sikka*—the right to issue coins and place his name on them.

In the Indian tradition, the currency of coinage seems to have been guaranteed by its resemblance to a generally accepted prototype rather than by the authority of the state or ruler. Thus, not surprisingly, we have copious instances of coins issued by non-royal or non-political authorities, including trade guilds. This curious, non-political attitude to coin design is exemplified by a majority of coins of the early south Indian dynasties discussed in this volume. This attitude may also partially account for these coins not being as artistic and carefully produced as the Greek and Roman ones, and those of the later Muslim kingdoms.

Reverting back to portraits on early south Indian coins, these were inspired by those on Greek and Roman coins but recreated by the Indian artists, according to their own sculptural style. As we are not too sure about the precise dates and genealogies of all the south Indian dynasties that issued portrait coins, it is hazardous to pinpoint any of them as the one that issued the first ones. However, generally, we consider the Sātavāhanas as the first south Indian dynasty to issue such coins. There are stylistic affinities between the portraits on the Sātavāhana and Sangam Pāṇḍya coins and, hence, one may surmise that the Pāṇḍyas designed their portrait coins on the Sātavāhana and, of course, the Roman models. On the other hand, the Sangam Chera portrait coins, are stylistically very different from the Sātavāhana portrait coins, and seem to have been solely and directly inspired by the Roman portrait coins, which, as per the latest studies, began to reach the Chera land as early as the third-second centuries BC. In any case, all the early south Indian dynasties considered portrait coins as special issues or commemorative coins, minted in limited quantities on special occasions, such as a coronation or a victory in war. This also accounts for the scarcity of these coins.

Graeco-Roman influences on Indian coinage were not restricted to royal portraiture alone. These variegated influences, that have hitherto been studied only in 'bits and pieces', extended to almost all aspects of coinage.[1] For instance, the Sātavāhanas and many of their contemporaries adopted the Greek-style figurative art on their coins. Even the technology of die-striking is believed to have been learnt by the Indians from the Greeks and Romans.

Graeco-Roman influences can even be seen in some of the legends appearing on early south Indian coins. On Indian coins, the earliest legends were written in a straight line and treated as though they were another punch-mark. With the coming of Greek coins, the Indians, like the former, placed the inscription in a circle or semicircle, as a border to the pictorial design on the coin. This positioning of the legend soon became very popular in many parts of India and continued for several centuries. Of course, every now and then, newer ways of positioning the legend were adopted. For instance, on some Sātavāhana coins, the legend above the elephant is neither in a straight line nor a curve but beautifully twists and turns in accordance with the bodily contours of the animal. The legend, thus, forms an interesting border just above the animal. Engraving the legends on the exergue, which is common on Roman coins, is, however, hardly known on south Indian coins.

It is, thus, obvious that the exchange of symbols, devices and other aspects of coins between different kingdoms was a complex and continuous process. With regard to symbols and devices, some kingdoms appeared to be more innovative and artistic than others. Thus, some of the coins inspired by those of the Sātavāhanas are artistically superior to the latter. The coins assigned to the Mahātalavaras (feudatories of the Sātavāhanas) of ancient Andhra, for example, bear the lifelike figure of the horse, mostly in high relief. Similarly, some of the issues attributed to the Andhra Mahāsenāpatis portray, on the obverse, the tree-in-railing with a beautiful representation of the taurine attached to the end of each of the six branches, as also to the central stem, of the tree. Likewise, the Pallava coins, too, exhibit a high level of artistry. The Pallavas used fairly pure metal for their coins and adopted an efficient process for manufacturing them in manually-controlled mints. Like the Indo-Greeks, the Pallavas employed skilled and imaginative sculptors for engraving dies to produce artistic coins. For the first time in south India, Pallava artists even embellished some of the coin legends with superb ornamental flourishes.

Many dynasties featured certain specific symbols and motifs not only on coins but also on other mediums of art, mainly stone sculptures. The Pallavas, in particular, appear to have regularly featured several symbols, devices and themes both on coins and in sculptures. Thus, one can discern various similarities between the figures on Pallava coins and their stone sculptures. Such a one-to-one comparison is not possible in the case of other dynasties like the Sangam Cōḷas and Sangam Pāṇḍyas, mainly due to the paucity of their surviving art relics.

A detailed comparative study of Pallava coins and stone sculptures has led to certain interesting observations. Coins of real artistic merit undoubtedly betray a stylistic relationship between coins and sculpture. These two media of art may also share common thematic and iconographic traits. As sculptural art is more pervasive than numismatic art, the latter appears to have felt the impact of the former. Often, figures on stone sculptures were reproduced on coins, without any change in the form or style of the figures. This is amply clear from the figures of animals such as the bull on Pallava coins. Here, it is sometimes seen standing on a pedestal similar to the one supporting the stone bull in Pallava temple sculptures. Of course, the pedestal serves no practical purpose on a coin. The artistic die-cutters and coin-makers faithfully reproduced, on a miniature scale, specimens of sculpture and architecture on to the coins.

Conversely, the portrayal of coins in stone sculptures is extremely rare. The *kārṣāpaṇas* are featured in early Buddhist stone sculptures such as those at Bharhut in central India and Amaravati in south India, and on a little-known terracotta plaque from Tāmralipti (Tamluk) in Bengal. Yet no early south Indian dynastic coin has been unequivocally identified in any stone sculpture. Rarer, still, is the portrayal of coins on coins. On some ancient Indian coins, especially those of the Viṣṇukuṇḍins, the *pūrṇakumbha* is shown overflowing with flowers and/or coins or coin-like objects that are too small and vague to be attributed to any particular king or dynasty. One may, however, assume that no king would normally feature the coins of another dynasty on his coin. Hence, the coins seen on the Viṣṇukuṇḍin coins should also belong to the same dynasty.

In the case of many of the dynasties covered in the present study, there have been specimens of unauthorized, imitation coins, produced by forgers during the period when the relevant, genuine coins were in circulation. These coins are generally made of impure metal and do not have much artistic value.

Future discoveries of new coin types and fresh specimens of the known coin types of the various dynasties are bound to change our perception of the numismatic art of those periods.

NOTE

1. Graeco-Roman influences on Indian coinage have been both direct and indirect. The direct influences are those exercised by ancient Greek and Roman coins on Indian coins. The indirect influences are those exercised by these Indian coins on later Indian coins. For a general survey of some of these influences on different Indian coin-series, see A.M. Shastri, ed., *Foreign Elements in Indian Indigenous Coins* (Varanasi, 1982).

APPENDIX I

Corpus of the Symbols and Devices on the Coins of Select Early South Indian Dynasties

This corpus is mainly based on a physical examination of the relevant coins in different museums and private collections in south India, Sri Lanka, United Kingdom, and in the National Museum, New Delhi. The information gleaned from various museum archives and catalogues, and secondary sources such as descriptive numismatic publications and unpublished theses, have also been incorporated.

Vague, confusing and indistinct symbols and devices have not been included in this corpus. The different interpretations and/or meanings of each symbol and device are beyond its scope. As far as possible, the corpus lists only the English names of the symbols and devices.

The division of the symbols and devices into various categories has been made for the sake of convenience. It may be noted that many of the categories overlap.

SANGAM CHERAS

Obverse

Landscape Devices: Canal; Hill; River or Sea; Tank.

Floral Devices: Flower; Tree (mainly palm tree); Tree-in-railing.

Faunal Devices: Bull; Cock; Elephant; Fish; Horse; Lion; Peacock; Snake; Tiger; Tortoise.

Human Figures: Commoner?; Warrior; King.

Everyday Objects: Dumb-bell; Flag mast; Lamp; Lamp-stand; Rope or Sling; Staff or Rod; Water-pot; Water-trough.

Dresses or Garments: Cap; Coat or Jacket; Neck muffler?; Sari?; Trousers.

Jewellery: Anklet; Bangle; Ear-ornament; Garland.

Weapons: Arrow; Axe; Bow; Dagger; Thunderbolt; Trident.

Architectural Devices: Beam; Column or Pillar; Door frame; Platform or Pedestal.

Deities: Yamuna.

Religious Symbols and Devices: Conch; Crescent; *Pūrṇaghaṭa; Śrīvatsa*; Star; Sun; *Svastika;* Taurine; Triskelion; Wheel.

Geometric Designs: Circle with a dot in its centre.

Subsidiary Decorative Elements: Beaded border.

REVERSE

Landscape Devices: Hill; River; Tank.

Faunal Devices: Fish; Lion; Tortoise.

Weapons: Arrow; Bow; Goad.

Religious Symbols and Devices: Svastika; Taurine; *Ujjain* symbol.

Subsidiary Decorative Elements: Dotted border; Linear border.

SANGAM CŌḶAS

OBVERSE

Landscape Devices: Canal; Hill; River; Tank.

Floral Devices: Coconut; Flower (including Lotus); Tree-in-railing.

Faunal Devices: Bull; Cow?; Elephant; Fish; Horse; Tortoise or Turtle.

Everyday Objects: Basin; Flag mast; Pitcher; Umbrella.

Weapons: Arrow; Axe; Bow; Spear; Trident.

Transportation Devices: Chariot.

Architectural Devices: Platform or Pedestal; Column or Pillar.

Religious Symbols and Devices: Conch; Crescent; Human footprint; *Śrīvatsa;* Sun; Taurine; Wheel.

Geometric Designs: Oval design; Quadrangular design.

REVERSE

Floral Devices: Leaf; Tree-in-railing.

Faunal Devices: Eagle; Peacock; Snake; Tiger.

Everyday Objects: Flag mast; Lamp.

Religious Symbols and Devices: Crescent; *Śrīvatsa*; Sun; Taurine; *Yajñakuṇḍa.*

Geometric Designs: Circular design.

Subsidiary Decorative Elements: Dotted border; Linear border.

SANGAM PĀṆḌYAS

OBVERSE

Landscape Devices: Hill; Pond; River; Sea; Tank.

Floral Devices: Coconut; Flower; Floral design; Foliage; Mango leaves; Tree; Tree-in-railing.

Faunal Devices: Bird (Vulture or Eagle or Some other bird?); Bull; Crocodile; Dog; Duck; Fish; Hare; Horse; Insect?; Tortoise or Turtle.

Human Figures: Warrior; King.

Everyday Objects: Caduceus?; Drum; Flag; Flag mast; Kitchen utensil; Lamp; Lamp post; Rope; Trough; Umbrella; Vase.

Dresses or Garments: Cap; Shawl or Blanket.

Jewellery: Chain or Necklace; Crown; Diadem or Head-band; Ear-ornament; Garland.

Weapons: Arrow; Axe; Dagger; Goad; Spear; Trident.

Transportation Devices: Anchor of a ship or boat.

Architectural Devices: Column or Pillar; Platform or Pedestal; *Stūpa*; Temple.

Religious Symbols and Devices: Conch; Crescent; Moon; *Nandīpāda; Pūrṇaghaṭa*; *Ṣaḍaracakra*; *Śivaliṅga*; *Śrīvatsa*; Star; *Svastika*; Sun; Taurine; Triskelion, Wheel; *Yajñakuṇḍa.*

Geometric Designs: Circle.

Subsidiary Decorative Elements: Beaded border (or Border of Pearls?)

REVERSE

Landscape Devices: Hill; River; Sea; Tank.

Floral Devices: Tree-in-railing.

Faunal Devices: Fish; Tortoise.

Religious Symbols and Devices: Taurine.

MALAIYAMĀNS

OBVERSE

Floral Devices: Oak-wreath; Tree-in-railing.

Faunal Devices: Horse; Bull.

Everyday Objects: Flag; Flag mast; Stool; Trough or Basin.

Weapons: Arrow; Bow; Goad; Staff or Stick.

Architectural Devices: Pillar.

Religious Symbols and Devices: Crescent; *Nandīpāda*; Sun.

Geometric Designs: Dotted lines.

REVERSE

Landscape Devices: Hill; Mound; River; Road.

Faunal Devices: Fish.

Weapons: Spear.

Geometric Designs: Lines parallel to each other.

SĀTAVĀHANAS

OBVERSE

Landscape Devices: Hill; Pond; River; Sea.

Floral Devices: Flower (such as Lotus, Lily); Plant; Tree (including banyan tree); Tree-in-railing.

Faunal Devices: Bull; Camel; Crab; Elephant; Fish; Horse; Lion; Snake; Tiger; Tortoise.

Human Figures: King; Warrior.

Everyday Objects: Amphora-like pot or Vase; Basin or Bowl; Flag; Flag mast.

Dresses and Garments: Cap?; Shawl?

Jewellery: Crown; Diadem or Head-band; Ear-ornament; Neck-band; Pearl necklace.

Weapons: Arrow; Bow; Goad; Sceptre or Staff; Thunderbolt?

Transportation Devices: Anchor of a ship; Ship.

Architectural Devices: Column or Pillar; *Stūpa.*

Deities: Lakṣmī.

Religious Symbols and Devices: Conch; Crescent; Moon; *Nandīpāda*; *Pūrṇakumbha*; *Śrīvatsa*; Sun; *Svastika*; *Triratna*; *Ujjain* symbol; Wheel; *Yajñakuṇḍa.*

Subsidiary Decorative Elements: Beaded border; *Prabhāvalī*-like ornamental frame.

REVERSE

Landscape Devices: Hill; Lake; River; Sea.

Floral Devices: Flower (mainly lotus); Tree-in-railing (including mango, palm, coconut and teak trees-in-railing).

Faunal Devices: Bull; Crab; Elephant; Fish; Horse; Snake; Tortoise.

Human Figures: Warrior?

Everyday Objects: Flag?; Flag mast?; Rope or String.

Weapons: Arrow; Bow; Spear; Thunderbolt?.

Deities: Vanadevatā (Goddess of the forest)

Religious Symbols and Devices: Conch; Crescent; Human footprints; Moon; *Nandīpāda*; *Śrīvatsa*; Sun; *Svastika*; Taurine; *Tritratna*; *Ujjain* symbol.

Geometric Designs: Square.

IKṢVĀKUS

OBVERSE

Faunal Devices: Elephant; Horse.

Everyday Objects: Rope or String.

Architectural Devices: Column or Pillar.

Religious Symbols and Devices: Ujjain symbol.

Subsidiary Decorative Elements: Linear border.

REVERSE

Floral Devices: Flower?

Faunal Devices: Elephant.

Religious Symbols and Devices: Ujjain symbol.

Subsidiary Decorative Elements: Linear border?

VIṢṆUKUṆḌINS

OBVERSE

Floral Devices: Flower.

Faunal Devices: Bull; Horse; Lion.

Human Figures: King?; Warrior.

Everyday Objects: Coin?; Slat; Vase.

Dresses or Garments: Cap; Coat; Shawl; Trousers.

Jewellery: Chain (beaded or spiked); Ear-ornament.

Religious Symbols and Devices: Crescent; *Pūrṇakumbha*; *Śrīvatsa*; *Svastika.*

Subsidiary Decorative Elements: Dotted border; Floral design; Linear border.

REVERSE

Faunal Devices: Flower (including lotus).

Everyday Objects: Coin; Lamp; Lamp-stand; Ploughshare.

Weapons: Sword; Trident.

Architectural Devices: Column or Pillar; Temple.

Religious Symbols and Devices: Conch; Crescent; Fire-pot; Moon; *Pūrṇakumbha*; Sun; *Śrīvatsa*; Taurine; *Ujjain* symbol; Wheel.

Subsidiary Decorative Elements: Rayed circle border.

PALLAVAS

OBVERSE

Landscape Devices: River; Sea.

Floral Devices: Flower; Sheath of corn.

Faunal Devices: Boar; Bull; Horse; Lion; Fish; Snake; Tiger.

Human Figures: King?

Everyday Objects: Flag; Flag mast; Umbrella; Vase?

Jewellery: Chain (beaded or perforated); Crown; Garland; Necklace.

Weapons: Arrow; Bow; Sword; Trident.

Transportation Devices: Anchor of a ship.

Architectural Devices and Furniture: Column or Pillar; Platform or Pedestal; Temple *vimāna*; Throne.

Religious Symbols and Devices: Conch; Crescent; *Śrīvatsa*; Star; Sun.

Subsidiary Decorative Elements: Dotted border; Linear border; Rayed circle border.

REVERSE

Landscape Devices: Hill; River; Sea.

Floral Devices: Flower (including Lotus); Leaf (including leaf of banyan tree); Plant or sprout; Sheath of corn; Tree (including Mango tree).

Faunal Devices: Beetle; Boar; Elephant; Fish; Lion; Peacock; Snake; Tiger; Turtle or Tortoise.

Everyday Objects: Flag; Flag mast; Fly whisk; Lamp; Lamp-stand; Slat; *Udukkai* (a musical instrument); Umbrella; Vase.

Weapons: Arrow; Axe; Bow.

Transportation Devices: Boat; Ship.

Architectural Devices: Cistern; Column or pillar; *Ghaṭikā* (university)?; Harbour walls?; Pillared temple; Platform or Pedestal; Triple-celled temple.

Religious Symbols and Devices: Conch; Crescent; *Pūrṇakumbha*; *Śivaliṅga*; *Śrīvatsa*; Sun; *Svastika*; Wheel.

Geometric Designs: Circle; Rectangle; Square; Triangle?

Subsidiary Decorative Elements: Beaded border; Floriated border; Linear border; Rayed circle border.

APPENDIX II

A Note on the Coins of the Aṇḍipaṭṭi Hoard (Tamil Nadu)

In Chapter 6, we had mentioned that besides the Cheras, Cōḷas and Pāṇḍyas—the three main Sangam age (300 BC-AD 300) rulers of ancient Tamiḷakam (Tamil Nadu-Kerala region), there were a number of smaller rulers or chieftains who ruled over small territories in this region. Among them, the Malaiyamāns of Tirukoilur minted their own coins. We are not sure whether any of the other chieftains had their own currency. A comparatively little-known hoard discovered at Aṇḍipaṭṭi in northern Tamil Nadu may be the issues of another chieftain named Chendan who ruled in this area around the first century AD. Some scholars, however, attribute these coins to the Kalabhras, a dynasty that ruled the region after the Sangam age.

The Aṇḍipaṭṭi hoard contains 143 lead coins in an extremely worn-out condition. These coins are mostly circular and, sometimes, oval in shape. Their average diameter is 2.32 cm. Each coin weighs around 8 grams. The obverse of these coins features a prominent gateway consisting of two vertical columns. At the middle of each column, there is a small circular structure or ring projecting outwards (away from the gate). A ploughshare or goad is seen above this gateway. The obverse also features a legend encircling the gateway. This is in the Tamil language and Tamil Brāhmī script. Unlike the legends on all the other early south Indian coins, this one has been engraved in the anti-clockwise direction. It features the name of the chieftain. The reverse portrays two wavy lines, parallel to each other. These obviously denote a river or stream. The river is flanked on either side by a row of five hills. The gateway on the obverse of these coins is somewhat similar to the doorway or gateway on the obverse of some of the standing warrior (king?) type coins of the Sangam Cheras. Similarly, the hills and rivers on the reverse are comparable to the same devices appearing on Malaiyamān coins. The legends on the Aṇḍipaṭṭi coins have been read and interpreted in different ways by various epigraphists and numismatists.[1] These coins have sometimes been regarded as the prototypes of later Sātavāhana coins.

NOTE

1. For a survey of the opinions of different scholars on these coins and a bibliography on these coins, see P. Shanmugam, 'Lead Coins of Chendan',

MCS Special Bulletin XI (2004), pp. 193-9. Also see I.K. Sarma, *Religion in Art, and Historical Archaeology of South India: Contacts and Correlations* (Madras, 1987), pp. 16-17.

APPENDIX III

A Note on the Coins of the Kalabhras

The Kalabhras are believed to have ruled over parts of the Tamil land some time between AD 300 and 500. In history, their rule is often referred to as the dark ages—a term justified more due to the scanty information available about their reign than because of a general decline in the politico-administrative and socio-economic systems of the period, as is generally believed. A small number of coins attributed to this dynasty have recently come to light.[1] Some of them have been found in and around Madurai in Tamil Nadu.

One of the Kalabhra coins is a small square specimen whose sides measure 2 cm. Made of copper, it weight 7.45 grams. The obverse portrays a well-built tusker to the right; the trunk of the animal hangs downwards and terminates in an inward twist. Above the elephant, there is a legend in the Tamil language and Tamil-Brāhmī script. It has been written in an anti-clockwise direction. The legend reads *Kalapirā*, the last letter *rā* being written in the same style as the letters in the Bhattiprolu inscription (Andhra). The reverse of the coin is blank.

It is not astonishing to note that the coins of the Kalabhras have been greatly influenced by those of their immediate predecessors in Tamiḷakam. The elephant device would have been borrowed from the Sangam Cheras, Cōḷas and Pāṇḍyas. Stylistically, the elephant on Kalabhra coins is closest to that on Sangam Cōḷa issues.

At this juncture, mention may be made of an epigraphic discovery from Pulankurichi in the Ramanathapuram region in Tamil Nadu. This large rock inscription has been dated to the fourth century AD and assigned to a Kalabhra king. Incidentally, this is the only stone inscription unequivocally attributed to the Kalabhras. Close to and coeval with it, there are sketches of a trident on a lotus and a battle-axe engraved on the rock. Both these symbols may be royal emblems. These are stylistically not very different from the same symbols or figures on *kārṣāpaṇas*. It may be recalled that the trident was not unknown on Sangam Pāṇḍya coins. Significantly, the site of the present Kalabhra rock inscription lies within the territorial limits of the Sangam Pāṇḍyas. Future discoveries of coins and other antiquities of the Kalabhras can throw further light on the history and art of this obscure dynasty.

NOTE

1. For more details about Kalabhras, their coins and their Pulankurichi inscription, see I.K. Sarma, *Religion in Art, and Historical Archaeology of*

South India: Contacts and Correlations (Madras, 1987), pp. 16-17. Also see R. Krishnamurthy, 'Kalabhra Coin With a Legend', *JNSI* XLVIII 1 & 2 (1986), p. 48. For the latest interpretation of the contents of the Pulankurichi inscription, see I. Mahadevan, *Early Tamil Epigraphy: From the Earliest Times to the Sixth Century AD* (Chennai, 2003), p. 136. For some more details about the history of the Kalabhras, see K.A. Nilakanta Sastri, *The Cōḷas* (Madras, 2000), pp. 100-2. K.A. Thirugnanasampandam (Erode) has, in his private collection, a few coins that he wrongly attributes to the Kalabhras. These coins feature various symbols and devices such as the fish, boar, deer, tiger, flower, bow-arrow and the wheel.

APPENDIX IV

A Note on the Art in Roman Coins and their Imitations Found in India

Researches on Roman coins and their imitations discovered in India have been invariably confined to their significance from the point of view of the history of early trade.[1] Hence, almost all published works on the subject are silent on the obverse and reverse devices of these coins. So far, there have been very few attempts to classify or catalogue these coins on a typological basis.

The study of the artistic value of Roman coins in India is beset with several problems. First, only certain specific types or varieties of Roman coins have been found in India and, hence, it would be hazardous to generalize on any aspect of Roman numismatic art solely based on these finds. Also, the Roman coins discovered in India and brought to the notice of archaeologists and numismatists constitute a very small fraction of the total Roman currency exported to the Indian subcontinent. This is because the Indians melted substantial quantities of Roman aurei and denarii for the manufacture of jewellery, coins and other objects throughout the ancient and medieval periods and even later. Even among the known Roman coin finds in India, especially those reported during the nineteenth and early twentieth centuries, precise details about the various coin types represented in each of these finds are rarely recorded, and the present whereabouts of many of these coins are not known. Another major problem is that good quality photographs and descriptions of only a very small number of these coins have been published. Further, as Indian scholars are mostly unfamiliar with Roman numismatics and art, many of the Roman coins published by them have been wrongly attributed to certain emperors, and their legends incorrectly read and understood.[2]

At this juncture, it may be noted that there have been quite a few attempts to analyse Roman numismatic art based on the finds within Europe.[3] Since all the Roman coin types known in India are also seen among the discoveries in Europe, studies on European collections may be considered to be fairly comprehensive.

It is not the intention here to repeat all the general characteristics of Roman numismatic art, except for some important observations pertaining to Roman coin types which occur in large quantities among the Indian finds. Our emphasis would be on the imitation Roman coins in India, which, though numerically not too large, form a little-known and distinct group, especially with regard to artistic merit.

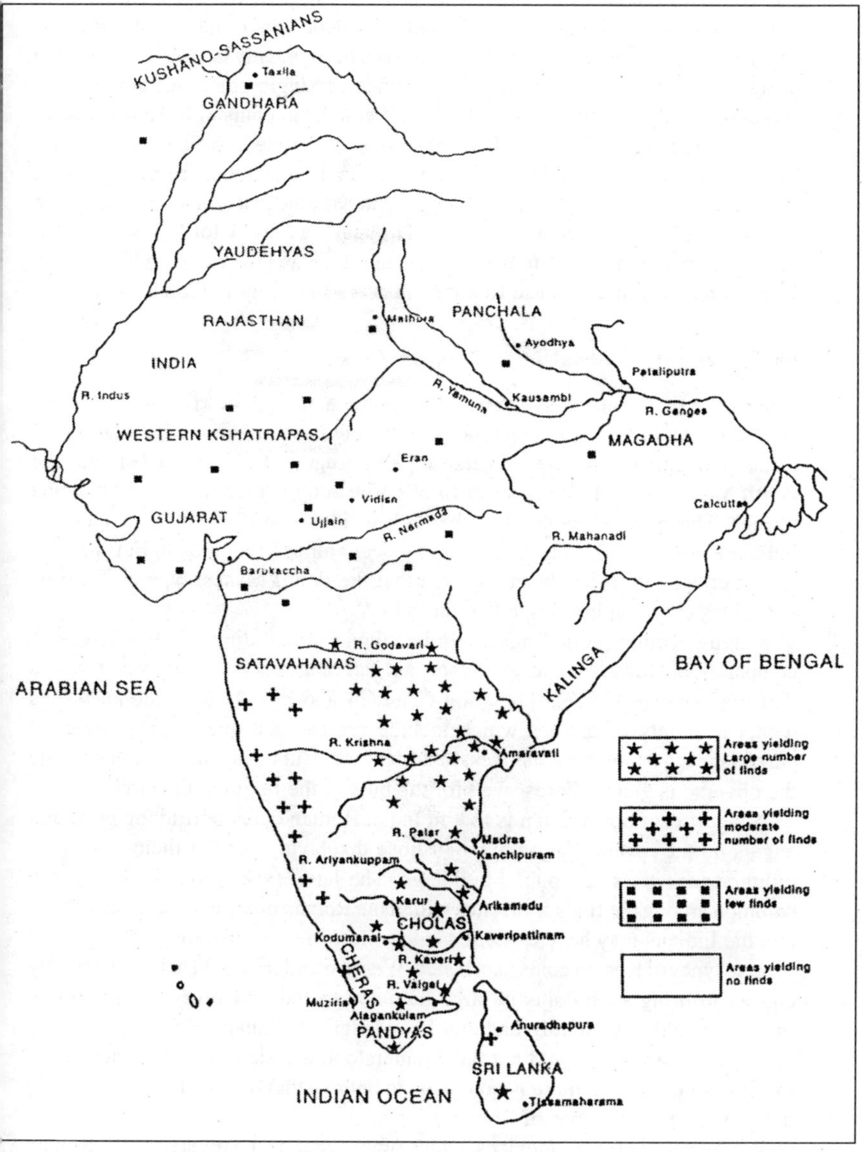

Map 2: Distribution of Roman coin finds in India

GENUINE ROMAN ISSUES

Republican Denarii

The earliest Roman coins found in India are the Republican denarii belonging to the second-first centuries BC—the period around which Indo-Mediterranean contacts are believed to have started. The coins occur mostly in large underground hoards and, rarely, as surface or stray finds of single coins but never in an archaeologically stratified context. These Republican coins in India are mostly so worn that the figures on them are often obliterated. Among the Roman Republican coins in India, the discoveries of single specimens from Ajaigadh in the Madhya Pradesh region, and Tiruppur and Krishnagiri(?) in Tamil Nadu, are noteworthy. The little-known coin from Tiruppur was struck for Julius Caesar in 46 BC at Africa. On this coin, the obverse and reverse devices are in high relief. The figures on some of these Republican coins betray early Greek influence.

Julio-Claudian and Post-Julio-Claudian Coins

Among the first century AD Roman coins in India, mainly in Andhra, Karnataka and Tamil Nadu, two common types, both in gold and silver, predominate—the Gaius and Lucius Caesares reverse type of Augustus (27 BC-AD 14), and the Pontif Maxim type of Tiberius (AD 14-37). The latter is more numerous than the former. The precise reasons for the high incidence of these two varieties in India are not clear. Both types frequently occur among the finds in Europe, too, but, interestingly, it has been reported that the Pontif Maxim type of Tiberius is far less common in Europe than in India.[4]

Among Roman coin finds in India, those post-dating Tiberius, though comparatively fewer in number, display a wider range of types. It may be recalled that the reverse of these late Julio-Claudian and post-Julio-Claudian issues depict a variety of themes which include princes and queens, mythological personages, architectural devices, historical incidents and war-weapons, while the obverse is generally reserved for the bust of the reigning monarch.

A significant observation is that in India, Roman coins portraying gods and angels on the reverse far outnumber those displaying secular themes such as military successes and public buildings. The latter types, are, however, very common among the finds from sites within the Roman empire. It has been opined that the Indians may have exhibited a definite preference for the god and angel reverse types of Roman coins and, hence, Western traders would have deliberately chosen to bring such coins in large numbers to India.[5] However, the ancient Indians would have hardly had any knowledge of Roman mythology, history or art and, therefore, could not have understood the significance of deities on foreign coins. Hence, there is no reason to believe that they had a special liking for certain specific types of Roman issues.

A few specific figures/devices, which often occur on the reverse of the Roman coins found in India, may be noted. The divine personages seen on them include

Peace-Nemesis, Jupiter, Minerva, Roma, Mars, Venus, Victory and Genius. It is interesting to note that two hitherto unknown coins—a badly worn Claudius (AD 41-54) issue of the Peace-Nemesis reverse type, and a broken and worn Nero (AD 54-68) coin of the usual oak-wreath reverse type—both belonging to the large Pudukkottai hoard (Tamil Nadu), have been traced to the collection of the Government Museum at Pudukkottai. These two coins have, however, recently been acquired by the Government Museum, Chennai.

A very limited number of Roman coins, mainly in gold, displaying architectural devices, have been reported from among the finds in south India, especially Tamil Nadu. Among these specimens, the majority are those portraying a triumphal arch surmounted by an equestrian statue on the reverse. Kottayam (Kerala), famous for its very large but poorly-documented Roman coin hoard (found in 1847), has recently yielded a stray find of a single, badly worn aureus of the triumphal arch reverse type, attributed to Nero (?). A rare aureus from the Nagavarappupadu hoard (Andhra) portrays, on the reverse, the frontal view of a large rampart. A shrine of Vesta is seen on a Nerovian aureus from Valuvally (Kerala). The temple of Janus appears on an aureus of the same ruler found in the Darmavaripalem (Andhra) hoard of 26 aurei.

Floral and faunal devices are uncommon among Roman coin finds in India. Two aureus types that are very rare in India—a Marciana obverse type issue of Trajan (AD 98-117) depicting an eagle on the reverse, and a Faustina obverse type of Antoninus Pius (AD 138-61) representing a peacock on the reverse—are known from the Valuvally hoard. The same hoard has also revealed a Sabina obverse type aureus of Hadrian (AD 117-38), portraying Juno and a peacock on the reverse. It is well known that the peacock was never found in Rome but was occasionally exported from south India to the west, where the bird was reared as a pet among ladies of the Roman aristocracy.

Roman coins displaying a royal bust both on the obverse and reverse are not unknown among south Indian finds. The Agrippina reverse aureus of Claudius from the Nagavarappupadu hoard may be cited as an example.

Metal

The earliest Roman coins to reach India were of silver. All the Republican issues, and the majority of Augustan and Tiberian finds in India, are of that metal. From the time of Gaius (AD 37-41), however, there is a gradual increase in the number of gold issues *vis-à-vis* silver ones. Apart from economic reasons, the insistence of Indians on the foreign gold money may also be linked to the fact that the aurei are artistically much superior to the denarii. Indeed, aurei looked so beautiful that a large number of these coins were pierced or looped to be used as ornaments, mainly pendants of necklaces, by Indians. Even the aurei hoard from Soriyapattu (Tamil Nadu) has revealed at least 12 coins with a rouleau loop attached to the top. Pierced and looped denarii have also been found in India but they are fewer than the pierced gold coins. Further, indigenous gold coinage was unknown in early historical south India and, hence, foreign gold issues were very much in demand, both for use as circulation money and jewellery, and also for preservation as objects of beauty or as curios.

Roman copper coins of the first two centuries of the Christian era are known in India but are very few in number. Those of the fourth-fifth centuries AD occur in substantial numbers in a limited number of sites such as Madurai and Karur in Tamil Nadu. The figures and devices on these small and unattractive late Roman coppers are often effaced because of the extreme corrosion of the metal. Most of these coins have not been correctly identified, studied or published. They have not attracted many coin collectors and museums.

IMITATION COINS

Distribution Pattern and Date

Imitations of Roman coins have been reported from nearly thirty sites, all confined to specific regions of western and southern India. It is plausible that a few more published finds also contained imitations, which were never identified and recorded. These occur in gold, silver, copper and lead. The copper imitations, though confined to the smallest number of sites, are the most numerous.

The earliest imitations in India are the silver copies of the common types of Augustus and Tiberius. Gold imitations of the Julio-Claudian period are extremely scarce. Imitations of the late first and second centuries AD are, however, all of gold and they represent a wide range of types. The copper imitations are mostly of the fourth-fifth centuries AD, and they often occur in association with genuine late Roman and Byzantine coppers at Madurai and Karur in Tamil Nadu.

Technique

Many of the known Roman imitation issues in India seem to have been die-struck. The existence of a possible die-link between various imitation coins of the Gumada hoard (Andhra) has also been suggested. A few imitations were also produced by the casting process.

It was originally believed that plated Roman coins or base metal coins plated with a silver or gold coating,—mainly the Gaius and Lucius Caesares reverse type denarii of Augustus,—were specially manufactured for the India trade. It has, however, now been confirmed that the majority of denarii in India, including those which have been identified as imitations, are not plated issues. Yet archaeological excavations at Peddabankur (Andhra) have brought to light, in stratified deposits, over 8 worn imitation Roman silver coins, some of them plated ones. Plated aurei are extremely scarce both in India and elsewhere, the only well-attested find of such a coin being the one from Kondapur (Andhra). This coin is artistically superior to most other Roman imitations in India.

Stylistic and Other Features

It would now be relevant to note a few important characteristics pertaining to gold and silver Roman imitations in India. Regarding the silver imitations, it may be said that all known denarii copies belong to the first century AD and are almost identical to the original ones in size, thickness, weight, and the purity and colour of the metal. Apparently, the makers tried their level best to reproduce all the features of the original coins on the copies. Yet they were incapable of correctly reading the legends on the genuine coins and this accounts for the few mistakes in the inscriptions on the copies. The main point of difference between the genuine and imitation denarii, however, is that the figures and devices on the latter are artistically of a lower standard than those on the former. This may again be precisely due to the fact that the manufacturers of these copies, being ignorant of Roman mythology and art, would have portrayed Roman rulers and divinities in a comparatively crude fashion.

Attempts to compare the imitation denarii finds in India and those reported from Europe have been made but there is no unanimity of opinion regarding the artistic value of the Indian imitations *vis-à-vis* those reported from the Danubian region and elsewhere.[6] There are opinions both for and against the theory that denarii copies in India are artistically superior to those reported from regions within the Roman empire. In any case, the Indian imitations differ from those discovered elsewhere with regard to weight and metallic composition.

The general characteristics of imitation Roman gold coins in India are a striking contrast to those of the denarii copies. Unlike the silver imitations, at least a few of the gold copies in India are totally different from the original Roman gold coins in size, fabric and weight. It is also pertinent to note that although the legends of both the gold and silver imitations are garbled, those on the denarii copies can be read and understood, and be matched with the legends on the corresponding genuine denarii. However, in the case of the majority of gold imitations, their legends hardly convey any meaning and, hence, cannot be unequivocally matched with those on any of the original Roman issues. This is most startlingly illustrated in the imitation aurei where the obverse legends consist of mere tiny, horizontal strokes and circles or dots, which have been engraved merely to indicate the presence of legends, without conveying any meaning whatsoever. Again, unlike denarii copies, the gold imitations often exhibit known obverse and reverse types but in impossible combinations. To cite an example, an imitation aureus discovered in south India, bearing an obverse type of Septimius Severus (AD 193-211) and a reverse type of Marcus Aurelius (AD 161-80).

Compared to the silver copies, gold imitations are more widespread. While all the denarii imitations in India are of the first century AD, the gold copies range in date from the first century AD to the fourth century AD and even later. Not surprisingly, the stylistic features and artistic value of all known silver imitations are almost identical, whereas the gold copies belonging to varied periods and regions exhibit wide variations in style.

One is able to observe a direct correlation between the artistic merit of the Indian imitations and that of the corresponding genuine Roman gold and silver issues. For instance, we have already noted that original Roman gold coins were artistically of a higher standard than the genuine denarii. The known gold copies are also of a superior level of artistic workmanship than denarii copies. Similarly, it is well known that compared to the obverse, the reverse motifs on genuine Roman coins were treated with less care by the minter because a mediocre standard of technical achievement was considered sufficient for the reverse themes. Hence, the reverse figures and devices are generally not as aesthetically appealing as the royal bust on the obverse. The same phenomenon is discernible in the case of the Indian imitations, too. Besides, the makers of imitations always reproduced the complete obverse or reverse types on the copies and did not, under any circumstances, add or alter the decorative features and/or attributes pertaining to any of the figures appearing on the genuine coins.

Regarding copper imitations, these form a distinct group. The dumpy figures on the worn, tiny copper copies are, in most instances, partially out of the flan and not of much artistic value.

SLASH-MARKS AND COUNTERMARKS ON ROMAN COINS

The two features peculiar to Roman coins discovered in India are the countermarks and slash-marks found on a few of the specimens. These marks occur both on the gold and silver issues, as also on the genuine and imitation ones. Small countermarks, some of them resembling the symbols on *kārṣāpaṇas*, have been noticed on some of the Roman coins found in Tamil Nadu and Andhra Pradesh (Plates 34, 35). The phenomenon seems to be far more widespread than is

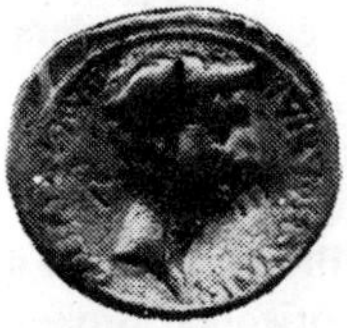

Plate 34: Roman emperor Augustus coin—bust obverse; vertical slash-mark, countermarked with the letters 'R' and 'E'.
(Photo: Department of Coins and Medals, The British Museum, London)

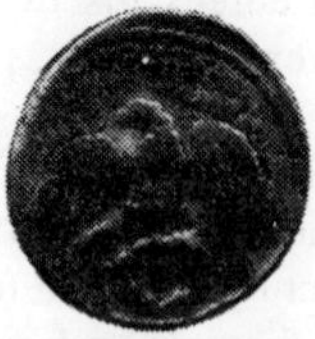

Plate 35: Roman emperor Augustus coin—eagle on oak-wreath reverse.
(Photo: Department of Coins and Medals, The British Museum, London)

generally believed. The exact purpose of these markings is not known. From the numismatic art point of view, these countermarks are not aesthetically pleasing to the eye. Many of them are small, irregular, asymmetrical and crudely executed. Often, the marks are placed right on the obverse or reverse figures, thus marring their main features.

Slash-marks effected by a knife or blade are seen on some of the Roman coin finds in south India. Several coins from the finds at Tondamanathan (Tamil Nadu), and Nandyal and Penuganchiprolu (Andhra), have been slashed. The reason for the defacement of these coins is still hotly debated. In any case, it is clear that the incisions, deliberately placed on the obverse bust, obliterate many of the finer details of the head. Many of the slash-marks are very deep and ugly-looking, and they often bend and even break the coin.

CONCLUDING REMARKS

The present study has confirmed that only a few of the many known types of genuine Roman coins occur in India. A physical examination of Roman denarii, aurei, solidi and copper coins in various collections has revealed that a muscular and robust physiognomy characterize the gods and kings depicted on them. The only remote precedent for this is, in isolated instances, from the early Hellenistic tradition. Objective naturalism also seems to have played a part in the delineation of figures and devices, especially during the Julio-Claudian period. The figures on the coins of subsequent centuries become increasingly stylized.

In Andhra-Tamil Nadu, the most beautiful and well-preserved Roman coins are the Nerovian aurei, displaying, on the obverse, the bust of the youthful and handsome Nero with a bare head. The typical Roman nose—protruding and pointed—is also best represented on the portrait coins of Nero.

A large number of the early Roman coins found in India were produced at Lugdunum, which was one of the most important eastern mints of the Roman empire. It may be recalled that Roman issues of these mints are considered aesthetically more appealing, probably because of the higher level of artistic skill of the minters in the east. Of course, Roman coins from other mints such as Rome and Tarraco are also known in south India.

Imitation Roman coins, whether in gold, silver or copper, are definitely of a lower standard of artistic merit than the genuine coins. In fact, the figures on the two imitation aurei attributed to Constantine I (AD 307-37) in the Gumada hoard (Andhra) appear to be like thumb-nail sketches, devoid of any illusion of depth or sense of movement. The busts on these two coins are stylistically akin to those on the gold issues of Theodosius II (AD 402-50) some of which have been found in south India.

Roman coins exercised immense influence on the coinage of ancient south India. The portrait coins of the Sātavāhanas, Sangam Cheras and Pāṇḍyas are believed to have been inspired by the royal busts on Roman coins.

NOTES AND REFERENCES

1. Bibliographies of the Roman coin finds in India have appeared in a series of earlier publications and, hence, are not repeated here. For a good bibliography, see P.J. Turner, *Roman Coins From India* (London, 1989), pp. 144-52; S. Suresh, *Roman Antiquities in Tamil Nadu* (Madras, 1992), pp. 88-94; idem, *Symbols of Trade: Roman and Pseudo-Roman Objects Found in India* (New Delhi, 2004), pp. 185-94.
2. In K.V. Raman, 'Roman Coins From Tamil Nadu', *SSIC* II (1992), pp. 19-34, a coin of Diocletian has been wrongly identified as an issue of Hadrian (?) (plate II, n. 17). In I.K. Sarma, 'Roman Coins From Andhra Pradesh: Their Contexts, Chronology and Cultural Significance', *SSIC* II (1992), pp. 35-50, an aureus of Claudius has been assigned to Constantine the Great (plate III, n. 1). Again, in V.V. Krishna Sastry, *Roman Gold Coins: Recent Discoveries in Andhra Pradesh* (Hyderabad, 1992), despite the author's admirable efforts, quite a few errors, mainly pertaining to the legends and figures on the coins, have crept in. The incomplete and often wrong identification of the coins, when they are initially published, has frequently led to confusion because subsequent researchers, who may not have access to the relevant coins, invariably rely on these published accounts.
3. For a brief survey of the literature on Roman numismatic art, refer to Chapter 1 of this volume.
4. Peter Berghaus, 'Roman Coins from India and their Imitations', in Amal Kumar Jha, ed., *Coinage, Trade and Economy* (Nashik, 1991), pp. 108-21.
5. T. Sathyamurthy, *Catalogue of Roman Gold Coins (In the Collections of Department of Archaeology, Kerala)* (Thiruvananthapuram, 1992), p. 8.
6. See P.J. Turner 1989 (supra n. 1), pp. 37-41 and Peter Berghaus 1991 (supra n. 4), pp. 108-21. Turner's opinion is that the imitations found in India are artistically superior to the Danubian copies. On the other hand, Peter Berghaus asserts that the Roman coins have been imitated in India in a rather barbarous style, which is very different from the style of the imitations from Europe. Also see Peter Berghaus, 'An Indian Imitation of an Augustean Denarius', in D.C. Bhattacharyya and D. Handa, eds., *Prāćī-Prabhā, Perspectives in Indology: Essays in Honour of Prof. B.N. Mukherjee* (New Delhi, 1989), pp. 101-5.

Select Bibliography

Allchin, F.R. et al., *The Archaeology of Early Historic South Asia: The Emergence of Cities and States* (Cambridge, 1995).

Beck, Elisabeth, compiled, *Sri Aurobindo on Indian Art: Selections from his Writings* (Ahmedabad, 1999).

Begley, V., 'Arikamedu Reconsidered', *AJA* 87 (1983), pp. 461-81.

——, 'Rouletted Ware at Arikamedu: A New Approach', *AJA* 92 (1988), pp. 427-40.

——, 'Ceramic Evidence for Pre-*Periplus* Trade on the Indian Coasts', in V. Begley and Richard Daniel De Puma, eds., *Rome and India: The Ancient Sea Trade* (Madison, 1991), pp. 157-96.

Berghaus, Peter, 'An Indian Imitation of an Augustean Denarius', in D.C. Bhattacharyya and D. Handa, eds., *Prācī-Prabhā, Perspectives in Indology: Essays in Honour of Prof. B.N. Mukherjee* (New Delhi, 1989), pp. 101-5.

——, 'Roman Coins from India and their Imitations', in Amal Kumar Jha, ed., *Coinage, Trade and Economy* (Nashik, 1991), pp. 108-21.

Berkson, Carmel, *The Life of Form in Indian Sculpture* (New Delhi, 2000).

Biddulph, C.H., *Coins of the Pāṇḍyas* (Varanasi, 1966).

Bopearachchi, Osmund, *Indo-Greek, Indo-Scythian and Indo-Parthian Coins in the Smithsonian Institution* (Washington, D.C., 1993).

——, 'Archaeological Evidence on Changing Patterns of International Trade Relations of Ancient Sri Lanka', in Osmund Bopearachchi and D.P.M. Weerakkody, eds., *Origin, Evolution and Circulation of Foreign Coins in the Indian Ocean* (New Delhi, 1998), pp. 133-78.

Bopearachchi, Osmund and Rajah M. Wickremesinhe, *Ruhuna: An Ancient Civilisation Re-visited: Numismatic and Archaeological Evidence on Inland and Maritime Trade* (Colombo?,1999).

Breglia, Laura, *Roman Imperial Coins: Their Art and Technique* (London, 1968).

Casson, L., 'P.Vindob G 40822 and the Shipping of Goods From India', *Bulletin of the American Society of Papyrologists* 23 (1986), pp. 73-9.

——, 'New Light on Maritime Loans: P.Vindob G.40822', in Ranabir Chakravarti, ed., *Trade in Early India* (New Delhi, 2001), pp. 228-43.

Champakalakshmi, R., 'From Kuṛiñci to Tamiḷakam: The Universalisation and Emergence of Sacred Geography in the Cult of Murukan', Paper presented at the first international conference seminar on Skanda-Murukan (Madras, 1998).

Chandra, D.K., *The Mystery of Art* (Delhi, 1995).

Chattopadhyaya, Brajadulal, *Coins and Currency Systems in South India c. AD 225-1300* (New Delhi, 1977).

Cimino, R.M. and F. Scialpi, *India and Italy (Exhibition Organised in Collaboration With the Archaeological Survey of India and the Indian Council for Cultural Relations)* (Rome, 1974).

Codrington, H.W., *Ceylon Coins and Currency: Memoirs of the Colombo Museum*, Series A, No. 3 (Colombo, 1924; rpt. 1975).

Das, D. Jithendra, 'Sātavāhana Coins From the *Mahā Stupa* Excavation at Kanganhalli in Karnataka', *SSIC* XI (2001), pp. 36-48.

Dasa, Asimakrishna, *Evening Blossoms: The Temple Tradition of Sāñjhī in Vṛndāvana* (New Delhi, 1996).

Deraniyagala, S.,'The Citadel of Anuradhapura 1969: Excavations in the Gedige Area', *Ancient Ceylon* 2 (1972), pp. 48-170.

Desakachari, T., *South Indian Coins* (Trichinopoly (Tiruchi), 1933).

Dhopate, Shashikant G., 'Half Denomination Silver Portrait Coin of Yajna Satakarni', *SSIC* XIII (2003), pp. 20-2.

——, 'Silver Portrait Coin of (Gautamiputra) Kumbha Satakarni', *SSIC* XIV (2004), pp. 41-3.

Gangoly, O.C., *Andhra Sculptures* (Hyderabad, 1973).

Gokhale, Shobhana, 'Junnar in Trade During Sātavāhana Period', in Amal Kumar Jha, ed., *Coinage Trade and Economy* (Nashik, 1991), pp. 55-7.

——, 'Elephant and Vase Type Coin of Kochhiputa Satakarni', *SSIC* II (1992), pp. 107-10.

Gopalachari, K., *Early History of the Andhra Country* (Madras, 1976).

Guillaume, Olivier, *Analysis of Reasonings in Archaeology: The Case of Graeco-Bactrian and Indo-Greek Numismatics* (New Delhi, 1990).

Gupta, P.L., *Punch-marked Coins in the Andhra Pradesh Government Museum* (Hyderabad, 1960).

——, *The Amaravati Hoard of Silver Punch Marked Coins* (Hyderabad 1963).

——, *The Early Coins From Kerala* (Trivandrum, 1988).

——, *Coins* (New Delhi, 2000).

Gupta. P.L. and T.R. Hardaker, *Ancient Indian Silver Punch-marked Coins of the Magadha-Maurya Kārṣāpaṇa Series* (Nashik, 1985).

Gurumurthy, S., *Ceramic Traditions in South India (Down to 300 AD)* (Madras, 1981).

——, *Deciphering the Indus Script (From Graffiti on Ancient Indian Pottery)* (Madras, 1999).

Harrauer, H., and P.J. Sijpesteijn, 'Ein neues Dokument Zu Roms Indienhandel: P.Vindob. G 40822', *Anzeiger der Akademie der Wissenschaften, Wien, Philologisch-historische Klasse* 122 (1985), pp. 124-55.

James, Josef, ed., *Contemporary Indian Sculpture: An Algebra of Figuration* (Madras, 1998).

Jeyaraj, V., 'A Technical Study on a Pallava Lead Coin', *SSIC* I (1991), pp. 121-3.

——, 'Physico-chemical Examination of two Punch-marked Coins', *SSIC* II (1992), pp. 159-63.

Kasinathan, Natana et al., *Alagankulam: A Preliminary Report* (Madras, 1992).

Kasinathan, Natana and A. Abdul Majeed, *Thirukkoyilur Excavation* (Madras, 1996).

Kasturi, Prema and S. Suresh, 'Women in Coinage: A Socio-iconographic Study With Special Reference to South India', *MCS Special Bulletin* XI (2004), pp. 235-44.

Knox, Robert, *Amaravati: Buddhist Sculpture From the Great Stupa* (London, 1992).

Krishnamurthy, R., 'Kalabhra Coin With a Legend', *JNSI* XLVIII 1&2 (1986), p. 48.

——, *Sanga Kāla Cōḷar Nāṇayangal* (Tamil) (Madras, 1986).

——, *Pāṇḍiyar Peruvaḷudi Nāṇayangal* (Tamil) (Madras, 1987).

——, 'Sangam Period "Malayaman" Coins', *JNSI* XLIX 1 & 2 (1987), pp. 41-3.

——, *Sangakāla Malaiyamān Nāṇayangal* (Tamil) (Madras, 1990).

——, 'A Rare Sangam Period Chola Coin', *SSIC* I (1991), pp. 31-2.

——, 'Oblong Copper Coin With "Mother Goddess" Symbol From Karur, Tamil Nadu', *JNSI* LIII 1 & 2 (1991), pp. 59-61.

——, 'Two More Pallava Coins With Legends', *JNSI* LIII 1 & 2 (1991), pp. 62-3.

——, 'Mākkōtai Coins', *SSIC* II (1992), pp. 89-93.

——, *Sangam Age Tamil Coins* (Madras, 1997).

——, 'A Note on Counterstruck Silver Coin of Mākkōtai', *SSIC* VIII (1998), pp. 35-9.

——, *The Pallava Coins* (Madras, 2004).

——, 'Sangam Age Pāṇḍya Coins With Legend Peruvaluthi in the National Museum, Colombo', *SSIC* XV (2005), pp. 58-63.

Krishnamurthy, R. and Mohd. Safiullah, 'A Satavahana Lead Coin With Bow and Arrow Symbol', *SSIC* XV (2005), pp. 35-8.

Lahiri, A.N., 'Numismatography of Punch-marked Coins', in C. Mani, ed., *A Macro Study of Early Indian Coins* (Delhi, 1999), pp. 33-44.

Lal, B.B., 'Śiśupālgarh 1948: An Early Historical Fort in Eastern India', *AI* 5 (1949), pp. 62-102.

Lockwood, Michael, *Māmallapuram: A Guide to the Monuments* (Madras, 1993).

Lockwood, Michael and A. Vishnu Bhat, 'The *Birudas* of Mahēndravarman', Paper presented at the third annual Congress of the Epigraphical Society of India (Udupi, 1977).

Lockwood, Michael, et al., *Pallava Art* (Madras, 2001).

Mahadevan, I., *Early Tamil Epigraphy: From the Earliest Times to the Sixth Century* AD (Madras, 2003).

Maity, S.K., *Early Indian Coins and Currency System* (New Delhi, 1970).

Mangalam, S.J., 'Satavahana Terracottas From Paithan', in P. Sitapati and V.V. Krishna Sastry, eds., *Satavahana Seminar Souvenir* (Hyderabad, 1981), p. 53.

——, 'New Discoveries of Viṣṇukuṇḍin Coins From Maharashtra', Paper presented at the Colloquium on *South Indian Archaeology* (Hyderabad, 1990).

——, 'A Unique Inscribed Viṣṇukuṇḍin Coin From Vidarbha', *SSIC* I (1991), pp. 81-6.

Mattingly, H., *Coins of the Roman Empire in the British Museum,* Vol. I: *Augustus to Vitellius* (London, 1965).

Minakshi, C., *The Historical Sculptures of the Vaikuṇṭhaperumāḷ Temple, Kāñchi* (Delhi, 1941).

——, *Administration and Social Life Under the Pallavas* (Madras, 1977).

Mukherjee, B.N., *Nana on Lion: A Study in Kushana Numismatic Art* (Calcutta, 1969).

——, *Kushana Coins of the Land of the Five Rivers* (Calcutta, 1978).

——, *Art in Gupta and Post-Gupta Coinages of Northern India* (Lucknow, 1985).

——, *The Indian Gold: An Introduction to the Cabinet of the Gold Coins in the Indian Museum* (Calcutta, 1990).

——, ed., *Numismatic Art of India,* Vol. I: *Historical and Aesthetic Perspectives* (New Delhi, 2007).

——, ed., *Numismatic Art of India,* Vol. II: *An Album of the Masterpieces of Indian Coins* (New Delhi, 2007).

Mukherjee, B.N. and P.K.D. Lee, *Technology of Indian Coinage* (Calcutta, 1988).

Mukherjee, Chhanda, *Gupta Numismatic Art: An Artistic and Iconographic Study* (Delhi, 1991).

Munirathnam, K., 'A Lead Coin From Andhra Pradesh', *SSIC* XII (2002), p. 16.

Nagaswamy, R., *Tamil Coins: A Study* (Madras, 1981).

——, 'Alagankulam: An Indo-Roman Trading Port', in C. Margabandhu, K.S. Ramachandran, A.P. Sagar and D.K. Sinha, eds., *Indian Archaeological Heritage, Shri K.V. Soundara Rajan Felicitation Volume* I (New Delhi, 1991), pp. 247-54.

——, *Roman Karur: A Peep into Tamils' Past* (Madras, 1995).

Nagaswamy, R. and A. Abdul Majeed, *Vasavasamudram (A Report on the Excavation Conducted by the Tamil Nadu State Department of Archaeology)* (Madras, 1978).

Narasimha Murthy, A.V., 'Numismatic Studies in Karnataka', *SSIC* I (1991), pp. 99-120.

——, *Some Aspects of Early Historic Archaeology and Numismatics of Karnataka* (Madras, 1991).

Narasimman, K.T., 'Recent Discoveries Made by Chennai Circle During This Decade', in K. Damodaran, ed., *Tamil Nadu: Archaeological Perspectives* (Madras, 1999), pp. 156-62.

Natarajan, Avvai and Natana Kasinathan, *Art Panorama of Tamils* (Madras, 1993).

Pal, Pratapaditya, 'A Sacrificial Horse and a Mysterious Script', *South Asian Studies* 3 (1987), pp. 47-52.

Pillay, K.K., *A Social History of the Tamils* I (Madras, 1975).

Pushparatnam, P., 'Sankam Age Coins Found in Sri Lanka', Paper presented at the international seminar on Tamil Nadu and Sri Lanka: New Evidence on Maritime and Inland Trade (Madras, 2004).

Radhakrishnan, P.V., 'A Punch-marked Die From Karur', *SSIC* IV (1994), pp. 51-6.

——, 'Chronology of Silver Punchmarked Coins in South India', *SSIC* VIII (1998), pp. 27-34.

Rajan, K., 'A Chronological Note on the Punch-marked Coins of Tamil Nadu', *SSIC* I (1991), pp. 17-22.

Rajavelu, S., 'A New Copper Coin of Satakarni From Madurai', *MCS Special Bulletin* XI (2004), pp. 200-2.

Rajesh, M. and T. Arun Raj, 'Some Observations on Seṅgamēdu: A Hinterland Trade Centre of Arikamēdu, Tamil Nadu, India', *Circle of Inner Asian Art, SOAS Newsletter* 17 (2003), pp. 17-22.

Ramachandran, C.E., *Ahanānūru in its Historical Setting* (Madras, 1974).

Raman, K.V., 'Excavations at Pumpuhar', in *The Handbook (II International Tamil Conference)* (Madras, 1968), pp. 238-40.

——, ed., *Excavations at Uraiyur (Tiruchirappalli) 1965-69* (Madras, 1988).

——, 'Further Evidence of Roman Trade From Coastal Sites in Tamil Nadu', in V. Begley and Richard Daniel De Puma, eds., *Rome and India: The Ancient Sea Trade* (Madison, 1991), pp. 125-33.

——,'Roman Coins From Tamil Nadu', *SSIC* II (1992), pp. 19-34.

——, 'An Early Chola Coin From Arikamedu', *SSIC* III (1993), pp. 87-8.

Raman, K.V. and P. Shanmugam, 'Terracotta Coin Moulds From Kanchipuram', *SSIC* I (1991), pp. 23-9.

——, 'Pallava Coin Moulds From Kanchipuram Excavations', *SSIC* V (1995), pp. 77-80.

Ramasamy, Vidwan I., 'Ancient Chera Coin Found (Globule)', *JNSI* LIII 1 & 2 (1991), pp. 64-5.

Rangarajan, Haripriya, 'The Significance of Ujjaini Symbol', *SSIC* IX (1999), pp. 14-22.

Rangarajan, L.N., *Kautilya: The Arthashastra* (New Delhi, 1992).

Rao, C. Somasundara, 'A Note on Bilingual Legends on Sātavāhana Coins', *SSIC* VII (1997), pp. 17-21.

Rao, M. Rama, *Select Sātavāhana Coins in the Government Museum, Madras* (Madras, 1959; rpt. 2000).

——, *Sātavāhana Coins in the Andhra Pradesh Government Museum Hyderabad* (Hyderabad, 1961).

——, *Viṣṇukuṇḍin Coins in the Andhra Pradesh Government Museum, Hyderabad* (Hyderabad, 1963).

Ravishankar, T.S., 'A Note on Three Ikshvāku Coins', *SSIC* X (2000), pp. 32-6.

Ray, S.C., *Stratigraphic Evidence of Coins in Indian Excavations and Some Allied Issues* (Varanasi, 1959).

Reddy, D. Raja, 'An Overview of Andhra Region Coins', *SSIC* XV (2005), pp. 7-29.

Reddy, D. Raja and P. Suryanarayana Reddy, 'Andhra Coins: A Bibliography', *SSIC* XIII (2003), pp. 91-125.

Sahay, B.K., 'Portrait Coins of Sātavāhanas: A Reappraisal', *JNSI* LIII 1&2 (1991), pp. 30-1.

Samuel, John et al., eds., *The First International Conference Seminar on Skanda-Murukan-1998 Souvenir* (Madras, 1998).

Santhi, R., 'Sangakāla Pāṇḍyarkalin Cheppu Kāśugal (Tamil)', *MCS Special Bulletin* VIII (2001), pp. 12-15.

Sarasan, Beena, 'An Unique Punch Marked Coin of Venad', *SSIC* XV (2005), pp. 30-4.

Sarkar, H. and S.P. Nainar, *Amaravati* (New Delhi, 1972).

Sarkar, H. and B.N. Misra, *Nagarjunakonda* (New Delhi, 1980).

Sarma, I.K., *Coinage of the Sātavāhana Empire* (Delhi, 1980).

——, *Religion in Art, and Historical Archaeology of South India: Contacts and Correlations* (Madras, 1987).

——, 'Sātavāhana Coins From Paithan and Connected Problems', *SSIC* I (1991), pp. 33-43.

——, 'Roman Coins From Andhra Pradesh: Their Contexts, Chronology and Cultural Significance', *SSIC* II (1992), pp. 35-50.

——, 'Viṣṇukuṇḍin Coins From Peddavegi Excavations and Related Issues', *ND* XVI (1992), pp. 95-111.

——, 'A Critical Study of the Numismatic Evidences From Nagarjunakonda Excavations', *SSIC* IV (1994), pp. 63-78.

——, 'An Appraisal of Recent Discoveries of South Indian Coins', *SSIC* V (1995), pp. 9-27.

——, 'Coins From Peddavegi Excavations (1985-87)', *SSIC* VI (1996), pp. 49-65.

——, 'Coins From Amaravati Excavations', *SSIC* VIII (1998), pp. 44-57.

——, 'A Critical Assessment of the Coinage of the Sātavāhanas: Sequence and Dating', *SSIC* XI (2001), pp. 18-27.

Sastri, K.A. Nilakanta, *The Cōḷas* (Madras, 2000).

——, *A History of South India: From Prehistoric Times to the Fall of Vijayanagara* (New Delhi, 2002).

Sastry, V.V. Krishna, ed., *Annual Report of the Department of Archaeology & Museums, Government of Andhra Pradesh, 1976-77* (Hyderabad, 1978).

Sastry, V.V. Krishna, *Roman Gold Coins: Recent Discoveries in Andhra Pradesh* (Hyderabad, 1992).

Sathyamurthy, T., *Catalogue of Roman Gold Coins (In the Collections of Department of Archaeology, Kerala)* (Thiruvananthapuram, 1992).

——,'Angamali Hoard of Silver Punch-marked Coins', *SSIC* IV (1994), pp. 45-50.

——, 'Numismatic Evidences From Archaeological Excavations: Chennai Circle', *SSIC* XV (2005), pp. 110-18.

Seneviratne, S.,'The Ecology and Archaeology of the Seruwila Copper-Magnetite Prospect, North East Sri Lanka', in Jonathan Mark Kenoyer, ed., *From Sumer to Meluhha: Contributions to the Archaeology of South and South West Asia in Memory of George F. Dales, Jr. (Wisconsin Archaeological Reports 3)* (Madison, 1994), pp. 261-80.

——, 'The Ecology and Archaeology of the Seruwila Copper-Magnetite Prospect, North East Sri Lanka', *The Sri Lanka Journal of the Humanities* XXI 1 & 2 (1995), pp. 114-45.

Seyone, K.N.V., *Some Old Coins Found in Early Ceylon (Sri Lanka),* Part III-XI (Colombo?,1998).

Shanmugam, P., 'Two Coins of Tamil Origin From Thailand', *SSIC* IV (1994), pp. 95-100.

——, 'Sangam Pāṇḍya Coins in Sri Lanka', *SSIC* XIV (2004), pp. 30-40.

——,'Tamil Nadu Coins: A Bibliography', *SSIC* XIV (2004), pp. 120-59.

——, 'Lead Coins of Chendan', *MCS Special Bulletin* XI (2004), pp. 193-9.

——, 'Two Inscribed Coins of the Sangam Age Cheras', *SSIC* XV (2005), pp. 53-7.

Shanmugam, P. and S. Raman, 'A River Goddess Coin From Karur', *SSIC* XI (2001), pp. 62-4.

Sharma, Savita, *Early Indian Symbols: Numismatic Evidence* (Delhi, 1990).

Shastri, A.M., ed., *Foreign Elements in Indian Indigenous Coins* (Varanasi, 1982).

——, 'Presidential Address (International Colloquium on Coinage, Trade and Economy)', in Amal Kumar Jha, ed., *Coinage, Trade and Economy* (Nashik, 1991), pp. XI-XXIII.

——, 'Sātavāhana Silver Coinage', *SSIC* I (1991), pp. 45-60.

——, 'Kondapur: A Sātavāhana Silver Coins Mint', *SSIC* III (1993), pp. 81-5.

——, 'Three Sātavāhana Mint-Towns', *SSIC* IV (1994), pp. 57-62.

——, 'On an Enigmatic Khaharata Coin', *SSIC* VI (1996), pp. 19-23.

——, 'An Unique Identity Ring From Karur', *SSIC* XI (2001), pp. 57-9.

Sircar, D.C., 'Silver Coin of Vasishthi-putra Satakarni', *Epigraphica Indica* 35 (1963-4), pp. 247-52.

Sitholey, B.S., 'The Art of Gupta Coins', *JNSI* X 2 (1948), pp. 119-31.

Sitaraman, Arumuga and Sankaran Raman, *Pallavar Kāśugal* (Tamil) (Tanjavur, 2002).

Sitrampalam, S.K., 'A Note on the Lakshmi Plaques of Sri Lanka', *SSIC* II (1992), pp. 151-8.

Sivaramamurti, C., *Mahabalipuram* (New Delhi, 1978).

——, *Numismatic Parallels of Kālidāsa* (New Delhi, 1983).

Srinivasan, K.R., *Cave Temples of the Pallavas* (New Delhi, 1964).

Srivastava, A.L., 'Use of Auspicious Motifs in Indian Epigraphs', *Bulletin of the Assam State Museum* V (1985), pp. 1-18.

Srivastava, Prashant, *Aspects of Ancient Indian Numismatics* (Delhi, 1996).

Subrahmanyam, R., *A Catalogue of the Ikshvaku Coins in the Andhra Pradesh Government Museum* (Hyderabad, 1979).

Suresh, S.,'Defence Architecture in the Early Tamil Country', *Proceedings of the Indian History Congress: Forty-ninth Session, 1988* (Delhi, 1989), pp. 657-61.

——, 'Roman Vestiges in Kanchipuram', in Nanditha Krishna, ed., *Kanchi: A Heritage of Art and Religion* (Madras, 1992), pp. 56-61.

——, *Roman Antiquities in Tamil Nadu* (Madras, 1992).

——, 'Early Roman Finds in Madras City', in G.J. Sudhakar, ed., *Aspects of Madras: A Historical Perspective* (Madras, 1993), pp. 13-16.

——,'Vishnu in South Indian Coinage', in G. Kamalakar, ed., *Vishnu in Art, Thought and Literature* (Hyderabad, 1993), pp. 273-8.

——, 'Recent Archaeological Discoveries and Studies in Tamil Nadu', *Quarterly Bulletin of the School of Historical and Cultural Studies, Calcutta,* I 3-4 (1994-5), pp. 11-16.

——, 'Roman Coins Found in India: A Study of the Countermarks', Paper presented at the international seminar on Trade and Economy of Ancient Sri Lanka, India and South-East Asia: Archaeological and Literary Evidence (Colombo, 1999).

——, 'Roman Denarii Hoard From Koneripatti, Tamil Nadu', *The Quarterly Review of Historical Studies,* XXXIX, 1 & 2 (1999), pp. 1-6. Same paper also published in S. Rajagopal, ed., *Kaveri: Studies in Epigraphy, Archaeology and History (Prof. Y. Subbarayalu Felicitation Volume)* (Madras, 2001), pp. 267-72.

——, 'Numismatic Studies: New Methodologies and Approaches (Summary of Presidential Address delivered at the Seminar of the Madras Coin Society)', *MCS, Chennai: Special Bulletin* VIII (2001), pp. 1-3.

——, 'Religion and Trade: Spread of Jainism in Ancient AndhraDesa and Tamiḷakam', in Haripriya Rangarajan, G. Kamalakar and A.K.V.S. Reddy, eds., *Jainism: Art, Architecture, Literature and Philosophy* (Delhi, 2001), pp. 321-7.

——, 'Countermarks on Roman Coins Found in India: Context, Chronology and Significance', *Indian History Congress: Proceedings of the LXII Session*, (2002), pp. 976-85.

——, *Symbols of Trade: Roman and Pseudo-Roman Objects Found in India* (New Delhi, 2004).

——, 'Kārtikeya in Early Indian Coinage', in K.V. Ramesh et al., eds., *Śrī Puṣpāñjali (Recent Researches in Prehistory, Protohistory, Art, Architecture, Numismatics, Iconography and Epigraphy) Dr. C.R. Srinivasan Commemoration Volume* I (Delhi, 2004), pp. 95-102.

——, 'A Note on the Temple Tokens of Late Medieval South India', *MCS, Chennai—Special Bulletin XI* (2004), pp. 162-6.

——, 'Muziris to Arikamedu: Roman Trails in South India', Paper presented at the international conference on Arikamedu Archaeological Heritage: Cultural and Technological Valorisation' (Pondicherry, 2004).

——, 'Early Roman Trade With South Asia: A Study Based on Recent Explorations in South India and Sri Lanka', Paper presented at the international seminar on Tamil Nadu and Sri Lanka: New Evidence on Maritime and Inland Trade (Madras, 2004).

——, 'The Devarāja Concept in Ancient Tamiḷakam: Numismatic and Art Historical Evidences', in Arputha Rani Sengupta, ed., *God and King: The Devarāja Cult in South Asian Art and Architecture* (New Delhi, 2005), pp. 129-37.

——, 'Counter-marks of Buddhist Symbols on the Roman Coins Found in Andhra Desa', in G. Kamalakar and M. Veerender, eds., *Buddhism: Art, Architecture, Literature and Philosophy,* Vol. II (Delhi, 2005), pp. 481-6.

——, 'Epigraphical Evidences for the Roman Trade and Roman Artifacts in Ancient India: With Special Reference to South India', Paper presented at the Second Symposium on Tamil Epigraphy: Historical Sources and Pluridisciplinary Perspectives (Paris, 2006).

——, 'Numismatic Art: A Survey With Special Reference to South India', in P. Chenna Reddy, ed., *Mahāsenasiri: Riches of Indian Archaeological and Cultural Studies (A Felicitation Volume in Honour of Dr. I.K. Sarma)* II (Delhi, 2006), pp. 525-8.

——, *Arikamedu: Its Place in the Ancient Rome-India Contacts* (New Delhi, 2007).

——, 'Devices on the Coins of Far South of the Early Centuries AD', in B.N. Mukherjee, ed., *Numismatic Art of India:* Vol. I: *Historical and Aesthetic Perspectives* (New Delhi, 2007), pp. 199-210.

——, 'Two Unpublished Roman Aurei from Pudukkottai Hoard, Tamil Nadu', *SSIC* XVII (2007), pp. 33-7.

——, 'The British Museum Collection of Roman Republican Coins Found in India', *SSIC* XVIII (2008), pp. 20-4.

——, 'A Rare Roman Republican Coin Found in India', *SSIC* XIX (2009), pp. 32-4.

——, 'Two Unpublished Roman Denarii Found at Kodumanal, Tamil Nadu', *SSIC* XX (2010), pp. 37-9.

Suresh, S. and M. Nambirajan, 'The Single Surviving Roman Coin From a Rare Hoard in Goa', *SSIC* XX (2010), pp. 44-8.

Suresh, S. and Prema Kasturi, *Cambodia: What it Got From South India? (A Historical-cum-Archaeological Survey)* (Madras, 2009).

Thirugnanasampandam, K.A., *Kanchi Pallava Coins* (Erode, 1989).

Tripathi, Alok, 'The Underwater Exploration of Mahabalipuram in Bay of Bengal', *Purātattva: Bulletin of the Indian Archaeological Society* 32 (2001-2), pp. 93-100.

Thakur, Upendra, 'Mints and Minting in India', in C. Mani, ed., *A Macro Study of Early Indian Coins* (Delhi, 1999), pp. 117-35.

Turner, P.J., *Roman Coins From India* (London, 1989).

Varma, Laxmikant B., 'Rare Portrait Coins of Skanda Satakarni', *ND* XVII (1993), pp. 25-27.

Venugopalan, T.R., ed., *History and Theory: National Seminar Papers* (Thrissur, 1997).

Vijayaraghavan, P., 'A Punch-marked Chera Silver Coin From Karur', *SSIC* X (2000), pp. 28-31.

——, 'A Further Note on the Silver Punchmarked Chera Coin From Karur', *SSIC* XI (2001), pp. 60-1.

Wakankar, V.S., 'Rock Art of South India', in C. Margabandhu, K.S. Ramachandran, A.P. Sagar and D.K. Sinha, eds., *Indian Archaeological Heritage: Shri. K.V. Soundara Rajan Felicitation Volume* I (New Delhi, 1991), pp. 63-90.

Wheeler, R.E.M., A. Ghosh and Krishna Deva, 'Arikamedu: An Indo-Roman Trading-Station on the East Coast of India', *AI* 2 (1946), pp. 17-124.

Williams Jonathan et al., eds., *Money: A History* (London, 1997).

Yazdani, G., 'Excavations at Kondapur: An Andhra Town *c.* 200 BC-200 AD', *ABORI* XII (1941), pp. 171-85.

Index